BEHIND HER BADGE

BEHIND HER BADGE

A Woman's Journey into and out of Law Enforcement

ANN MARIE DENNIS

ROWMAN & LITTLEFIELD
Lanham • Boulder • New York • London

Published by Rowman & Littlefield
An imprint of The Rowman & Littlefield Publishing Group, Inc.
4501 Forbes Boulevard, Suite 200, Lanham, Maryland 20706
www.rowman.com

86-90 Paul Street, London EC2A 4NE

British Library Cataloguing in Publication Information Available

Library of Congress Cataloging-in-Publication Data on File

ISBN 978-1-5381-7344-2 (cloth : alk. Paper)
ISBN 978-1-5381-7345-9 (electronic)

♾️™ The paper used in this publication meets the minimum requirements of
American National Standard for Information Sciences—Permanence of Paper
for Printed Library Materials, ANSI/NISO Z39.48-1992.

For my son, Tyler. My reason for living.

CONTENTS

ACKNOWLEDGMENTS

I would like to thank several people who helped me on my journey to make this memoir possible. As an undergraduate, Professor Margaret Murphy opened my eyes to a world I had been living in and didn't know existed. The first person to see potential in my story and start me on my path to writing this memoir was Professor John Freeman. He made me believe that not only was my story worth telling, but that I was capable of telling it. Professor Susan McCarty then came in and completely changed the direction I was headed. She was patient, supportive, and always working hard to keep me focused. It is because of her that this memoir is what it is. I thank Professor Albert J. Meehan for opening doors to opportunities that I never would have had access to on my own. He treated me like a colleague who had valuable insights to offer and pushed me to work harder and do more than I ever could have imagined. He was generous with his time and guidance, and offered never-ending support of all my endeavors. Without these professors and the administration at Oakland University, this memoir wouldn't be possible. I have been lucky enough to have had an unlimited source of encouragement and support that helped me overcome every challenge that interfered with my educational goals. I also thank members of the Police-Involved Shooting research group that I have worked with for the past three years: Dr. Carmen Nave, Dr. Patrick Watson, and Dr. Michael Lynch. Amy Ashton-Stewart, I am grateful and blessed to have someone to reminisce with about my friend, Tina. Thanks to David Weiner for my Pontiac PD photo, to Gil Garrett of Garrett Group Media for the photo contributions, including the cover photo, and to my sister, Katy, for her phenomenal editing skills. To all my former Pontiac Police coworkers—thank you for keeping me safe, making me laugh, and blessing me with some of the closest friendships I'll ever have. And, most importantly, to my family and friends who loved and supported me along the way—especially Neil and Tyler. And lastly, to my family who chose to be my family, not the family that shares my blood—I owe you my life. Thank you all for making this dream come true.

The stories in this book reflect the author's recollection of events. Some names, locations, and identifying characteristics have been changed to protect the privacy of those depicted. Dialogue has been re-created from memory.

PREFACE

The purpose of this memoir is to illustrate how overcoming difficulties and making something of yourself is possible, and to address my growing concerns with law enforcement. A word of warning: this memoir contains many topics that some people may find controversial, including race, gender, policing, abuse, rape, abortion, religion, immigration, suicide, and more. My hope is that readers will take my experiences for what they are. I have no hidden meaning, no agenda, no partisan statement to make. My intention is not to sway your opinion one way or another, nor is it to impugn anyone. Rather it is to share with my readers the struggles that I have gone through while coming to terms with who I was, what I've done, and who I've become.

I became a police officer because I wanted to help people; however, when I look back, I see that I was a part of the structural issues that exist in this country. While the police may not make a systematic effort to be a part of the system, there are many ways in which they unwittingly have. For example, how many times did I issue citations for having a suspended license or outstanding warrants, propelling people into the criminal justice world? I assure you, it's too many to count. Not only was I not helping them, but I further disadvantaged those that were hurting the most already.

Had this question been posed to me a few years ago, I would have told you that people need to take personal responsibility for their actions. If they get themselves into trouble, then it's their responsibility to take care of it. If they can't, then they shouldn't be driving or getting into trouble with the police. There lies my internal dilemma: can I still believe that both are true? How do I reconcile my newly discovered knowledge of inequity with my strongly held beliefs in personal responsibility? Some days this knowledge overwhelmed me with guilt and remorse. Maybe I wasn't the person, or the officer, I had always thought I was.

My hope is that when you finish reading this memoir you see the world just a little differently. That you see struggling children, people who've been arrested, drug addicts, those with mental illness, and police officers through a different lens. Maybe find a way to reach out, offer help, or just give them some grace. Lastly, we all have the power to advocate for change. Let's advocate for more police training and mental health funding.

1

WHORES, LOLLIPOPS, AND ROSIE

I wore an old pair of faded blue jeans that I had owned for more than ten years, and my tank top exposed just a bit of my bare stomach. On my feet were plain, dingy, white tennis shoes from high school. I had stopped washing my hair several days before and applied hair wax to intensify the greasy look. I had slept in my makeup and rubbed my eyes with my hands, smudging the mascara to make it look even messier. On the tips of my fingers, I used a combination of yellow highlighter and dirt to make them look stained from excessive smoking. The coup de grâce of my look was a burned-out crack pipe I confiscated from a prostitute the day before, sticking out of my shirt, held in place by my bra strap. I was as ready as I could be for my first undercover prostitution assignment.

I had been on the police force for about six months when the first significant opportunity came my way. Prostitution was a big problem in our city and the department was organizing an undercover group of female officers to hit the streets as prostitutes. Fortunately for me, not a lot of female officers were interested.

Over the years, veteran female officers had participated in the detail so frequently that they had grown tired of it. Many stated that they no longer wanted to deal with the "disgusting men" that came with it. I didn't completely understand what they meant, but I would learn later. With the shortage of female officers willing to participate, I was granted a spot, regardless of my rookie status. My enthusiasm was palpable, but I had no idea what I was getting into.

Everyone involved in the prostitution detail that day was to meet at the Vice Office about a mile from the police department on the west side of Pontiac, Michigan, the former automotive capital that was well past its glory days. I had never been there. Becoming a Vice officer required years of experience, and I was a mere rookie road officer still struggling to memorize the layout of the city. In fact, I still came to work at least an hour early every day to study my map of the city streets. Going to a new building, one shrouded in secrecy, only added to my jitters. As I pulled into the parking lot, I could feel my heart racing, and I thought seriously about turning around and driving home. With its graffiti, overgrown grass, and ten-foot-high fence, the building looked old and rundown. I don't know what I was expecting, but this wasn't it.

I approached the building entrance and was flooded with insecurity. I knew before I even walked in that everyone in that building was a veteran police officer. Other than me, no one had less than five years on the job. Working undercover is a dangerous assignment and part of maintaining your safety is not being seen at or near the police department. Because of that, I had on rare occasions observed some of these officers coming and going from the station, but I had not gotten to know any of them on a personal level. There were officers that had been involved in on-duty shootings and bought drugs undercover, and supervisors that had worked in every available unit over the years and were looking toward retirement soon. They all had years of experience under their belts, and I was a nobody with six months on the job. What was I doing here?

For police officers in Pontiac, their first four months or so are spent with a field training officer. Other than seeing other officers on police calls here and there, new officers were fairly segregated from everyone else. The first year on the job is spent on probation. Fear of getting in trouble during that time keeps most from partying and/or socializing with other officers. This makes the first year on the job feel a bit ostracizing, even if it is self-imposed. I was in my sixth month and most of the department was still relatively unknown to me. It made participating in this detail feel all the more overwhelming.

I finally got up the courage to walk inside the building. The main room was large and open with desks lining each of the north and south walls. Some of the desks were messy and piled high with paperwork, while others were neat and organized. Taped on the walls were various mugshots, photos of wanted vehicles, photos of large quantities of drugs confiscated in past raids, and, of course, drawings making fun of a fellow officer.

Making fun of and giving each other a hard time is expected in this line of work. The most popular pranks were moving someone's patrol vehicle so when they came out of the station they would have to search for it, and turning on all the lights and sirens so when an officer started their patrol car, it scared the hell out of them. I wouldn't take part in the pranks until several years later, but it was fun to watch them being played out.

I took a few deep, steadying breaths and stepped into the spacious meeting room. It seemed as if all eyes were on me. Of course, that wasn't really the case, but my insecurities followed me everywhere I went. I sat in the corner of the room and listened quietly to the briefing given by the commanders.

I couldn't believe how many people were involved in this detail. I was looking around the room at all the officers and supervisors and realized that most of them were complete strangers to me. When I was approached to be a part of the detail, I was told when and where to meet, but I wasn't given any other information about it, which intensified my nervousness. Sergeant Stern appeared to be leading the detail and doing most of the talking. He explained that the female officers would be sent out in pairs: one pair to Baldwin Road and Tregent Street to the party store parking lot and the other pair to Baldwin Road and Montcalm Street to the plaza parking lot. This area, Baldwin Road between Montcalm Street and Howard Street, was known as "Hooker Row."

Sergeant Stern went on to explain that one of the females in each pair would be wired with a recording device, which would allow her to tell the take-down officers when a transaction was completed and its details. *Could a panic attack be heard over a wire*, I wondered to myself? *Would they hear me stammering and stuttering and think I was a fool?* Relief washed over me like a tidal wave when it was decided that I would not be one of the female officers wearing the wire.

Sergeant Stern then went on to assign take-down teams to each of the pairs of female officers. These were groups of undercover officers in plainclothes driving unmarked vehicles who would stage in a nearby area, preferably where they could see the female officers. The johns would drive up to us and once a transaction was agreed upon, the female officer would tell the john that she would meet him behind the building. The take-down teams would descend upon the vehicle and block it from the front. Officers would quickly pull the driver out, handcuff him, and place him in the unmarked vehicle. One of the plainclothes officers would then get in the john's vehicle and follow the unmarked vehicle to the staging area. The take-down was always done behind a store, out of sight of the main roads, so that the cover of the female officers would not be compromised. The take-down officers were so efficient that the whole thing would be over within seconds and the female officers were on to their next customer.

The Mobile Command Vehicle (MCV) was parked at the staging area about a mile away. The MCV was a large recreational vehicle that could be outfitted with everything officers would need for undercover work: surveillance equipment, communication equipment, paperwork, weapons, ammunition, and coolers full of water to keep everyone hydrated. Once at the staging area, the johns were processed for arrest, their vehicles impounded, and then they were released with a summons to appear in court on a specified day. Another group of officers would remain at the staging area and write reports for each arrest, including details of the agreed-upon transaction.

The last, but most important, part of the detail was to clear the area of the real prostitutes before the undercover officers showed up. As one would expect, all the prostitutes in the area knew each other. If undercover female officers showed up, the real prostitutes would spot them and blow their cover within minutes and the entire detail would be a flop.

At that time, I didn't think about whether any of this was right or wrong—I just did what I was told. My early years in police work were characterized by assuming that the administration knew what and how things should be done, and my job was to do it. While we were able to arrest lots of people, we never addressed the core issues that led to the prolificacy of prostitution. No matter how many times we arrested a prostitute there was always another to take her place. No matter how many johns we arrested there was always another to take his place. It was a vicious cycle that never amounted to any real success. The problem with prostitutes and johns was the same at the end of my career as it was at the beginning. As the years passed and I became more familiar with the prostitutes on a personal level—learning about their struggles—I grew to regret more and more my participation in the prostitution details. Not because of the johns, but because it necessitated arresting the prostitutes first. Right or wrong, I have never developed any sympathy toward the johns.

With everyone clear on where they were going and what they were doing, it was finally time to hit the streets. I was sure they could all hear my heart beating as we walked outside to the unmarked cars. It sounded like thunder in my ears. Our first stop was a local party store. Sergeant Stern gave us money to go inside and buy whatever we wanted. I didn't know what I was supposed to be buying, but I followed the lead of the other female officers.

Each of them bought a forty-ounce beer and a pack of cigarettes. A couple bought lollipops. For a moment I hesitated, but then asked one of them, Officer Moore, why they were buying beer. "Prostitutes are always drinking and smoking, so if we want to be believable, then we needed to be drinking and smoking too," she replied. Taking the further risk of looking stupid, I asked why they were buying lollipops. She laughed and said, "A lollipop is the best way, besides a banana, to look slutty on the street." Lollipops would be in my future, but I wasn't ready for them at that moment. Each of the other officers wrapped their beers in a brown paper bag. I always hated beer, so I bought a fruity wine cooler, wrapped it up in my own brown bag, and got a pack of Marlboro Lights.

As we were driving to our location, I thought for a moment that drinking on the job without a weapon wasn't a great idea. What if something went wrong? What if someone grabbed one of us quickly, pulled us into their car, and drove away? What if someone pulled a weapon on one of us? There were a million things that could go wrong, but the reality is that police work is full of dangerous situations. It's part of the job—the job I wanted so badly. And why did I want this job so badly? I was desperate to prove myself as a female officer. I wanted to be part of every opportunity that the department had to offer. More than that, I was determined to be successful. I don't know where my hard-headed determination and competitiveness came from: maybe it all stems from my desire to earn the love of my parents when I was a child. Regardless of the origin, these traits were front and center when it came to doing my job.

Almost immediately I pushed all doubts out of my head. I had a job to do, and to do it I had to trust my coworkers to take care of me. A few blocks later, I was walking up and down Baldwin Road between Howard Street and Tregent Street, mostly staying in the parking lot of the party store. The area was dirty, rundown, and, due to the shelter just a few blocks down the road, had a large population of homeless people hanging around. The surrounding neighborhood was full of abandoned houses that were frequently used by the homeless, drug addicts, mentally ill, and prostitutes. Graffiti was everywhere, as were empty beer and liquor bottles, used needles, and other drug paraphernalia. While I had felt perfectly at home in this area when I was in uniform, I suddenly felt naked and vulnerable, unarmed in my regular clothes. I hadn't realized it before, but in my head, my uniform gave me a feeling of invincibility that was now gone. The thundering of my heartbeat continued to get louder and more powerful as it threatened to send me into a panic attack.

Initially, I stood near the edge of the parking lot and wondered what I should do next. I took a large gulp of my wine cooler hoping it might take the edge off. Then I reminded myself to sip it slowly so that I didn't get tipsy right away. I needed to keep a clear head. I thought about what

I saw the prostitutes doing when I was on patrol. *Don't just stand here like a fool*, I thought to myself, *MOVE*. I took a deep breath and began to stroll back and forth on the sidewalk near the roadway. As I strolled, sipped my drink, and smoked cigarettes, I felt myself calming down.

Over the years I would learn the nuances of solicitation, but in that moment, I knew absolutely nothing. The most universal thing I would come to learn is that it's common for johns to drive by a prostitute several times, observe her, then finally stop to make a deal. As a perceptive police officer, I had noticed a man in a particular truck drive by three times, but without any idea about what this meant. I just assumed he lived in the area. It didn't take long before he turned into the parking lot of the store, pull to the side of the lot away from the store, and jerk his head as a summons toward me. He was my first john. My heart began racing again. For a second, I wondered if the man might actually hear my heart beating if I got too close to him.

The john was a Black male in his fifties. He had a fade haircut, his black hair sprinkled with touches of gray throughout. He was driving a pickup truck, I don't remember the color. It wasn't new, but it was in decent shape. The man didn't approach me with a smile or try to flirt—he was all business. Over time I would discover that nearly every conversation with a john was basically the same and went something like this first one.

"Hey, baby. Wanna date?

Whatchu lookin' for?" I asked in best come-hither slang. I approached the driver's window, leaned against the car with my forearms on the open window so that my cleavage was in full view for him, and stuck my ass out.

"How 'bout you suck my dick," he said.

"So, what's in it for me?" I asked as I batted my eyelashes and licked my lips suggestively.

"This," he said smiling as he showed me a plastic bag with an off-white substance that looked like a rock. I recognized it immediately as crack cocaine.

"Ok, baby. But I've seen the cops around so meet me behind the store." I smiled, turned, and started sauntering toward the back.

This was the point when my job was basically done. The john would drive to the rear of the store to wait for me, and the takedown team would seem to appear out of nowhere. I would instantly turn around and walk back to my spot in the parking lot as if nothing had happened. Two officers from the takedown team would jump out of their car and quickly pull the john out of his car, handcuff him, and place him in their undercover car. A third member of the takedown team would jump into the john's car and drive it away. Within seconds, the john, his vehicle, and the takedown vehicle were gone.

There were exceptions, but the standard fee was twenty dollars for a blow job and fifty dollars for sex, or an equivalent in drugs. The key to a prostitution sting is that the john must state what he wants and what he's going to give you for it. It doesn't matter if he offers you money or drugs, as long as he proposes to give you compensation for a sex act. If the officer makes suggestions, then it's entrapment. It took me a while to get comfortable with the subtleties of this dance, but eventually, I became a pro.

I'm not sure that undercover work is something that can be taught. Certainly no one stepped forward to teach me anything. Either an officer is able to step directly into the role of an undercover prostitute or not. I could have been a complete failure at it as much as a success. Certainly, there were many other officers that were unsuited for this type of work, but if I was going to be given opportunities, then I was going to do my best to make the most of them. While I've never been a prostitute or a drug addict, I was able to put myself in their mindset and try to act and talk like I thought they would. Not only did I pick up slang terms and mannerisms from working in Pontiac, but I had briefly lived there as a teenager. I'm not sure why I turned out to be good at this work, but maybe it's as simple as this: I'm a good liar. I'd spent many years as a child lying to my parents and telling them what they wanted to hear to keep myself out of trouble, lying to my friends to save myself from embarrassment, and lying to family friends, teachers, and doctors to keep my parents out of trouble.

There were times working undercover that I made mistakes and slipped out of character, but I managed to improve with each detail. One of my many mistakes was made during that first detail.

One day a full-sized pickup truck driven by an African American male in his thirties pulled up next to me. I smiled and turned toward his truck.

"Damn girl! You got a big 'ole Black girl bootie," he exclaimed.

"What the hell does that mean? Are you calling me fat? What the fuck is your problem?" I yelled at him. I didn't just slip out of character I plummeted out of character. The man looked at me totally confused, shook his head, and drove away without another word. Officer Moore couldn't stop laughing. Seconds later one of the takedown cars drove up next to me. All four of the officers inside the vehicle were laughing hysterically.

"What? What's so funny?" I asked. I didn't understand what the hell was so funny and why they would risk approaching me during the detail.

"He wasn't calling you fat, dumbass, he was complimenting you," Officer Henry replied, still laughing, as they drove away. Apparently, Officer

Moore had been standing close enough to me for the takedown car to hear the whole thing on her wire. All part of the learning curve.

Working the prostitution detail is where my alter ego, Rosie Jacobs, came to life. Over the years I would perfect Rosie, slipping into her as easily as one slides into an old pair of sweatpants. Rosie's emergence came about completely by accident. It was that first day undercover when I was approached by a john, and after a few minutes of small talk he asked for my name. I hadn't thought that far ahead. I wasn't going to use my real name. How could I not have planned for this? I wonder if he saw the surprise in my eyes. At the time, I had a small tattoo of a rose on my left breast, which has since been removed. The tattoo was visible thanks to the small tank top I was wearing that cut deep into my cleavage. Always quick on my feet, I blurted out, "Rosie." From that day forward Rosie became a part of who I was.

Having alter egos was nothing new to me. I've been wearing a variety of masks since early in my childhood. From behind the mask of brave police officer I hid the truth of child abuse, molestation, rape, spousal abuse, armed robbery, burglary, and assault. I was embarrassed by my victimhood, and I often took great pains to bury it, even from those closest to me. The only difference now was that this mask had been given a name. Somehow, it made this mask more powerful. From that day forward I wore my "Rosie mask" with pride. I was resolute; I would not let Rosie fail.

Sometimes the hardest part of being an undercover prostitute is finding a way to stay in character when the johns do or say the most shocking things. Some memories I have blur together, but there are three encounters that I'll never forget.

The first of these memories is of the man who drove up to me with no clothes on. Next to him, on the seat, was a jar of Vaseline. He masturbated while speaking to me. It took everything I had to hide the shock and disgust I felt and continue to play my part in securing the arrest. I have never thought of myself as prudish, but this scene appalled me in a way I couldn't have imagined.

The second memory I have is of the guy who grabbed one of my breasts as we were talking. I had been grabbed or touched before, but never this aggressively. I didn't have time to think, but only react. I slapped his hand and sternly said, "You haven't paid for that yet!" Ultimately, he was able to get away from the takedown team, which led to a long car chase. When the man was finally caught, four cities away, a variety of weapons and bondage implements that he had been planning to use on me were found in his car. I don't remember if he had admitted that he planned to kill me or if that was an assumption made by the officers later and relayed to me. I was very unsettled after this incident and took a break from the prostitution detail for a bit.

The third incident I'll never forget was when I was approached by a well-dressed pair of White men in their thirties, wedding rings on and golf clubs in the back of a newer model Cadillac Escalade. The men solicited both me and the other female officer on the detail for an orgy. I remember thinking they could be my neighbors, friends, even family members. They seemed so "normal." I couldn't help but think about their wives at home. I wondered if this was their first time picking up hookers or one of many? Did they use condoms or risk catching diseases that they would then take home? In fact, I don't remember the exact words I used, but I asked them what their wives would think about this. Officer Moore, who was standing on the passenger side of the car, glared at me when I asked it. I knew I was messing up the bust, but I was irked in a way that I hadn't been before.

Somehow, I worked through my nerves and was able to secure many arrests during that first detail. For the next four years, I was selected for the undercover assignment every time it came up. My arrest stats grew more impressive with each prostitution detail I worked, but there was a downside to being a good undercover prostitute. Though everyone worked together seamlessly, there were times that we would get so many arrests we would be forced to stop early because the arrest paperwork would get backed up.

I was surprised when I was selected for the prostitution detail, but even more so when I was approached by someone from the vice unit about a year later and asked if I wanted to participate in some undercover drug buys with them. Of course, I immediately jumped at the chance. Soon after, I found myself driving around with Officer Henry looking to buy drugs. He explained to me that people are more apt to sell drugs to a couple rather than two men, and since there were no women in vice, they needed someone to partner up with them. For several hours Officer Henry and I drove around together trying to buy drugs from random dealers on the streets. We made a few buys, but in the end, it was all rather routine and uneventful, but it was yet another opportunity to expand my skills.

As much as I enjoyed being a part of the prostitution detail, it was equally frustrating. It didn't matter how often we conducted the detail, or how many johns we arrested, it never made a difference in the grand scheme of things. The number of prostitutes working the streets didn't decrease nor did the number of johns we arrested. Police officers want to make a difference, and it seemed that no amount of hard work ever amounted to success. Arresting people seems to be the one-size-fits-all solution to problems. Unfortunately, arrests don't always work. Some societal issues are so big that other solutions must be sought and implemented.

An unexpected result that came from my work as an undercover prostitute was my compassion for the real prostitutes that worked in Pontiac. I began to realize how difficult their lives must be interacting with some of the world's most repulsive men, let alone performing sexual acts on them. I understood why these women used drugs to help them get through the day. I felt sorry for them knowing how fearful they must be getting into each vehicle and hoping that they wouldn't be raped, assaulted, or robbed. These realizations would shape my interactions with prostitutes throughout the rest of my career.

I arrived home from working that first prostitution detail full of emotions. As I pulled into the driveway of my little three-bedroom house, I became overwhelmed. I needed a moment to process and transition from the environment I had just "lived" in to where my "real" life was. This was my first house, and I was proud that I was able to buy it on my own, giving my son a stable home in a good neighborhood in a city whose motto was "Where living is a vacation." Everything in my life was about providing the best for my son, Tarec.

When I started with the Pontiac Police Department, I knew I had to find a house nearby. I couldn't commute ninety minutes each way from East Lansing forever, but I also knew I wanted to put Tarec in the best possible school system. I had gone to many schools growing up and my favorite had always been the Lake Orion school district, so I focused my house hunting there. There weren't many houses in my price range, but I was lucky and found a cute little house only two blocks away from Pine Tree Elementary School, which was recognized as a State of Michigan Blue Ribbon School.

I knew that moving my five-year-old son across the state, away from his father and his friends, was going to be tough on him. Searching for ways to make Tarec feel at home became my top priority. His bedroom walls were covered with all things sports, and I bought him a sports-themed bedding set. Tarec loved sunflowers and wanted to plant them in front of the house. Soon after moving in, I called Tarec into the spare bedroom where I had set up my desk. I turned on the computer, Tarec jumped up on my lap, and we searched for the most unique sunflower plants we could find. He settled on four different varieties: Cherry Rose, Gypsy Charmer, Terracotta, and Golden Cheer. The day the sunflowers arrived in the mail, Tarec jumped up and down, eager to plant them. We were both excited at the prospect of watching our newly planted sunflowers turn from seed to tall plants.

Sitting in my driveway, several months after planting them, I realized how fast those sunflowers were growing. Each plant was around three feet tall and would soon be taller than me. Our house had a fenced-in backyard where Tarec had room to run and play. I had a real career, and it was allowing me to live a life I never expected to have.

Growing up hadn't been easy for me. I had never been the priority in either of my parents' lives, nor had my happiness ever been more than an afterthought. If someone had told me years before that I would have a child someday, and that he would be the most important person in my life, I would have laughed in their face. Conversely, if someone had told me that I would end up living paycheck to paycheck in a dead-end job, married to a man who abused me, and someday dying of a drug overdose or in prison—now, that I would have believed. It seemed much more plausible than the happy state of my current life.

As I opened my car door, I saw Tarec's little face in the front picture window. His babysitter, Jenny, stood behind him. By the time I reached the front door, he was standing in the doorway. I opened the screen door and he jumped into my arms and gave me a big hug.

"I missed you, Mommy!"

"I missed you too, buddy. Have you been a good boy for Jenny?" I asked him.

"Yes!" he yelled with a big smile.

"He's always a good boy," Jenny said as she picked up her purse.

I thanked Jenny for babysitting and handed her some cash as she left. For the time, I forgot all about work and enjoyed the evening with Tarec. I made him dinner, watched *SpongeBob SquarePants* on TV with him, gave him a bath, and read two stories before tucking him in for bed.

Once Tarec was asleep, the house was overcome with a deafening silence. I struggled to find something to distract me—the gentle ripple of water flowing through the fish tank, the faint ticking of my bedside clock—but nothing could stop the deluge of thoughts and insecurities that washed over me. I was a fraud. If my coworkers and supervisors knew who I really was, where I had come from, the things I had been through, would they look at me differently? Would they see that I was an imposter? A weak, insecure, damaged child pretending to be a fearless cop? Would they realize that all my outward confidence was a well-constructed front to hide the fact that I was afraid of everything? Afraid of failure. Afraid of weakness. Afraid of being seen for who I really was. After so many years, memories of my childhood still seemed to sneak up on me at the most unexpected times.

It was 1985. The summer before I turned twelve. President Ronald Reagan was in office, Coca-Cola introduced "New Coke," the wreckage of the *Titanic* was found, and singers from all genres were singing "We Are the World" together at a Live Aid benefit concert to provide relief from the famine in Africa. Half of my friends were listening to Madonna and Wham! and the other half were headbanging to Metallica and Megadeth. I loved it all. My clothes were mostly hand-me-downs from my cousins or gifts from other family members. My hair was long, and my bangs were teased a mile high. I was considered part of the "stoners" group at school, but that wasn't because we drank or smoked; it was because of where we lived.

My family lived in a trailer park. I was still too young to realize that I was supposed to be embarrassed by that. Instead, I reveled in the fact that I had so many friends within walking distance. During the summer, kids left their houses in the morning and didn't come home until the streetlights came on in the evening. We would stop in at someone's house here and there like little scavengers searching for food throughout the day. Then off we would go again into the freedom of the summer sun. I didn't care where I was during those days, as long as it wasn't at home.

My trailer was the third from the corner on Apple Street. It was small and old, but it was better than an apartment, which we had lived in before. The trailer had three bedrooms and I was grateful to have my own room. In the past, I had been forced to share a room with my brothers, and I hated the intrusion into my space.

It was a typical summer evening in the trailer park, and I was out with a group of friends walking the neighborhood. For hours we had been playing kickball in a field and everyone was exhausted. The sun was just beginning to crawl toward the western sky as we walked, and the group got smaller as kids broke off to head for home. Eventually, it was just a boy named Wesley and me laughing and walking. As we approached my street, my stepfather drove by, arriving home from work. He didn't stop, wave, or even acknowledge that he saw me. He must have had a bad day at work, I thought. Shortly after, I said goodbye to Wesley and turned toward home.

I no sooner walked into the trailer when I was slammed against the wall. My stepfather leaned down into my face screaming obscenities at me. It came on so suddenly that I couldn't comprehend what he was saying. Instead I focused on the rancid odor of fresh beer on his breath. He told me that if I wanted to roam the neighborhood like a whore with a boy, then I could sit on the corner like a whore. As my mother stood by and watched, he grabbed me by the arm and threw me back out the front door. He yelled at me for the whole neighborhood to hear, "Go sit on the corner like a whore and don't come back."

I walked to the corner slowly, sobbing uncontrollably. When I got to the corner, I didn't know what to do. I hadn't seen anyone looking out their windows, but in my mind, the whole neighborhood was staring at me. I had been branded a whore and I was sure that now everyone knew it.

I sat on the sidewalk at the corner and tried to slow my breathing, gather my thoughts, and replay the events of the last few days trying to remember anything I might have done. Had all this really been over my stepfather seeing me walking with Wesley? Wesley, someone I had been friends with for years? It seemed implausible, but I couldn't think of anything else that would have incited such anger.

Watching my mother fawn over my stepfather and make excuses for his behavior had incensed me over the years, but this seemed like too much to excuse, even for her. She had already lost one child, my older brother, who moved in with our maternal grandparents due to the abuse of my stepfather. Rather than do something about her husband's behavior she continually made excuses. I lost count of the times when my mother would quietly whisper, "I know he's wrong, but let's just keep quiet. We don't want to make him angry." Even as a child it was wildly frustrating, and hurtful, to know that my mother cared more about my stepfather than she did about her own flesh and blood.

As the sun disappeared below the horizon and darkness overtook my exhausted little body, I began to wonder what would happen to me now. Would I be allowed to go home to sleep? Would I be forced to sleep on the sidewalk? Goosebumps covered my arms and legs. I was wearing only shorts and a tank top, and the night air was becoming chilly. As the hours passed, I moved further off the sidewalk onto the grass of the neighbors' yard, hoping it would provide some heat and shield me from the ongoing embarrassment of passing eyes.

Eventually, I cried myself to sleep curled up in the grass. I don't know how much time had passed, but it was dark when I was abruptly jerked up off of the grass. I was face-to-face with my stepfather, again. The odor of beer on his breath was stronger and mixed with the stale smell of cigarettes. He dragged me over to the car and threw me into the back seat next to two full garbage bags and a notebook—my journal. He shut the door and got into the driver's seat. My mother reached back, grabbed the notebook, and shook it in my face. "You ungrateful little bitch! You don't deserve to live under our roof," she shouted.

I had been writing in my journal for nearly a year about the miseries of living with my mother and stepfather. I opined about how great it would be to live with my father—the man I didn't know. In my young mind I couldn't imagine anything worse than where I was.

Why am I stuck here? I have a father. Why can't I go live with him? Just because my mother hates him doesn't mean that I will! Anything has to be better than living in this HELL! Someday, I'll leave this house and never look back.

I had no idea where we were driving to, but deep down inside I knew I wasn't going back home. I wouldn't be saying goodbye to my friends. I wouldn't be kissing my cat goodbye. I wouldn't be saying goodbye to the lady I babysat for, Carol, or her kids. I sat in the back seat and cried softly to myself.

What I didn't know was that while I had been relegated to the corner like a whore, my mother had contacted my father. Some sort of arrangement was made between them. I was never told exactly how it occurred or how my mother even knew how to contact my father. Regardless, my mother threw some clothes in garbage bags, loaded me up in the car, and dropped me on his doorstep in Lake Orion about fifteen minutes away.

So many years had passed, but sometimes, I still felt like that scared, insecure little girl. As a means of survival, I had become a well-versed master of denial. For now, at least, my secret was safe from my coworkers. I was determined not to waste this undercover opportunity by wallowing in the self-doubt that my past often plunged me into. It was ironic, however, that as an adult I would choose to work as an undercover prostitute. My thoughts turned to the first time I was called a whore, to how much it hurt. I wondered why I was putting myself in a position where my past could unsettle me so completely. I reminded myself that I wasn't a whore. It was a job. A part that I was being paid to play, just as Julia Roberts had in one of my favorite movies, *Pretty Woman*. As I drifted off to sleep, I reminded myself that I was no longer a child. But that word—*whore*—wouldn't leave my mind.

2

LOVE IS STRONGER THAN DNA

I didn't grow up wanting to be a police officer. In fact, I can remember distinctly being four years old telling everyone who would listen that I was going to go to Michigan State University and be a lawyer someday. How and why this came to be, I have no idea, but the thought planted roots and grew like a tree over the years. As with most childhood dreams, things change.

When I was seventeen years old, I moved to East Lansing to attend Michigan State University. Unfortunately, I wasn't ready for life at a big university or to make decisions regarding my future. I dropped out due to poor academics after a year. Maybe I had spent so much of my childhood trying to be responsible that college became an excuse to finally let loose and be a kid. Young, impulsive, and a lack of grounding—all good descriptions of me and a recipe for certain failure.

One important thing did come out of that year at Michigan State, though, was I discovered that I didn't really want to be a lawyer. I didn't want to prosecute criminals, and I certainly didn't want to defend them. I wanted to be a part of finding the criminals, although at the time I didn't know what that would look like or how it might come to be. In the coming years, that desire to find the criminals would slowly develop into a desire to become a police officer.

Instead of correcting my life, which had clearly gone off track, I left college and floundered around for the next several years trying to figure life out. I loved living in the college town of East Lansing so much that I stayed in the area and tried to build a life there—even though I had no direction as to where that life was headed. I took a few classes at the community college, worked a few random jobs, and hung out with friends.

My carefree life took a dramatic turn when I was twenty. A friend of mine, Andrea, worked at a local big chain hotel in Lansing, just across the border from East Lansing, and was asked to cover the night shift for a week while the night manager went on vacation.

"It's so hard to stay awake. Please come hang out with me and help me stay up," she had begged me. I didn't have to work the next day, I had nothing else to do, and wanted to be a good friend, so I agreed.

The hotel was nice: four stars. The entryway had two large glass doors that opened into the lobby and the front desk was immediately to the right. Andrea had rolled a television set out into the breakfast area to give us something to do between guests checking in. I sat in a chair with my back to the hotel entrance and Andrea sat to my left so that she could see if anyone came in.

It was about ten minutes before midnight when Andrea commented that it was almost time to lock the front doors. After midnight, guests would have to be buzzed into the lobby. Only moments later I heard the lobby doors open and Andrea got up and walked toward the front desk. It should have struck me as odd that I didn't hear her greet the incoming guests, but I was too tired to think about it so I didn't even turn around.

Then I felt it: the cold, hard steel of the barrel of a gun pushed against the right temple of my head. "Get up!" an unknown man yelled at me. My mind and body froze. The man pushed the gun harder against my temple and yelled again, "Move it!" I slowly stood up as he continued to push the gun against my head, leading me behind the front desk.

As we rounded the corner, I saw Andrea lying on the floor behind the desk, on her stomach. There was another man wearing a black ski mask standing over her with a gun in his hand. "Get on the floor!" the man behind me yelled as he pushed me to the ground. Andrea and I lay on the floor facing one another. We reached out and held hands as we cried. The man that had been behind me knelt down and kept the gun pointed at us. I couldn't see it, but I could hear the second man taking money from the hotel cash register.

Suddenly, the man pointing the gun at us reached out and grabbed one of my hands away from Andrea's. I instinctively pulled away and he grabbed my hand again and told me not to move. The man then removed the rings I was wearing, one by one. He then grabbed my other hand and did the same.

"Please don't take my rings! Isn't the money from the hotel enough?" I pleaded.

"Shut up!" he screamed at me.

The two men stood up and whispered to one another. A thousand thoughts ran through my head in a split second: *Were they going to kill us? Rape us? Kidnap us?* But mostly I thought about how helpless I was in that moment.

I have no idea how much time passed before Andrea and I realized that the only sounds we could hear were our own sobs. The men were gone. We continued to lay there too paralyzed with fear to move. Eventually, we decided it was time. We jumped up and ran down the hallway behind the front desk toward the guests' rooms. We started banging on all the doors as we screamed for help. A bewildered and sleepy man finally opened his room door, and we ran inside. "Call 911!" we cried.

The police arrived a few minutes later and took a report. We gave them as good a description of the men as we could, which was very little since they had been wearing masks. It's hard to describe, but the officers seemed as if they didn't want to hear from me at all. They didn't care about what was stolen from me. They questioned Andrea about the money that was taken from the hotel register but left me off to the side, crying and alone. Finally, I pushed myself into their faces to make them listen to me. I described all the jewelry that was stolen from me, as well as my purse that had been stolen from behind the desk. Maybe they felt like I didn't work there and shouldn't have been there to begin with? Maybe they simply felt that the money stolen from the hotel was more important? Either way, the officers were not kind or compassionate. We were both so young, yet the officers didn't ask if we needed anything, if we had anyone to call, or anywhere to go.

There was no doubt that Lansing was a busy city and that the Lansing police were accustomed to dealing with these types of crimes, but Andrea and I weren't. We were traumatized and afraid. I knew that I would never treat victims of a crime this way if I was a police officer and I was disgusted that we weren't taken care of better. I would replay their behavior over and over in my head over the next couple days.

Without my stolen purse, I had no money, no credit cards, no identification, and the robbers knew where I lived. I was scared to death to go home alone. I sat in my car in the hotel parking lot and cried. Where would I go? What was I supposed to do now? There was only one place that I felt safe enough to go to.

Since I was eleven years old, I had been bouncing around from home to home. I had run away from my father several times to return to my mother. I'd been sent back to my father by my mother several times, lived with my maternal aunt briefly, moved in with a lady named Carol that I babysat for as kid, and lived with a few friends along the way. My life had been nonstop chaos for five years. I attended different schools up to three times a year, as each move required a change of school. Over time the schools have blended into a blur, and it has become impossible for me to keep straight in my head exactly when I went to which schools and for exactly how long. Throughout my childhood my pursuit of academia had been an attempt to garner love and attention from my parents. I grew up with the mistaken belief that being a good student would make my parents love me. After nearly a decade of trying, it had become clear that this was a futile pursuit and I had long since stopped caring about school or grades. Instead, I had begun to see life as something I had to endure rather than envisioning a better future for myself.

When I was sixteen I was back at my father's house in Lake Orion. Nothing had curbed his abuse and trying to escape it was a strong contributor to the reason I had moved around so much. Fortunately for me, by this time I had met someone, and we were dating exclusively. His name was Peter, and he was two years older than me. Peter was friends with my older brother, and we had met a few months earlier at my brother's house. I never lived with my older brother, but his house was a constant party, and my cousin and I hung out there frequently. For the first time in my life, it felt like I had someone who I could depend on completely.

Peter was unlike anyone I had dated before. He wore his hair in a mullet and had the kindest brown eyes. He was quiet, somewhat reserved, and had an incredible sense of humor. That's what attracted me to him—he had a way of always making me laugh. For the first six months of our "relationship" we insisted to anyone and everyone that we weren't boyfriend/girlfriend. "We're just friends" was our mantra, even though we spent every day together. Finally, we gave in and admitted to our friends, and ourselves, that yes, we were dating.

Peter came from an upper-class family. His mom was a surgical nurse and his dad was a patent attorney. They lived in a large, beautiful house on private Lake Voorheis and had several boats. His parents had bought him a new truck when he turned sixteen. This was a different lifestyle from anyone who had previously been in my life, and I felt embarrassed of my upbringing and unworthy to be around people whose social class was so far above mine. The first time he drove me by his house I freaked out. I told him to keep driving. I wasn't ready to walk into a home so grand and meet his family—a family that I knew was not going to be anything like mine.

Over time I had confided in Peter about some of the abuse that I suffered at the hands of my father. Peter was frustrated that he couldn't do anything to stop it, but he did his best to keep me out of the house as much as he could. He picked me up each morning for school and we would go back to his house at the end of the school day. I would stay at Peter's house as late as I could and then he would drive me home. His basement became my home away from home. We would do our homework and play *Super Mario Bros. 2* on Nintendo NES or pool. Summers were the best. We would while away the days taking out his boat, water skiing, tubing, or just throwing out the anchor and swimming around.

One day while I was home doing chores around the house, my father came home early clearly intoxicated or high or both. "What the fuck have you been doing all day?" he screamed in slurred speech as he began to walk toward me unsteadily. I could see that he wasn't in a good mood and this wasn't going to end well for me.

"Cleaning the house," I stammered. I knew what was coming next. I began to back away from my father as he approached me. He kept coming toward me until my back was against the wall. Then the beating began. Punches came from all directions. The odor of beer and marijuana oozed from his pores as he hit me. But something was different for me this time. Maybe enough was enough because Peter's family had shown me how life was supposed to be. Maybe it was because I had realized that all parents don't abuse their kids. Maybe I just didn't want Peter's parents to see me covered in bruises and be forced to explain where they came from. Whatever it was, I decided this was the last time my father would hit me.

I dropped to the floor and scurried away from my father's grasp. I ran toward the front door to escape. I pushed open the screen door and walked out to safety. My father would be too intoxicated to follow me, or so I thought, but I heard the door open behind me. Turning around I saw my father running toward me with a baseball bat in his hands. He wasn't carrying the bat down at this side. He had it gripped tightly with both hands up on his right shoulder like he was preparing to hit the game-winning homerun.

The look in his grayish-blue eyes made my heart stop. There was nothing but pure evil in them—anger and hate boiling to the surface from the deepest core of hell. I knew, right at that moment, that if he caught me, he would kill me. I turned around and ran as fast as I could. I had no shoes on and every pebble and rock seemed to slow me down, but I kept running. I knew that I couldn't stop.

Shortly after I reached the end of our road and turned the corner, I saw that my father had fallen behind. Now was my chance to disappear, so I ran between two houses and crawled under the deck of a stranger's house. After a few minutes, I crawled out and slowly made my way through six backyards and to my friend Sue's house. I checked the sliding glass door to her basement and found that it was open. I ran inside and hid in a closet. Not long after, I heard Sue's brother in the basement. I came out of the closet and ran, crying, into his arms.

I had met Sue shortly after moving in with my father when I was eleven. We had become good friends and I had confided in her about some of my father's abuse. I didn't tell her everything, but she knew enough. My friendship with Sue was sporadic. I had moved many times over the years, and it was difficult, if not impossible, to maintain friendships, but whenever I moved back to my father's house, Sue and I always picked up where we left off.

Sue came downstairs when she heard me and asked what happened. Tearfully, I told her my father had chased me down the street with a baseball bat. She sent her brother upstairs to peek out the front window of their house to see if my father was anywhere in sight. He reported that my father was walking up and down the street with the bat.

After about an hour, Sue's brother said that my father wasn't outside, so we figured he must have finally gone home. I had no idea what to do next, but all I could think about was getting to Peter. Sue gave me a pair of her tennis shoes and put me in the backseat of her brother's car that was parked in the garage. I laid down in case my father was still out there looking for me and they drove me to Peter's workplace.

Peter had graduated from high school the prior year and had taken a job at an equipment rental business in Auburn Hills, which was only about ten minutes from my father's house. I told Peter what happened, and he said that he still had several more hours left of work, but I didn't care. I felt safer there with him than anywhere else.

I went out to the parking lot and climbed into Peter's truck—a Chevy S-15 with manual transmission. The inside of the truck wasn't big, but I curled myself up on the floor of the passenger side into the smallest ball I could, locked the doors, and waited for his shift to end. My arms and legs cramped up and my back ached. I had loved learning how to drive that truck, but at that moment I wished the truck was an automatic so I could stretch out across the floor. Regardless of the discomfort, I wasn't coming out. As the hours ticked by, I couldn't stop imagining the awful scenarios that would take place if my father found me there.

After work, Peter took me back to his house and we occupied our-selves with video games and billiards. Peter wanted to tell his parents what had happened, but I was embarrassed. I didn't want them to think I was a trashy person from a trashy home. The abuse I suffered was a humiliating secret. For most of my life the blame and guilt I heaped on myself were my closest companions. Peter's parents and sister had been kind and welcoming to me from the day I had met them, but I was afraid of how they would perceive me if they knew my truth. I begged and pleaded until finally he agreed not to say anything.

Hours went by as we tried to figure out what to do next. It was get-ting close to 11:00 p.m. when Peter's mom said it was time for him to take me home. Grudgingly, we left. As we approached my street, I asked him to drop me off a few houses down. Going home simply wasn't an option at this point. I knew what I was going to do, but I didn't want to tell him.

When I stepped out of his truck the cool night air threatened my resolve. It was late fall, and I wasn't wearing a jacket, so Peter gave me his.

"What are you going to do? Are you going to be OK?" Peter asked, worry dripping from each word.

"I'll be fine, I promise," I replied with a fake smile.

"Call me tomorrow—first thing."

"I will."

We said our goodbyes and he drove away, his face unable to disguise his anxiety. I walked slowly toward my house. As irrational as it was, I still worried my father could be stalking the streets searching for me all these hours later. I entered our yard from the furthest point away from the house and did my best to avoid all windows. I tried to remain silent as I walked, panicking with each rustle of a leaf or snap of a twig. I reached the back of the house, undetected, and peeked through the kitchen window into the living room. The rooms were dark, and I assumed that my father and his wife, Caroline, had gone to bed for the night.

My father had married Caroline a few years prior after only know-ing her for a very short time. Caroline and I did not get along. She was materialistic and selfish and hated whenever I lived with them. After my father married Caroline two things changed for me immediately. The first was that the physical abuse by my father resumed and the second was that Caroline made it her mission to eliminate me from their lives. Caroline had been single, working as a waitress, and struggling financially for many years. My father was her golden ticket and she saw me as someone who was taking money away from her. She was now a woman of leisure, she didn't have to work, she had all the drugs she wanted, and my father gave her anything she desired. Caroline's only remaining problem was me. She took every opportunity to create a problem so I would get another beating.

Not long after my father and Caroline were married, I came home from school and went to work doing my chores. Caroline was watching TV and didn't really say much of anything to me. After I finished my chores I went to my room and started on my homework. About an hour later I heard my father come home from work. He didn't acknowledge me, but instead went straight to the bath that Caroline had ready for him. I heard Caroline talking to him in the bathroom but couldn't make out what they were saying. I continued working on my homework and didn't give them another thought.

In the distance I heard my father come out of the bathroom and walk into the kitchen. The click of the microwave opening echoed into my bedroom. It seemed as if everything was moving in slow motion. I knew what was coming next. The microwave door slammed shut and my father stormed into my bedroom. He grabbed me by my long, sandy-brown hair and dragged me into the kitchen. I couldn't get my feet under me no matter how hard I tried. I could feel the stinging of my hair being pulled out of my head into his large hands as he continued to drag me across the floor. We finally got to the kitchen, and he pulled open the microwave door again. He shoved my head into the microwave and slammed the door on it. The door crushed my head like a vise and then ricocheted back open. My father was yelling the whole time, but my ears were ringing, my scalp was burning, and I felt dizzy. I couldn't focus. I couldn't concentrate on what he was saying.

The next thing I knew my father threw me down on the floor and walked away. I curled into a fetal position on the floor, held my head in my hands, and waited for what was coming next. With an open concept layout, the kitchen and living room were connected. It was only seconds later when my father grabbed me by the arm, jerked me up off the floor, and pushed me over the side of the couch. My father had retrieved from the kitchen wall a hanging three-foot decorative wooden spoon. He began striking me, repeatedly, on the back with it. I couldn't tell you how many blows, but it didn't take long until the spoon broke in half across my back. My father dropped the pieces of the spoon on the floor and threw me across the room.

The beating was finally over. My father sat down at the table and Caroline served him dinner. I crawled to my room, laid down on my bed, and cried myself to sleep. My tiny body, broken and battered, couldn't stay awake for long. I found out later that I had missed a small spot of food on the top of microwave when I had cleaned it. Caroline could have told me about the spot and allowed me to clean it. Instead, she waited to tell my father, knowing it would result in a beating.

My strong will, supported by fear, kept me from going inside the house after Peter dropped me off. Instead, I took two lawn chairs from the yard, placed them facing one another, and positioned them close against the house under the kitchen window to help block some of the wind and keep me out of sight if my father or Caroline looked out into the backyard. I sat in one chair and propped my feet up on the other one. I zipped Peter's jacket all the way up, pulled it up around my head as far as I could, wrapped my arms around myself with hands tucked inside the sleeves, and tried to go to sleep.

The temperature continued to drop and my whole body shivered uncontrollably. My mind raced. Could I stay out here all night? Would my father find me tomorrow dead in these chairs? Considering the alternative, I decided I had no choice but to risk it.

I was exhausted, mind and body, but sleep eluded me. As the hours passed, the shivering stopped. My feet and hands were tingling, burning, as if I were being pricked repeatedly with red-hot needles. Eventually, my body settled into numbness, and I no longer felt anything. My racing thoughts slowed until there was nothing. I couldn't think. I couldn't feel. I could barely breathe. I don't think I slept that night, rather I fell into periods of unconsciousness.

After what felt like an eternity, I finally stretched my head up and looked through the kitchen window again. I saw the bold red numbers of the clock on the microwave read 5:41 a.m. I knew my father would be getting up for work soon, so I needed to find somewhere else to go. I tried to stand up and discovered that I couldn't. My legs were numb but throbbing in pain at the same time. I looked at my hands and realized that they were a deep red color. My fingertips were a pale bluish white. I needed to get out of the cold as soon as possible.

If walking wasn't an option, then I would crawl. I got down on the ground and used my knees and forearms to crawl through the backyard, into the wooded area, and out near Sue's house. It was still early, but I was relieved to see lights on inside her house. I crawled to the front door and knocked with my forearms. Moments later, Sue's mom opened the door.

"Oh my God! Are you OK?" she exclaimed with fear in her eyes. "What's happened to you?" I must have looked worse than I thought.

"I—I sle-slept outside. I'm s-so cold," I stuttered.

Sue's mom helped me into the house and lay me down on the couch. She took off my cold jacket and covered me with several blankets. Over and over, Sue's mom asked me what was going on and why I had slept outside. Answers were something I knew I couldn't give her. If my father was abusive now, I could only imagine what he would do if the police were involved. My father hated the police. He never said why, but I always assumed it had to do with him being a drug dealer.

Sue heard the commotion and came into the living room. She didn't need to ask what happened. She knew that whatever it was it had to do with my father. Sue sat down on the floor next to me, slid her hand under the blankets, and put her warm hand on top of mine. It was this kindness and gentleness that allowed me to trust her over the years.

After a while Sue's mom came back into the room with two basins of water. She told me to sit up and placed one basin on my lap and one at my feet. She gently took off my shoes and socks and I saw that my feet looked much the same as my hands. She placed my feet into the lukewarm water in the basin on the floor and then placed my hands in the basin on my lap. As the blood began to return to my hands and feet, the numbness turned to burning and tingling all over again.

Within the hour I was able to stand up again. I took a shower and Sue gave me an outfit of hers to wear. While I was in the shower, Sue and her mom had a huge argument about calling the police. Sue's mom didn't know what exactly was going on, but she knew that a teenage girl sleeping outside was not normal. I have no idea what Sue said to her mother to convince her not to call, but I was grateful that it worked.

For a long time I had begged people to call the police on my father and no one ever did. Now someone wanted to call the police and I had never been more afraid. If the police sent me back to my father, he would kill me. If I was sent back to my mother, then I would be away from Peter. If the police got the courts involved who knows where I would end up. But no matter what happened, I knew that getting the police involved would cause Peter's parents to find out what was going on. I couldn't take the humiliation. They were good people. I was sure they wouldn't understand my life, nor would they want their son to be a part of it.

Sue's brother drove us to school, and I went straight to the office of a trusted counselor. Through a flood of tears and humiliation, I told her everything. The next few hours were filled with a flurry of phone calls. The first call was to my mother. The counselor explained what had occurred and requested that my mother come to the school to pick me up. My mother's reply was succinct and unwavering, "I'm done with her. Call social services. She can go to a foster home. I don't care what happens to her."

After the robbery at the hotel, I went to the only place I knew I could feel safe—Peter's parents' house. I barely remember the drive; my mind was numb with fear. While Peter and I had broken up a couple years before, neither he nor his parents had abandoned me. Peter and I hadn't broken up because of any type of argument, but because I had gone off to college and was acting irresponsibly. I was too busy partying and too stupid to appreciate the relationship I had with him. Fortunately for me, before we dated, Peter and I had a solid, platonic relationship that was steadfast over the years. As the decades passed my relationship with Peter morphed into that like a brother and sister. As for his parents, I had been completely wrong about them. When they found out the truth about my life during the three years that Peter and I were together, they didn't judge me—they embraced me.

When I was seventeen years old Peter's dad, who was an attorney, took my father to court to force him to pay for oral surgery that I needed. After the surgery, Peter's mom cared for me during my recuperation. When I was accepted to college Peter's mom told me to make a list of everything I needed. I made a very conservative list that covered just the basics. Peter's mom added lots of things to the list, gave us her credit card, and told Peter to take me shopping for everything I needed. When the dorms closed for the holidays and I had nowhere to go, Peter's parents let me stay with them even though Peter and I had broken up. No matter what has happened to me or how much I screwed up, Peter's family has always supported me. Over the years the relationship with Peter's family grew stronger. Peter's sister, Katy, became like a sister to me, and his parents became the parents I never had. I eventually started calling them Mom and Dad.

I showed up at their house early in the morning after the robbery and let myself in with my key. I took off my coat and shoes and went upstairs to one of the extra bedrooms. I was just crawling into bed when Mom walked in. She wasn't upset, but completely bewildered. I told her all about the robbery and how frightened I was to go home. She comforted me, hugged me, and told me that I was welcome to stay. I was finally safe.

The next day Mom gave me some money for gas for my car. When I went inside the gas station to pay, I couldn't breathe. My heart felt like it was going to beat out of my chest, my head began to spin, and I thought I might pass out. My hands were shaking uncontrollably, and it felt like someone was stabbing me in the chest. I didn't understand what was happening, but I felt trapped and strangled with fear.

I threw a twenty-dollar bill at the clerk and ran out of the gas station without a word. Jumping into my car to safety, I pulled out into traffic without checking if it was clear, tires squealing as I sped back to Mom's house. I ran inside, up to the bedroom, and back into bed. I had never had a panic attack before.

Images of the robbery continued to swim around in my head. Nights were filled with dreams: the gun pressing against my temple, being pushed to the ground, the violation at having my rings being ripped off my fingers. Every man I saw was potentially the one that robbed me. I stayed at Mom and Dad's house for a week before I could finally pull myself together and go home. As I had done for many years, I fell back on my tried-and-true method for dealing with difficult situations—I forgot about it and didn't speak of it to anyone after that day.

I was never contacted by the police for follow-up. My jewelry was never located, and to my knowledge, the suspects were never caught. Looking back with years of police experience, I realize that the officers turned the case over to the detective bureau and it would have been the detective's responsibility to contact me about any future updates with the case. I understand now that we were able to provide very little in the way of a description of the suspects, so it's not surprising that no one was ever arrested for the crime. I can only hope that I was never that cold and callous to a robbery victim, but unfortunately, I'm afraid I probably was.

3

BEING DUPED

When I finally went back to my apartment, I had several messages on my answering machine from Andrea. She hadn't heard from me since the night of the robbery and was concerned. I called her and told her that I was fine and had spent some time at my parents' house. We made plans to meet for dinner that night.

We laughed and joked and never mentioned the robbery. After dinner Andrea asked me to stop by the hotel with her to speak to the night manager who was back from vacation. A cold bolt of lightning sent a shock through my body, but I remained outwardly calm. I smiled and said, "Sure."

We entered the hotel lobby, and I could feel my hands shaking. I silently repeated to myself that nothing happened. Everything was fine. I was safe. Andrea introduced me to the night manager, Mohamad, an older Lebanese man with salt-and-pepper hair. He smiled at me and said, "Just call me Mo."

"So, tell me what happened," Mo said.

"It was crazy," Andrea replied with a tinge of excitement in her voice. "It was right before I was going to lock the doors. These two guys came in—" I interrupted Andrea and excused myself. Hands shaking, breathing heavy, I hurried to the bathroom down the hall. I slammed into the door so hard that it hit the wall behind it as I stormed into the room. I was grateful to see that there was no one else in the bathroom. I stood in front of the mirror, tears in my eyes, admonishing myself. *You're fine. Damn it! Nothing happened. It's just a hotel. Get ahold of yourself!*

I splashed my face with some water, plastered on my best fake smile, and went back to the desk with Andrea and Mo. Thankfully, they had moved on to another topic of conversation. We stayed there chatting with

Mo for about thirty minutes before Andrea said we were leaving. "Wait," Mo said. "Can I talk to you alone for a minute?" I realized that he was talking to me. Andrea walked out to the car and Mo asked me if I would go to dinner with him. I was shocked. I didn't even know this guy. I wouldn't say I was particularly attracted to him but looks aren't everything and he did seem nice. But was he too old for me? I was only twenty and he had gray hair.

In retrospect this was just more impulsive behavior, chasing yet another distraction from my trauma and the reality of my directionless life. Mo appeared nice enough, and Andrea said nothing but good things about him, so I gave him my phone number. A few days later we made plans to get together. Mo and I spent nearly all our time together after that dinner. He was always very polite to me, never raised his voice, and was a perfect gentleman. I was young and naïve and knew very little about the cultures and practices of the rest of the world. Talking to Mo about his culture and religion was fascinating. I had never dated someone who treated me so well: paying for meals, buying me gifts, wanting to spend all our time together, showering me with affection.

Mo started talking about getting married within the first couple months. I was twenty-one and he was twenty-eight, which was rather late to get married in his culture. I was insecure, lacked any sense of confidence in my decisions, felt unlovable, and thought that maybe being married would somehow settle my life down into something resembling calm and normal. My childhood had made me a walking disaster, so I trusted him because he was older, wiser, and more worldly than I was. If Mo thought what we had was good enough to jump into marriage, who was I to disagree? I had been through so much in my life that I just wanted to have the fairy-tale happy ending. Was it too much to ask to have the marriage that my mother and father were never able to find? I decided that I was going to think positive. I was going to get married.

In January 1995, only eight short months later, Mo and I married. It was a small wedding, mostly family. Regardless of their doubts, my mom and dad supported me and came to the wedding. Not only did they support me, but I spent the night before the wedding at their house and Mom helped me get ready. The little girl I had babysat for, who had become like a sister to me, was my maid of honor and my maternal younger brother walked me down the aisle. At that time, my biological mother and I were in the middle of a brief reconciliation period and her and my stepfather also attended the wedding. However, she was not given the usual important role of "mother of the bride." By this time, Peter and his family had become my family and they were all in attendance as well as Carol and her husband, Ryan. Those were the family members I most cared about, not my mother and stepfather.

All the positivity in the world couldn't "warm" my feet just before the wedding. I was standing in front of a mirror in the dressing room, and I began to cry. I was having doubts. Not little doubts, but all-consuming doubts. *What the hell was I doing?* I stood in front of that mirror staring in horror at myself. My hair was styled in a beautiful updo with long tendrils hanging down in the front that framed my face, my makeup was perfect, and I was wearing a floor length, off the shoulder, fitted, champagne-colored wedding dress that had a large bow on the back. A champagne-colored veil fell to the middle of my back and on my feet were satin ballet slippers. I should have been happy, but photos from that day show a red-faced, scared, and deeply conflicted woman.

I knew that I was broken. I could deny it all I wanted, but my past had created indelible scars on my psyche. I had been making impulsive, terrible choices for years. Why did I think this wasn't another one? Peter had once again become my best friend. I trusted him implicitly to always tell me the truth, even if I didn't want to hear it. I called him the night before the wedding, and we talked for a long time. I didn't come right out and ask him, but I had hoped that he would tell me not to go through with it. If he had, I would have listened. I trusted him more than I trusted myself. But he didn't and here I was.

The guests were seated. The music started, and I was frozen in place. Someone peeked in the room and said, "It's time." I snapped out of it, grabbed a tissue, and dried my tears. It was too late to back out now. I chided myself for being selfish and irresponsible. *It's a little late for doubts now. What the hell is wrong with you? The money is spent. Everyone is here and waiting. Stop acting like a child.*

The day is a blur. I couldn't tell you what songs were played, what words were exchanged, or what we ate at the reception at Mom and Dad's house. I felt trapped. Looking back, I now realize the trap was of my own making and I have no one to blame except myself. Up to that point, I'd spent the majority of my life making stupid, irresponsible, and avoidable mistakes, and this marriage was another for the list.

After we were married, Mo and I got an apartment together. I looked forward to starting an adult life and leaving behind the impulsive and irresponsible person I had been. Two weeks later, I came home from work and grabbed the mail on the way up to our apartment. "Hi," I said, "How was your day? Did you sleep well?" I asked.

"What the fuck is this?" Mo yelled as he snatched the mail out of my hand and shook it in my face.

"It's the mail. What do you mean?" I was confused. Why was he so angry?

"Who do you think you are getting the mail? If the mail needs to be collected, I'll do it," he yelled as he turned and walked away.

I stood there, speechless. Mo had never yelled at me before. What kind of masculine bullshit was this about for checking the mail? I would figure out later that this was the real Mo that he had hidden from me and waited until we were married to show. A few days later things got even more weird.

"We need to go down to Detroit and fill out some paperwork," Mo said casually during dinner.

"For what?"

"It's just some silly paperwork the Lebanese embassy requires because I've married an American," he said as he shoved a piece of pita bread and hummus into his mouth. I had never been through anything like this, so I trusted that he knew what we needed to do.

We went to the Lebanese consulate in Detroit the next day. I didn't even understand why I had to go. Couldn't he take the marriage certificate to them himself and fill out whatever paperwork was necessary? This is when I found out he was an illegal alien. Mo had been given a student visa to come to the United States for college, but never went home or reapplied to stay. He had been in this country illegally for more than eight years.

Now that we were married, he was granted a green card. If we stayed married for three years, then he could apply for citizenship. *Did he marry me just for the green card?* I began to wonder if I was nothing more than a pawn in his immigration game. Anger and confusion fought one another in my mind for days while I considered my options. I wanted desperately not to feel like a failure, like the girl who was constantly making stupid decisions. I thought back to the doubts I'd had just before the wedding. *Maybe I should have walked away. Maybe I knew all along that something didn't feel right.* I pushed the thoughts aside. I wasn't going to be like my mother and father who treated marriage like a passing hobby. My marriage was going to last—no matter what. What's done is done, I told myself, time to move forward.

Over the next few months life settled into a routine. Mo continued to complain any time I would assert independence. I tried my best to become the quiet, timid wife that he wanted. I never imagined myself being that type of person, but I didn't see any alternative. I was married, and for the sake of peace I was willing to try to be the woman that he wanted me to be. I was reverting back to the defense mechanisms of my childhood. When it came to my father and stepfather, I had always shut my mouth and put my head down to try to maintain peace in the house. When things got tough, I got quiet. Making a marriage work is one thing, but trying to make yourself invisible for the sake of the marriage is something entirely different. No one should have to live like that.

One day Mo and his brother, Fadi, approached me with the bright idea that we should all move in together. Mo and his brother were very close and relied on each other since they only had each other in the United States. Fadi had held on to his strict Muslim views and had no intention of marrying an American woman. I never knew him to date or go out and do things with anyone other than Mo. Fadi had always been nice to me, so when he said he found a great house for us all to live in I kept an open mind. A few days later Fadi took us to view a large duplex about three miles from our apartment. It was set up almost like two apartments with a shared kitchen. The upstairs had two bedrooms and the downstairs had one. There was a large backyard and a big deck off the kitchen. The house was spacious and beautiful, and it seemed feasible that we would all have our own space, so I agreed. Mo and I took the downstairs and Fadi took the upstairs.

I regretted the decision to move in together almost immediately. Not only did I have a husband that was unkind to me, but Fadi had no problem joining in. The two of them often ganged up on me yelling and complaining. Sometimes I felt like I had two husbands. It began small, with Fadi interjecting himself in conversations between Mo and I. Then it moved on to Fadi asking Mo, in front of me, if he was going to let me say or do certain things. Within a couple months it had moved on to Fadi directly telling me what to do.

They told me that I couldn't go out with my friends, drink alcohol, make a long-distance call to my mom or Carol, or go back to school. My world became isolated as my only interactions were with Mo and Fadi. I received a welcome respite when the two of them decided to go to Lebanon for a month to visit family. I was lucky enough to stay home because Mo and I couldn't afford the trip, and since Mo hadn't seen his parents in so many years, Fadi paid for Mo's travel expenses.

Prior to Mo leaving our marital intimacy had become strained. As controlling as he was in every aspect of my life, Mo never tried to force sex on me. We were quickly becoming two people who lived together but interacted as little as possible, which reaffirmed my fear that he married me only for a green card. During the month that he and Fadi were gone,

I realized that I had no one to spend time with. I had become distanced from all my friends, and without Mo I was completely alone. However, as so frequently happens in abusive relationships, it becomes easy to forget the bad stuff when you are away from your abuser for even a short period of time. By the time Mo came back from Lebanon, I was happy to see him.

Within weeks of their return, I began to feel tired and sick. I was hungry but couldn't eat without vomiting. Even the smell of coffee made me want to throw up. No matter how much I slept, I was always exhausted. I also noticed that I was short of breath and having chest pains regularly. A visit to the doctor cleared up the mystery. I was pregnant. It was very early; I hadn't even missed my period yet.

The pregnancy was not planned. I didn't think I even wanted kids. Regardless of the circumstances, there was a baby growing inside me and I knew that I could never abort it. It was time to wrap my brain around what was happening.

I told Mo and Fadi but neither said much. I called my mom and dad, and they couldn't have been more excited about the news. After I hung up the phone, I sat on my bed and thought about how lucky I was to have parents that loved me, supported me, and would do the same for this child. It didn't matter that they weren't my biological parents. They were the only people I would ever call Mom and Dad again. I also called Carol and her husband, Ryan. They had been in my life since I was a child and had grown to be like second parents to me. They were equally as excited at the prospect of a grandchild. My thoughts were broken suddenly by Mo walking into the room.

"Can we talk?" Mo asked gently. I couldn't get a read on his facial expression. It was unusually soft. It was like he was measuring every step, every word, every thought.

"Sure, what's up?"

He sat down on the edge of the bed. "We need to talk about this . . . this pregnancy," he began hesitantly. "My brother and I talked . . . and . . . well, we think it would be best for you to get an abortion."

I couldn't respond. I sat there silently as tears began to roll down my cheeks. He continued talking.

"It's just that in our culture it's customary for the oldest brother to get married and have kids first." He hesitated. Was he waiting for me to offer encouragement?

"Well, we already messed that up for him by getting married first. We really shouldn't have kids first too. It's not fair to him."

Mo sat stoically, his eyes pleading with me, waiting for some type of response. Suddenly, I snapped.

"You've lost your fucking mind!" I screamed. This was the last straw. I had put up with so much from the two of them and now I was expected to abort my child? I reached for the phone and called my mom back. Through my tears I pleaded with her to come and pick me up. I told her that he wanted me to get an abortion. My mom and dad were strict Catholics. I knew that she would help me.

Mo realized that his ticket to citizenship was about to run out and he began to apologize profusely. He begged me to hang up the phone and said that we would work it out. Finally, I told my mom that I was OK and that I would call her tomorrow. The word "abortion" was never mentioned in my presence again, but Fadi grew more hostile and angrier with each passing day. Fadi and Mo moved all our stuff to the two bedrooms upstairs, which didn't go over well with Fadi either.

My pregnancy was a difficult one. The reason I had experienced so many problems early on was because of a genetic heart condition. While my body was able to support me fairly well, it was unable to keep up with the added stress of a baby. On top of the heart and breathing problems, I suffered from abnormal bleeding. My doctor suggested restrictions only a few months into my pregnancy.

Besides the argument about whether or not to have an abortion, Mo and I were also having daily arguments about what to name the baby. I had agreed to give the baby a Lebanese name, but I still wanted whatever we chose to have an American spin on it. I was looking for a way to combine Lebanese and American heritage. We finally came to an agreement: Hala if it was a girl and Tariq, spelled Tarec, if a boy. The problem came when we discussed the middle name. I don't know if it's a cultural or religious practice, but Mo told me that regardless of the gender of the baby, that the middle name would be his—Mohamad. I was adamant that I would not name my daughter Hala Mohamad. She was going to be born and raised in the United States and should be named accordingly. Maybe that was wrong of me, but it felt hypocritical for him to have demanded an abortion and then expect that child to be named after him. I can't explain how I knew, but I began to *feel* confident that I was having a boy. I tried my best to let the subject go, knowing in my heart that it was a boy, and that arguing about its name was pointless. It was all for nothing as my son would be adopted by my future husband, Neil, and legally change his name to Tyler Dennis when he turned eighteen, severing the last remaining tie to his biological father.

Around the fifth month an ultrasound revealed that I was indeed having a boy. It was the first time my husband seemed to show any excitement or interest in my pregnancy. The first boy born into a Muslim family is a big deal and he couldn't help but be proud that it was *his* son that was to be first. It was also around this time that I started to panic about having a baby. Some people say that you will be the same type of parent as your parents. Nothing scared me more than the idea that I could turn out like my biological parents. I was determined to make sure that didn't happen. I knew that if I told Mo about my concerns, he would see it as an excuse to bring up abortion again, so I kept them to myself.

I couldn't work during my pregnancy, so my days were spent home alone while Mo and Fadi went to work. After talking to my doctor about my concerns, I was given the name of a therapist who would come to the house during the day to meet with me. We talked about my childhood and some of the awful things I'd been through. We talked about what it was going to be like to have a baby and methods to remain calm when I would be tired and frustrated. I didn't need Mo's help. I was going to do whatever I had to for me to become a good mom.

For me, childhood was always a roller-coaster ride. I rode the highs with a smile and braced myself for the downhills and many sharp curves. My stepfather was an abusive alcoholic, and my mother was an insecure woman whose main priority in life was keeping her man happy—even at the expense of her children. Adding to the tension in the house was the fact that we were poor. To say that we lived paycheck to paycheck would be generous.

There was always a struggle for food—not only from a lack of it, but also because my older brother somehow managed to become overweight. Obesity ran in our family, so it wasn't surprising that he overate, but trying to finish my food fast enough to keep him from eating it off my plate was nearly impossible.

We almost never ate out. If we did it was because our aunt and uncle or our maternal grandparents took us. We were not allowed to snack between meals or eat anything without asking first. All food was purchased for a specific reason and eating something without permission could lead to being an ingredient short for an upcoming dinner. Even getting caught with a glass of milk between meals could lead to punishment. Sneaking into the house and chugging milk straight from the gallon was all too common for me. It was a way of satiating my hunger while getting around my parents' questioning a dirty glass in the sink. If you didn't like what was for dinner, then you went hungry, which I often did. Dinners were cheap and boring—lots of Banquet frozen meals, boxed scalloped potatoes with kielbasa, or sometimes fried bologna sandwiches and chips.

Everyone's favorite dinner was when my mother would make homemade pepperoni pizza. There was just something about having pizza. We couldn't afford it often, so for a moment we were just like everyone else, indulging in what we saw as the finer things. We never had seafood, nor was there much meat served in our house. During the school year I was sent to school without a packed lunch or money for lunch. I always hated lunchtime at school. Watching everyone eating and coming up with excuses for why I wasn't hungry was an ongoing challenge. For years my friends thought I was anorexic. It was better to let them think that then to admit we were too poor to afford lunch.

The story of my parent's relationship is a mystery to me, but I do know that they separated long before I was old enough to remember anything. My father was my mother's second attempt at marriage, having already divorced my older brother's father. My earliest memories, at age four, included my stepfather. As I got older and began to ask questions about my father, it was made clear to me that the topic was off-limits. My mother would simply tell me that he was a "piece of shit," "abusive," or that he was a "drug-dealing asshole." Beyond that, I knew nothing of my father or their short-lived marriage. I don't know if I ever saw my father when I was growing up. If I did, I don't remember it. His absence would lead to me mythologizing about the man my father was. I built him up in my head to be the greatest man that ever lived. I just knew that he was a wonderful, compassionate man and that my mother had hatched a nefarious plot to keep us apart. Someday, I thought, he would rescue me from the hell that I was living in.

My mother gave birth to my younger half-brother when I was six and that's when everything changed. My stepfather had his own son now and my older brother and I were just extraneous burdens.

As the years progressed the treatment of my older brother and I became increasingly harsh. My stepfather hit us often, grounded us regularly, and yelled at us daily. My younger brother, on the other hand, got away with everything. This is not to say that my older brother and I never did anything wrong, but the punishment never matched the crime.

When I was around seven or eight, I got caught smoking a cigarette. We were living in an apartment complex at the time and a neighbor said she had some cigarette butts and asked if I wanted to try smoking them with her. We went to the farthest corner behind the building (not exactly a good hiding spot) and sat on the ground. It was a hot summer day. Frogs in the small, dirty pond behind the building croaked as we lit up a cigarette butt. We had each taken one puff and were coughing loudly when my mother walked outside and caught us.

"What in the fuck do you think you're doing?" my mother screamed at me. I didn't answer. If I could have stopped coughing, I probably would have stopped breathing out of fear. I was in big trouble. My mother stormed over, jerked me off the ground, and dragged me into the house.

I sat on my bed reading a book until my stepfather came home. I could hear my mother telling him what I had done. Then, I heard the heavy thud of angry footsteps coming down the hall toward my bedroom. Fear gripped my tiny body and tears began to fall down my cheeks as I waited for what was to come. My stepfather was already removing his belt as he entered my room.

"Stand up and pull your pants down," he said. I slowly scooched to the edge of the bed and hesitantly stood up. Crying, I turned and pulled my shorts down. After the beating, which left me in pain for days, he dragged me into the living room and told me to sit on the couch.

"You wanna smoke? Then you'll smoke till you hate it," my stepfather said. He handed me a pack of Kool menthol cigarettes and a lighter and demanded that I smoke them until they were gone. I coughed nonstop with each puff and wondered why anyone would enjoy smoking. As usual, my mother stood by silently. Afterward, I was grounded to my room for a week. My resentment boiled over. They both smoked cigarettes and marijuana in the house so it seemed hypocritical for them to be so angry at me for trying it.

As a parent, reexamining this situation, I could never imagine hitting my son with a belt or forcing him to smoke a whole pack of cigarettes. My anger toward them over the incident has lessened over the years, but it certainly hasn't dissipated completely. I don't believe it ever will.

My mother wanted no contact with me after she dropped me off at my father's house when I was eleven—at least that's what my father told me. The first few weeks with him were great. Finally getting to know my father and living in a beautiful house was more than I had hoped for. He looked so young to me, which made sense when I learned later that he was only fifteen when I was born. He looked like every other member of my family: average height and overweight. He had short brown hair, a bushy mustache, and thin lips that gave him a stern appearance. What struck me most was his blue eyes that looked just like mine. My mother had brown eyes and I always wondered how I ended up with blue eyes. Now I knew.

My father and I had the same mysterious blue eyes that changed color with our mood or surroundings. Sometimes they were cornflower blue, sometimes aqua blue, and sometimes grayish blue.

I didn't know exactly how my father paid for the beautiful house he lived in, but he worked as a large-machine repairman in industrial plants. Whatever it was, he was some sort of specialist in his field, which seemed odd to me because he never went to college. I had no idea what type of salary he earned, so I didn't know if his legitimate work paid for his lifestyle or if his illegitimate work did. My father wasn't rich, but what was immediately clear was that he was not strapped for cash the way my mother and stepfather were. One of the biggest surprises for me was all the food that was in the house. I was allowed to eat as much as I wanted whenever I wanted it. Being allowed to snack between meals and not asking for permission to eat something was shocking to me. My father ate a bowl of cereal nearly every night before bed. It became my favorite indulgence too. To this day, I love cereal and often eat it for dinner.

Initially, my father was so nice to me, and I was excited that he had a live-in girlfriend, Diana, who was nine months pregnant. I would have a baby sister soon. I learned that I also had a younger half-sister and half-brother that I never knew existed. Lastly, I was introduced to my paternal grandparents, my paternal aunt, and her three sons. I had a whole family I didn't even know about.

My paternal grandparents lived only about five miles away from my father's house, so I got to see them frequently. My grandfather and I became especially close. He was a kind and gentle man whose life fascinated me. He had fought in World War II, retired from General Motors, built his home with his own hands, tended an enormous vegetable garden in his backyard, took great pride in his extraordinary rose garden, baked homemade pies with pumpkins from his garden, and spent hours a day crocheting blankets. I found him to be a man with a unique combination of strength and softness.

It didn't take long before life in my father's house began to abruptly change for the worse. I noticed that there was a constant flow of visitors: the lesbian couple in their forties who always had smiles on their faces, the middle-aged white guy in dirty work clothes, the twenty-something Hispanic guy that showed up late at night. I didn't understand the constant parade of visitors that came to the house at all hours of the day and night, but eventually it became clear that they were there to buy drugs from my father. I would come to learn that my father dabbled in various drugs—cocaine, mushrooms, and LSD—but the main drug that he both used and sold was marijuana. My biggest irritation was that my bedroom was next to the living room, and I was constantly interrupted from sleep and reading by the overly gregarious laughter of guests. I didn't get the impression that my father would be too keen on being lectured about drugs by his young daughter, so I endured it all silently.

As he relaxed with my continued presence, he and his friends began to smoke marijuana and ingest various pills in front of me. I would watch as large, black garbage bags full of marijuana were carried into the house, weighed, divided, and placed into sandwich bags. The open use and sale of drugs became such routine that I began to forget it was unusual. I realized that my father was not the man that I had spent years building up in my head. He was not kind, wonderful, or compassionate. Behind those blue eyes was a monster whose moods changed as quickly and frequently as their shade.

As I settled into my new life, my father gave me a list of chores that had to be done daily. The list became longer and longer as the days passed. It felt like I was the maid brought in to serve them. Worse yet, the punishment for failing to complete those chores perfectly became physical: fists, belts, wall hangings, or anything within arm's reach. Failure didn't necessarily mean not doing the chores; it could be as simple as missing a small spot when cleaning the microwave, forgetting to line up the shoes by the door, not having the dishes done quickly enough, or forgetting to replace the toilet paper roll.

After Diana gave birth to my baby sister, Amber, life took another turn for the worse. Now that Diana was no longer pregnant, she was also a target of my father's abuse. Rather than suffer abuse from just my father, I was now subject to beatings from both of them as Diana took her anger and frustration out on me.

Each remaining day of my pregnancy seemed to blend in with the next. My relationship with Mo was strained at best. While the revelation that we were having a boy had softened his heart a bit, he still remained relatively aloof. My relationship with Fadi was hostile on good days and insufferable on others. He rarely spoke to me, and we were never in the same room for more than a passing moment. Mo had switched jobs during my pregnancy and now worked most evenings, so I was left home alone doing my best to stay out of Fadi's way. When Mo wasn't working, he and Fadi often went shopping, to the movies, or swimming together leaving me home alone.

During the sixth month, I went into premature labor. The doctors were able to stop the labor, but I continued to dilate. If I needed help getting into and out of the tub or off the couch, then I could usually count on Mo to help. But between him working and going out with his brother, I was mostly on my own. Even though I was supposed to be on bed rest, I still kept up with day-to-day household duties, grocery shopping, and cleaning the best I could. I reminded myself every day that nothing else was important as long as my baby was OK. My son was all that mattered. After having contractions and dilating for three months, my late July due date came and went. *Had the doctors stopped the labor too well?* By this time I just wanted to have the baby.

On Friday, August 2, 1996, I went to the doctor who said I was dilated to five and that I should spend the weekend doing things to get labor going, such as walking and having sex. I was enormous. My fingers were so swollen that I couldn't wear my wedding ring and only one pair of sandals would fit my inflated feet. The last thing I wanted to do was walk or have sex, but I was willing to do nearly anything to have this baby.

The tension between Fadi and I had continued to escalate over the months. By this time he wasn't speaking to me at all. I ate dinner alone and kept myself secluded to my bedroom to avoid arguments. Getting away from him and relaxing for a couple days was exactly what I needed. I decided to spend the weekend at my mom and dad's house. Mom and I walked around the neighborhood as much as I could handle, and I floated in an inflatable tube on the lake to stay cool. Even while contractions came and went throughout the weekend, it was still a much needed mentally relaxing and stress-free weekend. I went home Sunday night, physically exhausted, and went to bed around 10:00 p.m.

I tossed and turned endlessly. Not quite asleep, but not quite awake, my brain floated in the space somewhere in between. It felt like I was standing outside my body watching everything that was happening around me. I saw myself sitting in the corner of the kitchen, on the floor crying, hand over my mouth, trying to muffle my heaving sobs in an effort not to wake up anyone else in the house. Scared and alone, I had never felt so much pain. There was no doubt that I was in full-blown labor. How had I ended up in a marriage that was so bad that I couldn't wake up my husband when I felt like I was dying? I hated myself for bringing a child into the world in these circumstances. I don't know how long I sat on the kitchen floor crying, but eventually Fadi woke up for work and found me in the kitchen. Even through his hatred he could see that I was in bad shape. He ran into my bedroom and woke his brother up.

A short time later I found myself in a room that was brightly lit with bare white walls. There was a bed near the door, an armchair, and a small coffee table next to it in the far corner. The room wasn't warm, yet I could feel sweat pouring off my forehead. There was an overwhelming odor of disinfectant, incessant beeping from machines attached to my body, muffled swooshing sounds like whales heard through sonar, reassuring words spoken in hushed voices, and screams coming from deep inside me as I lay in the hospital bed.

I could swear there was a giant in the room, and he was ripping my body in half by my legs. There were so many people coming in and out that it was impossible to keep track of who and what they were there for. After eight long hours, the doctor proclaimed, "It's time." Suddenly, the chaos that surrounded me ended. Everyone became quiet. Focused. The moments seemed to move in slow motion. I felt my skin begin to shred apart.

Mom and Dad had arrived at the hospital, as well as Ryan, Carol, and her daughter, Taylor. I may not have had a great biological family, but these people had come to be all the family my son and I would ever need. While it was true that my son would never know my biological mother and my father, I knew that he would have grandmas, grandpas, aunts, uncles, and cousins that would love him even more.

That night, when everyone had left the hospital, I sat in my room staring at my newborn son. I had just finished breastfeeding, and the room was silent. The only light came from a small fixture from across the room. I was amazed at how beautiful he was. I couldn't believe that I, someone so broken and damaged, had created this perfect little baby. I knew that my life would never be the same again. In that quiet moment I made a vow to my son, Tarec. I gently stroked his face as he slept in my arms and I whispered, "I promise to be a good mom to you. I promise that I will always do my best to take care of you and give you a good life. I promise that I will only let people into your life that will love and protect you."

Life at home after my son was born went from bad to worse. Unfortunately, the first six months of his life was difficult. He didn't sleep regularly, and he wanted to be held all the time. When I put him down, he cried incessantly until I picked him back up. It was frustrating, and I blamed myself. I had no idea how to be a mom, but I was doing the best I could.

Fadi and Mo hated when my son would cry—especially in the middle of the night. They both yelled and complained at me constantly to "shut that kid up." I tried, but sometimes there was nothing that would make him stop.

The relationship, what was left of it, between my husband and I fell apart. Mo and Fadi ate dinner together every night and excluded me. I was not allowed to sit with them, nor would they cook enough food for me.

If I walked into the kitchen while they were eating, they would stop talking. I no longer felt just alone, I felt unwanted. To make matters worse, I was breastfeeding my son and he refused to take a bottle, so Mo would not allow me to leave the house without taking my son with me. Neither Mo nor his brother helped take care of him. My frustration level, along with exhaustion, had reached its peak.

I realized that my marriage was over, and yet, I was trapped. Mo had made it clear to me prior to getting married that no one in his family had ever been divorced and neither would he. At the time, it made me happy because I didn't want to be like my mother and cycle through marriages like most people change their socks. I wanted a marriage like the one the people I now called Mom and Dad had. I wanted my marriage to last forever. Unfortunately, I didn't know what kind of marriage I got myself into and now realized that more than ever there was no way out. I had a child, no friends, nowhere to go, no job, and no money. I focused on my son and did my best to tolerate the situation. Some days were harder than others—especially as an exhausted new mom.

One afternoon when Tarec was about two months old, I reached a breaking point. It was a sunny fall day and I found Mo sitting on the back deck talking with his brother. I felt like I was going to collapse if I didn't take a nap. Exhaustion overtook my common sense, and I walked outside.

"Mo, please, can you take care of the baby so I can lie down for a bit? I'm so tired," I begged.

"Get away from me. This is not what I signed up for."

"Are you kidding me? He's your son too!"

"You wanted him; not me," he replied as he stood up and walked by me.

"If you keep treating me like this I'm going to leave!"

Mo stopped suddenly, turned around, and glared at me. I'd never seen this look before. It was filled with more rage than I had ever seen. He said slowly and methodically, "Where the fuck do you think you're going? You have no job, no money, and a baby. You're stuck here. Shut up and deal with it." With that he turned back around and walked downstairs to his brother's first floor living area. Fadi said nothing but stood up and followed him.

I had been through a great deal in my life, and I knew that I could handle whatever abuse they dished out. That is, until the abuse affected my son. I didn't care what Mo said or thought, I would never be trapped anywhere that endangered my son.

When my son was only a few months old three incidents occurred that changed everything. The first took place one night around 3:00 a.m. Tarec wouldn't go to sleep, and he had been crying for at least an hour. I had tried everything, but nothing seemed to help. In an attempt to quiet him, I walked around the living room bouncing him in my arms. Fadi walked upstairs to the second floor living room screaming at me to make him stop crying. Not only was I frustrated at feeling like a failure for not being able to soothe my son, but I was exhausted. The thin line that was the last of my patience snapped.

"I'm doing the best I can. Take your ass back downstairs and leave me alone," I said through gritted teeth. Fadi suddenly grabbed me by the shoulders and threw me against the living room wall.

"Shut that kid up or I'll do it myself," he screamed in my face. I was too stunned to feel any pain or react to the sudden aggression. I wasn't surprised that Fadi would throw me around, but that he would do it with Tarec in my arms. Although they didn't help take care of him, he was still seen as the "golden child" because he was the first boy. The sound of my body slamming against the wall woke Mo, who got up and came into the living room to see what was going on. I told him that his brother had just thrown me against the wall with our son in my arms. Mo said nothing. He turned around and went back to bed. Fadi glared at me for another moment—knowing he had won—and walked back downstairs.

I held my crying son and cried along with him. I cried for Tarec—that I had given him such a terrible father. I cried for myself—that I had made such terrible decisions that had led me to another abusive relationship. The choices I had made, the choices I hadn't made, and the unknown future that lay ahead for both of us—I cried for them all.

The second incident occurred shortly after. It was early evening and Tarec was crying. I placed him in a bouncy chair on the living room floor and was trying to play with him. Nothing helped, and the crying continued. Mo had been downstairs watching television with his brother. He came upstairs and started screaming at me for not being able to make Tarec stop crying. I stood up and yelled back. I was a new mom who was getting zero help and almost no sleep. My threshold for bullshit was low and it didn't take much for me to snap.

Mo grabbed a throw pillow off the couch and threw it at me as he turned to walk back downstairs. I didn't realize it, but by moving out of the way the pillow flew straight toward Tarec and hit him in his bouncy seat. Yes, it was just a pillow, but I was incensed. I couldn't believe that he was now throwing things in the vicinity of our son. What was going to be next?

The last straw came about a week later. Once again it was evening, Tarec was crying, and I couldn't get him to stop. Fadi stormed upstairs screaming. I met him at the top of the stairs, bouncing my son in my right arm. I looked Fadi straight in the eyes and said, "Go back downstairs. I'm done listening to your bitching. If you think you can do better, feel free to try. Otherwise, go away." In a flash, Fadi grabbed me by the left arm and jerked me toward him, throwing me down the stairs. As I stumbled and tripped down the stairs, I realized that I had to protect my son. I covered his head and body with both of my arms, leaving myself completely exposed. I felt my body bounce off the walls as my feet flailed below me, unable to find footing on the carpeted steps as I continued to tumble down. A million thoughts rushed through my mind at once. *Tarec's head is still soft and can easily be crushed. How will I explain this to a hospital doctor? How will I take care of Tarec if I break my leg? What if Fadi kills me? What kind of life will Tarec have with Mo?* Finally, I hit the floor of the stair landing. One of my legs curled awkwardly under by body and the other leg stretched out in front of me, my head smashed into the corner between the wall and the front door. I felt pain shooting through various parts of my body, but I could only think about my son. I immediately began checking my crying baby for injury and was relieved to find him unharmed.

That was the day I knew that I was leaving. I didn't know how or when, but I knew that my marriage was over. It was one thing to hurt me, it was quite another to hurt Tarec. Even if they managed not to hurt my son, I didn't want him growing up thinking it was acceptable to abuse women. I'll never know for sure if Mo began to suspect that I wanted to leave or not, but it was around this time that he suggested a family trip to Lebanon. Mo had threatened in the past that he would take Tarec away from me and send him to Lebanon, so I knew that if I took Tarec there that he would never come home with me. The clock was ticking. I had to get out.

I finally told Mom and Dad what was happening, and they were devastated. Mom told me that they would do whatever was necessary to get me out of that house. I was ashamed that I had put off telling them how awful things were. I knew that if it was just me, I would have stayed and endured whatever came. However, I refused to allow Tarec to be taken away from me or to grow up in this environment and someday end up treating another woman the way that I was being treated. I had to break the cycle.

It took several months for me to get things lined up to be able to leave. During those months I had limited contact with Mo and Fadi. It was as if we were strangers—roommates at best. Mo and Fadi went to work, and I made calls to find an apartment, a job, and a daycare provider.

At the same time, Mo was planning our family trip to Lebanon. He had gotten passports for Tarec and me and was finalizing travel arrangements. I knew in my heart that my son would never come back from Lebanon if we went. The whole trip felt like a ruse to steal him. When Mo and Fadi came home from work they would eat dinner together and spend the rest of the evening downstairs watching television. I stayed upstairs and took care of Tarec. By this time, Tarec had gotten through his constant crying phase, so on rare occasions Mo and Fadi took him downstairs to play with him or would spend time with him on the deck outside.

When Tarec was eleven months old, the day before the airline tickets to Lebanon were to be purchased, we moved out. Mo and Fadi left to go to work in the morning and within minutes Mom, Dad, Carol, and Ryan came to Lansing to move me and my son to our new apartment. Mo knew nothing about us moving out; nevertheless, I was scared to death the whole time. I couldn't get out fast enough. I took only what was absolutely necessary: clothes and personal items, a couch, a chair, a bed, television, and all of Tarec's belongings. Everything else I left behind and Mom took me shopping to replace all the necessities: towels, dishes, silverware, garbage can, food, and more. I thought about leaving a note but decided that Mo didn't deserve one. He knew why I had left. Instead, I left the house key on the first stair just inside the front door. The trip to Lebanon that had been so important for him was cancelled after I left.

Mom and Dad hired a divorce attorney before I moved out. The personal protection order my attorney secured blacked out our new address and went into effect the day we left. I didn't have to worry that Mo would find us in our new apartment, which brought a feeling of safety that I hadn't had in a long time. That night I put Tarec to bed and sat down in the living room, looked around my new apartment, and softly cried. Those tears comprised a myriad of emotions: relief, disappointment, failure, sadness, hope. I had wanted to be a responsible adult and deal with my problems alone. I felt horrible that, once again, I had to resort to asking for help to fix a situation I had gotten myself into. But mostly, I thought about what would have happened to me, and where I would have ended up, without Mom, Dad, Carol, and Ryan.

The days, months, and years to come would prove that Mo had married me only for a green card. Every time my divorce attorney would come to some type of agreement with Mo, he would then claim to change his mind and force negotiations to start over. He fought the divorce long enough to show that we were married for three years so that he could gain his US citizenship. No matter how I tried, I was unable to stop it.

4

L.A.C.S.T.A.B.

After leaving my husband when I was twenty-three, I found myself separated, unemployed, living in East Lansing, and the mother of a one-year-old little boy. I had to figure out my next steps quickly. I found an office job working as an assistant, as well as good daycare for Tarec. Although my life had changed dramatically, I was happy. Tarec was too young to really know what was going on and I was grateful for that. Now he had little kids to socialize with and I was back to work and supporting us, by myself. I loved that Mom and Dad had done so much for us, but I hated having to take money from them to survive.

I moved into a government-subsidized, low-income, two-bedroom townhouse. The rent was cheap, and I couldn't have been happier to have so much space for my son and me. The basement had a washer and dryer, which was helpful with a messy toddler who went through several outfits a day. The second floor had a large kitchen with an eat-in dining area, a half bathroom, and living room. The upstairs had a full bathroom and our bedrooms. Outside we had a patio area and across the parking lot was a playground. It was perfect for the two of us.

After realizing that I would not be able to stop my soon-to-be ex-husband from getting citizenship, I decided to make peace with him for the sake of Tarec. I didn't want our son to grow up in the tumultuous setting that I had—wondering about his dad and mythologizing him as a great man the way I had with my father. I was generous with visitation and let Tarec call Mo every night.

It seemed to work for a while. Mo and I would meet for dinner occasionally so that he could spend time with Tarec. Eventually, I let Mo come to my house to pick him up. I even gave Mo a key to the house in case Tarec needed anything while in his father's care while I was at work.

Everything seemed to be improving and I thought maybe we had turned a corner. But, as I should have expected, it fell apart.

Mo decided that he wanted to stop divorce proceedings and give our marriage another try. I said no. It had been hard enough to leave and start my life over the first time. I wasn't going to risk being forced to do it again. Mo didn't take the news well.

Not long after turning down Mo's request to get back together, I picked up Tarec from daycare after work and drove home. At first, I didn't notice anything unusual in the house. As I began to clean and put the laundry away, I noticed a few things missing. Soon, I realized that there were many items missing.

I had locked the doors when I left that morning, and it was clear that no one had broken in. The only other person who had a key to my house was Mo. I was instantly furious and decided to call him and demand my property back.

"What the hell is wrong with you?" I screamed into the phone.

"What? What are you talking about?" he said innocently, which just infuriated me even more.

"You broke into my house and stole my things? Why would you do that?"

"I bought those things. Technically, they're mine. I was just retrieving my property," he calmly replied.

"Are you kidding me? What the hell do you need my roller skates for? You certainly can't use them. And my leather jacket? Are you suddenly a size small?"

I was growing more enraged as I listed off my stolen items.

"My photo albums? Do you really need all the photos of when I was pregnant? You didn't leave me a single photo! It was my pregnancy—my body to remember not yours. And all of Tarec's baby pictures? I don't get a single photo from the first year of his life? What kind of person are you?"

Mo didn't reply. He didn't say a word. I couldn't control my escalating anger. Soon, my emotions hit a point where anger turned to sadness, and I began to cry.

"I have been trying so hard to make peace with you. I let you see our son whenever you want. I gave you a key to my house to make things easier for you in case he needs something. You haven't paid a dime in child support. What else do you want from me?" I said.

I felt helpless. I hated that feeling and I hated him for making me feel that way. It wasn't about what he had stolen—it was about control. He took things that he had no use for and would piss me off. It worked.

I knew that calling the police would cause another rift in the relationship, but at that point, I didn't care. I called the police and said I wanted to report a burglary. Officer Jason Spano arrived at my house a short time later. I told Officer Spano what happened, and he gently broke the news to me. Unfortunately, Mo and I were still technically married, and all my property was his as well. I was angry, frustrated, and sad all at the same time. Officer Spano felt bad for me, so he told me to write a statement and he would see what he could do.

When I sat down to write my statement and looked up, Officer Spano was playing cars with Tarec on the floor. My heart melted. After I finished my statement, he continued to play with my son as we chatted. I couldn't help thinking how odd, yet sweet, it was that he was spending so much time at my house and playing with Tarec.

The next day, Officer Spano called me and reiterated that he was sorry, but there was nothing he could do about the theft of my property. At the end of the conversation, he asked me if I would be interested in getting together sometime. "I'll be at the Silver Dollar on Saturday if you're interested in stopping by," I replied. The Silver Dollar was a local nightclub that my friends and I sometimes went to. I thought it was the perfect place for a first meeting—there would be no pressure with all my friends around.

Jason and I hit it off and began dating exclusively. We dated for two years before my divorce was finalized. Afterward, I began to think about what was next for me. What would I do with the rest of my life? How would I support my son? I realized that in some ways I was still thinking and seeing myself as a victim. Someone who life happened to, not someone who made life happen. I wasn't being the strong, take-control person that I wanted to be, and it was time for a change. With some encouragement from Jason, I decided the best way to do that was to follow my dreams of becoming a police officer. After all, cops don't get victimized . . . do they?

The first step I took toward working in law enforcement was getting a job as a police dispatcher with Ingham County Central Dispatch in Lansing. I should have loved being a dispatcher. The starting pay was more than any other job I ever had, and the benefits were amazing. I was able to go on unlimited police ride-alongs and gain valuable insight into the profession. Throughout the hiring process, I never concealed the fact that my ultimate goal was to be a police officer, which didn't seem to be a problem for anyone involved in the hiring process. However, that was not the case for the people in dispatch. During conversations with my new coworkers I didn't hide the fact that I wanted to be a police officer at some point. After word got around, a few supervisors got together and decided that since I wasn't planning on staying in dispatch long term there was no reason to waste their time training me at all the stations.

The first couple weeks of employment were spent in training. Dispatchers need to learn many basics, such as the phonetic alphabet, the "ten codes," and department call signs. The phonetic alphabet is used by officers and dispatchers to help eliminate possible confusion with letters. Instead of saying, "I need to run a White male, Allan Jefferies, 5-4-54," officers will say, "I need to run a White male, Allan, adam-lincoln-lincoln-adam-nora, last name Jefferies, john-edward-frank-frank-edward-robert-ida-edward-sam, 5-4-54." Without this clarification, Allan Jefferies could be mistaken for Allen Jeffreys, Alan Jeffries, or any number of other spelling variations.

Ten codes are numbered 1–100 and each stand for a different request or situation. While the phonetic alphabet has very little variations between departments, the ten codes have substantial variations. Examples of ten codes would be: a license plate check, 10-23; a lunch break, 10-7; a mentally unstable person, 10-96; acknowledge, 10-4. Call signs are the unit numbers that each officer is assigned, and they vary by patrol location. For example, Williamston PD was 1100 units meaning officers could be assigned 1110, 1112, 1113, and so on.

My first day in dispatch was a sensory overload. There was so much going on: phones ringing, people talking, radios squawking, machines beeping, sirens blaring. I wondered how anyone could concentrate. As the supervisor walked me through the room, I realized the process of police dispatching, as well as the setup of the room, was similar to an assembly line. The room was windowless and nondescript. The walls were plain and there were no decorations of any kind anywhere. It was all business.

The first stop in the "assembly line" was at the furthest end of the dispatch room where call takers answered emergency calls and entered the information into the computer. The information was retrieved by either the police or fire dispatcher who would then relay it to the officers or firefighters on the road. In this dispatch center there was a dispatcher for Lansing North, one for Lansing South, one for County Deputies, one for Lansing Fire, and one for County Fire. The last stop on the assembly line was with the LEIN dispatcher. It is here where my training began and where I would be doomed to remain indefinitely.

LEIN stands for Law Enforcement Information Network, the database where all the information an officer needs is kept. LEIN has in-state and out-of-state driving records, license plate records, criminal arrests and convictions, stolen property records, and more. In 1998, police officers didn't have computers in their patrol vehicles, so they called in to the LEIN dispatcher via the radio every time they wanted to run a check on someone. LEIN was a network that you worked alone, and if you were good at multitasking it was the easiest to master quickly.

Between my numerous ride-alongs and dispatcher training, I was already feeling comfortable with LEIN. I put my headphones on and waited for the radio to come to life. Within seconds of placing the headphones on, I heard the sound of an officer calling. Those calls would continue almost nonstop for the next eight hours.

The hardest part of the job was keeping all the requests in order. It wasn't uncommon for two officers to call one right after another or for several to call while I was already running information for someone else. I realized quickly how lucky I was to be a quick typist and have excellent multitasking skills.

I'm not sure if it was hatred of the job or frustration with the people and environment, but I began to dread going to work each day. I realized that officers would call me on the radio and request information to only later hear them clear the call without explanation from the dispatcher station that was behind me. Clearing the call was how an officer notified the dispatcher that they were done with their current call and available for the next one. I found myself unable to stop thinking about what happened on their call. *What did the person say when the officer was there? What was the resolution? Did anyone fight? Get arrested?* The unanswered questions haunted me.

It wasn't unusual for me to ask the officers over the radio to call me at the LEIN desk after they cleared. When they would call, I would ask eagerly, "What happened?" Sometimes, I just couldn't help myself. Many of the officers had gotten to know me through my frequent ride-alongs and would laugh at my excitement. The dispatchers were a different story. They were annoyed that I wanted details. "It's not your job to worry about what happens on the calls," a supervisor once admonished me. But the more ride-alongs I went on, the more my curiosity was peaked.

Going to work every day became a necessary chore between ride-alongs. I dreaded it and couldn't wait for each day to be over. Somehow, my coworkers viewed my disinterest in the job as a personal insult to them. I didn't like them, and they didn't like me. I did my job but kept to myself and made no friends. Unfortunately, this would not be the last time in my life this issue would rear its ugly head.

After less than a year as a dispatcher, I decided to go to the police academy. The Lansing Police Department told me they would sponsor me if I waited until the following year. Sponsorship meant a paycheck and benefits throughout the academy and a job upon graduation. As logical as the proposition seemed, I just couldn't wait. Call me impatient—call me stupid—but the idea of another year working in that miserable environment was more than I could imagine. I jumped in with both feet and took one of the biggest risks of my life. I quit my job. Everyone thought I had gone completely insane.

With the decision made, it was time to figure out how to support myself and my son. I took out student loans to pay for school, equipment, uniforms, rent, childcare, car payments, groceries, and bills. Putting myself into this kind of financial debt was difficult for me. I struggled with whether I was being egotistical or risking my son's best interest to satisfy my own selfish desires. But I knew, in the end, I was doing what was best for both of us. Continuing to live with a victim mindset, settling for the easiest path, being a bystander in my own life was not good for me. More importantly, it was not a good example to set for my son. If I wanted him to grow up to be a strong person, then I needed to show him what that looked like.

The police academy was slated to start in July 2000. I had a few months to prepare for the rigors that lay ahead. I wasn't exactly sure what to expect, but Jason had stressed that physical fitness, shooting proficiency, and running were important. I had always worked out and thought of myself as being in pretty good shape, but I had never been a runner. So I started running a couple miles every day. Sometimes I would put Tarec in a stroller and go for a run with him. Other times Jason would stay home with him while I got a good run in by myself.

One of the things that worried me the most was that I had never held a gun before, let alone shoot one. With Jason's help, I bought a gun and practiced shooting at least once a week. Jason knew of a range in the middle of the woods that didn't have a rangemaster, so we were able to take our time and practice from a variety of angles and distances. Jason was patient and taught me well. We even bought three-year-old Tarec goggles and earmuffs so that he could go to the range with us. Jason and I were engaged by this time, and we decided that my son needed to be familiar with guns if we were both going to be carrying them. Several times we took pumpkins with us to the range to demonstrate how much damage a gun could do. We set the pumpkins up, helped Tarec hold the gun, talked to him about how to aim it, and helped him pull the trigger. He was never holding or in control of the gun by himself. When the bullet hit the pumpkin and caused major damage, it clearly demonstrated, even to his young mind, that guns weren't toys and not to be played with. Over the years this training paid off a hundredfold. If Tarec saw a gun sitting on the table, he would run to me and say, "Mommy, there's a gun on the table." Never once did he pick it up. I completely understand that some people would be horrified by this, but I believe that curiosity is what makes kids pick up guns, so we took curiosity out of the equation. By the time July started, I felt like I was as ready as I was ever going to be.

The police academy that I attended was the Mid-Michigan Police Academy located on the Lansing Community College campus. Mid-Michigan Police Academy was known for being one of the toughest academies in the state. State laws mandate that police academy recruits receive 594 hours of training to graduate. Mid-Michigan far surpassed the minimum requirements by putting their recruits through well over 700 hours of training over sixteen weeks.

Jason had given me some information about what to expect, but it did nothing to calm my nerves. I woke up early on the first day of the academy, got Tarec ready, and dropped him off at preschool. Walking into the academy's classroom filled me with anxiety and excitement. Mostly it was fear of the unknown that was messing with my brain. Here I was. I made it. I was a recruit in the 67th Mid-Michigan Police Academy.

Jason warned me about morning uniform inspections, so I had perfectly ironed my uniform, shined my shoes, and put my hair in a neat bun. Looking around the room, I didn't recognize anyone, but quickly surmised that I was one of the oldest recruits there at twenty-seven-years-old. I breathed a small sigh of relief though when I realized I wasn't the only female recruit.

The room looked like a typical college classroom. There was a blackboard and several rows of long tables with four chairs at each. Two tables were positioned in each row with a space in between them for a walkway. On top of the desks were name cards seating us in alphabetical order. After a few minutes of milling around chit-chatting everyone took their seat and waited. "Who the fuck told you to sit down?" an unknown man in a police uniform bellowed from the doorway. Everyone jumped out of their seats and stood up. "Line up! Alphabetical order!" I had no idea who the man was, but it was clear from his demeanor that he was in charge.

One thing you learn quickly is that instructors don't talk—they yell—all the time. No one knew each other's names, so it took a minute to figure out who was supposed to be standing where. "Attention!" We all stood up straight with our arms to our sides. The instructor/police officer walked over to the first person in line and stood directly in front of him. The instructor looked him up and down and began shouting out everything that was wrong with his uniform. "Tie isn't straight. Spot on the left shoe. Drop and give me twenty-five pushups!"

The male recruit got down on the ground and began to do pushups. "What the fuck do the rest of you think you're doing? You're a team. Get the fuck on the ground with him!" Everyone stood there for a moment in stunned silence looking around at one another. "Now!" We all threw ourselves on the ground and did twenty-five pushups then stood back in line at attention as the instructor moved to the second person in line.

"Your name tag is crooked. Twenty-five pushups." We didn't need to be told again. We all immediately dropped to the ground and did twenty-five pushups as ordered. We were only on the second person and my arms were already feeling like Jell-O. I don't know how many pushups we did that morning, but it was a lot. My only saving grace was that I didn't personally cause us to do any pushups. It was going to be a long sixteen weeks and I was already doubting whether or not I would make it or not.

After our harsh pushup laden introduction to police academy inspections, we were told to sit. All of us walked back to our seats shaking and rubbing our sore arms. The instructor looked at us and shook his head, "L.A.C.S.T.A.B.," he yelled. I looked at him and then I looked around at the other recruits. The looks I got in return were as quizzical as my own. "Life is a crap sandwich, take a bite!" the instructor yelled. "This is only the beginning." L.A.C.S.T.A.B. became our academy mantra. Rarely did a day go by when it wasn't spoken by someone—recruit or instructor.

The instructor brought in several more police officers in different uniforms and introduced them to the class. It seemed that the instructors were all police officers from local departments: Lansing, East Lansing, Ingham County, Lansing Township, Meridian Township, and Michigan State Police.

After introductions were complete the instructor launched into our first lecture, which lasted several hours. About an hour into class one of the recruits dozed off and was unlucky enough for the instructor to see him. The instructor walked over to the recruit, bent down close to his face, and screamed, "Sleep on your own time." The recruit jumped out of his seat and fell on the floor. Twenty-five pushups.

After that session was over, we took a ten-minute break, and a different instructor came in and lectured until lunch. The lectures covered things like laws, the elements of a crime and how police officers establish them. My brain felt like it was smoking, my arms were still shaky, but thankfully, no one did anything to give us more pushups. I couldn't believe how much information had gone into just the first few hours. We were given a thirty-minute lunch break and most of the class went to a small campus eatery. We didn't have much time, so we ate quickly and headed to the training room. The next session of the day was physical training. "Head to the locker room and get changed!" No one hesitated. We moved with purpose. After we changed into our academy shorts and t-shirts, we met two instructors on a large field just to the east of the training building.

"Line up. Count off." We quickly lined up and counted off: one, two, one, two, and so on. "Ones come with me. Twos stay here." I was a two. I stood motionless as I watched half the recruits following one of the instructors back toward campus. The remaining instructor laughed and yelled, "Follow me!" He turned and started running toward the river walk. I fell in line with the rest of the group and ran.

I noticed immediately that the pace we were running was much faster than the pace I had been running on my own. The recruits were not running in a large group, but rather in a staggered line. I took solace in the fact that I wasn't at the end, but rather somewhere in the middle. The instructor wasn't saying anything to us as we ran except, "Let's go! Keep up!" I could hear the whispers of my fellow recruits around me questioning each other about how far we were going to have to run.

At the beginning of the run, I didn't pay attention to the markers along the river walk that designated how far we had gone, but eventually, I couldn't help but look. THREE MILES. I watched recruits run toward the edge of the river walk and vomit in the bushes. They would then run to catch up with the group again. My stomach was cramped up and I could feel my lunch churning, threatening to come up too. FOUR MILES. *Will this run ever end?*

I saw the instructor come to a stop up ahead of me and yell, "Catch up! Run, run, run!" Thinking that we were finally coming to the end, those of us that weren't at the front of the line picked up the pace and gave it all we had to get to the end. FIVE MILES. When the last person reached the instructor he yelled, "Alright, let's go back!" The collective groan was loud and frustrated. I had no idea how I was going to make it another five miles. My breathing was ragged and heavy and my head was spinning.

The second five miles was torture. Even the best runners struggled to finish. I had never run ten miles before and I couldn't believe that I had just done it. As we slowly walked over the bridge that led from the river walk to campus, I couldn't help but think to myself, *If we had to run ten miles on the first day what's the rest of the academy going to be like?* I put it out of my head immediately and focused on my breathing.

Another female recruit came up next to me, leaned in, pointed to the running instructor, and whispered, "Did you notice that he's not even sweating?" I hadn't, but now that she mentioned it, I wondered how that was possible. We found out later that he was a college running coach. Ten miles was probably a warm-up for him.

We got back to the campus training building and exchanged places with group one. They left with the running instructor and my group followed this instructor into an expansive gym filled with every piece of weightlifting equipment one could imagine. "Let's build some muscles, recruits!" I was more physically exhausted than I had ever been in my life. Now we had to lift weights? My legs were so shaky they felt like the bones had been removed. I decided the best course of action was to focus on my arms. Maybe that would give my stomach time to settle down.

After group one returned from their run, which was only two miles, we were released to shower and change back into our uniforms. We were required back in class in thirty minutes. Group one was shocked to hear that we had run ten miles. We all wondered why the difference, but no one was going to question it. That would be asking for pushups that no one wanted to do. If it was hard to focus and stay awake during the morning lecture, the afternoon lecture was worse. Our bodies and minds were shutting down.

Jason picked Tarec up from preschool that day and they were waiting for me at home when I arrived. It was late, and Tarec's bedtime. I got him ready for bed and read two bedtime stories to him. I fell asleep halfway through the second book when he woke me up.

"Mommy, Mommy, wake up," he whispered as he gently shook my arm.

"I'm sorry, sweetie. Mommy is so tired."

"It's OK, Mommy. You don't have to finish," he said with a smile. I kissed him on the forehead and told him that we had to finish so we could find out what was going to happen to Winnie the Pooh. Somehow, I managed to get through to the end. Pooh finally got his head out of the honey jar.

I thanked Jason for taking care of Tarec and he asked me how my day went. I told him that I was sorry, but I was too tired to talk. He understood. I went to bed and fell into a deep, coma-like sleep. Tomorrow was going to come entirely too soon.

Our days began between 6:00 a.m. and 8:00 a.m. and ended as late as 11:00 p.m. Training was mostly five days a week, but there were plenty of Saturdays and Sundays added into the schedule. Every day in the academy was essentially the same with minor variations in tasks and the order they were completed. Mornings always started with uniform inspections. We learned quickly what was expected and we would all arrive early and inspect each other prior to the arrival of the instructors. Creases had to be perfect, ties straight and in line with the belt buckle, shoes shined like mirrors, name tags pinned on symmetrically over the right breast pocket, men freshly shaved and women's hair in a neat bun or braid off the collar. The smallest imperfection on behalf of anyone would lead to pushups for all.

Classroom instruction would usually follow inspection. It's amazing how many laws are expected to be learned and absorbed in such a short amount of time. Just learning the many elements of all the crimes was daunting, but so important. Officers need to know exactly what constitutes a crime in order to know if someone is guilty. Then the officer needs to be able to write a report that effectively shows that a person did violate those elements. We spent a great deal of time mastering the knowledge and then practicing writing reports. It was often tough to stay awake during some of the dry and boring sections, but we did our best to keep each other awake with subtle punches under the table if someone started to doze off.

There was some sort of physical training every day: weightlifting, defensive tactics, subject control, boxing, running, and calisthenics. The physical training was always after lunch. Early on it was common to see people vomiting along the river walk or running out of the sparring room to vomit in the bathroom. It didn't take long before we learned that eating lunch was a bad idea. This habit of not eating and drinking would often lead to other problems.

After a seven-mile run on a 90-plus degree day we were walking over the bridge from the river walk back to the locker room when I passed out. I don't remember going down, but I woke up to find several of my fellow recruits and the running instructor surrounding me on the ground. The instructor wanted me to go to the hospital, but I convinced him that I was just hungry and dehydrated. I promised that I would eat a snack on the way back to the classroom and I would drink lots of water for the rest of the day. He finally relented and allowed me to continue on. Calculating nutrition with not wanting to vomit was a delicate balancing act.

By the time graduation arrived, everyone in the academy lost weight. Some had lost as much as seventy pounds. I started the academy at a healthy 125 pounds. Throughout the duration of the academy, my weight went down to 110 pounds, but I ended at 118 pounds by building muscle. Never in my life had I been so physically strong. Strength and control had seemed like mythical concepts—pillars to the heavens that I couldn't climb. Now, for the first time in my life, I felt like no one would ever victimize me again.

When growing up my grandparents always said, "Times were different back then," referring to their younger days. Today, I find myself saying these very words regarding child abuse and how it wasn't talked about when I was young. It was seen as a "family issue." Some family members choose to look the other way to avoid facing the problem head-on. As a young child into my teenage years, I wore visible signs of the physical abuse I endured, but no one reached out to help. Not my father's friends, my grandparents, or school counselors. I attended school with bruises on various parts of my body regularly. On many occasions I was unable to lean back against the classroom chairs because the welts on my back made it too painful. Sometimes teachers noticed and sent me to the office.

Eventually, I confided in my school counselor, Mrs. Schneider, about the physical abuse I was suffering at home. Mrs. Schneider was in her forties, had kind eyes, and a smile that lit up her face. She spoke in a soft, quiet voice that always made me feel at ease. The day I went to her office was the day that I stood up for myself. I was going to tell her absolutely everything that was going on in my house.

It was hard to tell her the things that I had been holding in for so long, to build up the courage to share the secrets of my shameful life, but finally I did. Everything came rushing out of me like an avalanche cascading down a mountainside. I could no longer hold back. I told Mrs. Schneider that my father beat me up almost every day. That he used drugs all night long and sold it to people that came to the house. That he grew marijuana plants in the backyard and hung them to dry in the shed. How a drawer in the kitchen was full of pills. That the top shelf of my father's bedroom closet had a box with cocaine in it. The drug scales and pipes in the laundry room cupboard. I begged her for help. I begged her to call the police, have my father arrested, and save me from the hell that I was living in. Mrs. Schneider hugged me and told me not to worry. She said everything would be all right. I was desperate to believe her.

After school that day, I went home and spent the night sitting on my bed staring out the window. I knew the cavalry would arrive at any moment. Surely Mrs. Schneider had called the police and they were just taking some time to get organized before they busted into the house and took my father away. Alas, no one ever came. That day changed everything for me. Looking back, I realize that was the moment when everything became crystal clear—I was hopelessly alone. I stopped seeking help from anyone at school and simply tried harder to hide my injuries.

When my sister was six months old, Diana reached her limit. She packed everything up and moved out while my father had gone fishing for the weekend. She didn't leave a note. My father never found them. Honestly, I don't remember my father even looking. One day they were there and the next day they were never spoken of again. As much as I hated her for physically abusing me, for not protecting me, I still cried when she left. I had no idea what my life was going to be like with just the two of us.

After Diana left, I quickly learned that it was my responsibility to be the woman of the house. I had to run a bath for my father when he got home from work and then have dinner on the table. All the chores and laundry were my responsibility on top of going to school. I had thought my life couldn't get worse than it had been suffering through the abuse, but now, I had no idea what was coming. I was terrified. I prayed to God every night before I went to sleep. I prayed to ask God to have my father arrested. I prayed to ask God to kill him. And sometimes, I prayed to ask God to kill me.

In between our regular academy schedule were days that focused on specialized training: pepper spray, tear gas, firearms, emergency vehicle operations, and first aid. Tear gas training was hands down the worst day of the entire academy. It's been over twenty years and it still makes me cringe thinking about it.

We were in a large open area beside a small shed. We lined up and were divided into groups of eight or so. I was in the first group. We were handed old gas masks that looked like they were from World War II and told how to properly adjust them. The mask felt awkward on my face and slightly claustrophobic. The ironic thing was that it was meant to help you breathe, but I found I couldn't get a good, deep breath.

We walked into the shed and found it completely empty aside from one bench on each of the north and south walls. We sat down, four to a side, close together. From outside, the instructor threw in a canister of tear gas and quickly closed the door. I watched the tear gas spew from the canister and fill the room. Suddenly, I was grateful for the claustrophobic mask. Someone outside began yelling through the door. "Listen up. When I say 'now' you are to take off your mask and call out your last name. When everyone has said their name then I will open the door."

I couldn't see the reaction on the faces of my fellow recruits, but I imagine they had the same look of horror that I had. I had hoped to hold my breath long enough to get out of the building without breathing in the tear gas, but clearly that wasn't going to be possible if we had to speak. "Now!" the voice called out. I closed my eyes, ripped off my mask, and yelled out my name when it was my turn. It only took seconds before the door opened, but I was already feeling the effects of the tear gas. I ran out of the shed coughing, choking, spitting, my nose and eyes watering uncontrollably. I couldn't see anything right away, but I could hear the rest of my group coughing and vomiting. I could also hear the rest of the recruits and instructors laughing. I'm sure we were quite a sight. Within a few minutes my eyes stopped watering enough to be able to see somewhat and the coughing lessened. I knew it then and I feel it now—I never want to go through that again.

A full week of training took place at the shooting range. We were given safety glasses and earplugs, which were required to be worn at all times. Being caught, even momentarily, without either would mean certain punishment. If you were already employed by a police department, then you were allowed to use whatever duty weapon your department used. Otherwise, everyone was assigned a 40-caliber Glock handgun. Prior to the academy, I practiced with a SIG SAUER 9-mm handgun. I had no idea what the difference would be, but I hoped that I would be equally as proficient.

We were each stationed in our own shooting lane and told when to shoot at the target. Most of the time the target was a picture of a man holding a gun pointed toward me. This was supposed to prepare us for shooting at a person. Police aren't trained to shoot at small areas like arms or legs, which are hard targets to hit under stress, even more so when a person is moving. Police are trained to shoot center mass—the torso of a body, which presents the largest target and the place most likely to stop an approaching threat.

We practiced shooting at different distances, sometimes timed and sometimes not. We were learning to shooting accurately and quickly. Unfortunately, I was not as experienced a shooter as others were, and I let the difference in guns get in my head. I struggled to become proficient at shooting a 40-caliber. I hit the bull's-eye with every shot when I was practicing, but official testing made me fall to pieces. The worst part was that official testing was no different than practice. It was the exact same course of fire. The only difference was that the instructor would say, "OK, this is the official test," and I would get nervous and fall apart. It was frustrating because I knew that I could shoot well. I had a good stance, steady breathing, and a smooth trigger pull.

I decided to devote a great deal of extra time practicing. My instructor didn't understand why I only missed shots when it was for a test. "Damn it! You can do this. Get out of your fucking head and shoot!" he screamed at me. Thankfully, he saw my potential and didn't give up on me. By the end of the week not only did I pass my final test, but every shot hit the small round orange sticker that my instructor placed on the center of the target.

Safety at the range was incredibly important and being caught pointing the gun, even unloaded, in the wrong direction would result in certain punishment. Finger on the trigger when not shooting—pushups. Shooting an extra round by accident—pushups. Shoot too soon—pushups. Walk away without making sure the gun was unloaded with the slide locked open—pushups. The instructors told us that infractions would start at twenty-five pushups and double with each subsequent infraction.

By the end of the week enough mistakes had been made as a group that we owed the instructors eight hundred pushups. On the last day, we did four hundred pushups before lunch and another four hundred before we went home for the day. As much as my arms ached day after day, I loved the muscular definition the pushups were giving my upper body.

The most fun part of the academy was the week of driving instruction. We learned a variety of emergency vehicle driving techniques and practiced them over and over. We drove police cars forward and backward, around and between obstacles, as fast as possible. I have always been a bit of an aggressive driver, so this training was right up my alley. That was the only week of training where everyone in the academy let their guard down slightly and enjoyed themselves.

My favorite driving maneuver was called the Serpentine. Orange cones were set up in a straight row at intervals of a few feet. The goal was to drive backward and forward as fast as possible, weaving in and out of the cones without knocking them down. It sounds easy, but driving fast in reverse, weaving in and out of cones, can be disorienting. Nearly everyone knocked down cones the first time they tried it.

I pushed my body and mind to the breaking point during those sixteen weeks. Aches and pains, mental exhaustion, and sleep deprivation became all too common. On top of everything else, the man who had encouraged me to follow my dream of becoming a police officer ended up making the process significantly more difficult to complete.

Jason and I had become engaged prior to my entry into the police academy, but I never mentioned it to anyone. Police officers are a tight knit-group, and I knew that many of the academy instructors either worked with Jason at East Lansing PD or knew of him. I didn't want to be treated differently, whether it be positive or negative. I should have suspected that they would find out somehow.

About four weeks into the academy, I began to notice Jason behaving oddly. I would wake up in the middle of the night and find him on the computer talking to people in chat rooms. When I caught him, there was always some innocent story behind it. Frankly, I was too exhausted most days to try to investigate further.

One night Jason said he was going to work on some electrical stuff at a house he had recently purchased. The plan was to fix up the house and move in together after we got married. Since Jason worked the night shift it wasn't unusual for him to be wide awake when I was falling asleep. Later that night I woke up at 3:00 a.m. and Jason still wasn't home. I called him, but there was no answer. As the minutes ticked by, my level of worry increased. *Did he electrocute himself? Was he in a car accident? Did someone go into the house and assault him while he had his back turned?*

I knew I wouldn't be able to get back to sleep until I checked on him. I got out of bed and dressed, gently picked Tarec up out of his bed, loaded him into his car seat without waking him, and drove over to the house. On my way over I called again; still no answer. My anxiety was increasing, and I realized I was speeding. As I approached the driveway, I saw that there were only dim lights on in the house. That made sense because he was supposed to be working on the electrical lines. Then I noticed that there were two cars in the driveway. I pulled in behind the second car, which I didn't recognize, and parked. Had Jason called one of his friends to come over and help?

Tarec was still asleep, so I left him in his car seat and locked the doors. I walked toward the house and heard the faint sound of music playing inside. The front door was open, and I could see through the screen door that there were several lit candles in the living room and a single red rose lay on the coffee table in front of the couch. Jason was lying on the couch and under him was a girl. I stood there motionless, speechless, watching Jason kissing this unknown girl.

I opened the door and walked inside. I wanted to yell at him. I wanted to beat the shit out of him. I wanted to grab Jason's gun and shoot them both. Instead, I stood there, unable to formulate words. I started crying and ran back to my car.

Before I could pull out of the driveway, the girl ran outside and stopped me. She apologized profusely and said that she didn't know about me. Through my anger and hurt, I thought about it and decided that she was probably telling me the truth. This wasn't her fault—it was Jason's. He was the asshole. It would be unfair to mistreat her. Besides, she looked so young.

We stood in the driveway for several minutes. I could see Jason standing in the doorway of the house watching us, but he was smart enough not to dare come outside. I was not in control of my emotions, and I could have snapped at any moment. I didn't know this girl at all, but she seemed pissed off too. She saw Tarec in the back seat and, somehow, that upset her even more.

"You have to know the whole truth," she said. "You need to know who I am and how we met. I don't want him to be able to lie and talk his way out of this later." For only being twenty years old, she was a smart girl.

"My name is Tiffany and I'm an MSU student. I met Jason in a chat room online a few weeks ago and we've been talking on the computer and phone since," she explained.

"How many times have you been out with him?" I asked, unsure if I really wanted to know the answer.

"Tonight was our fourth date." Her voice dropped as she said it. I could see the shame in her eyes. How could I feel so bad for her when I was so hurt myself? "Jason told me that he was single and had been for several years." Then came the worse part. "I came over here last weekend and saw you mowing the backyard. Jason ran out of the house and told me that you were a friend of his just helping him out with the house. He said he was super busy and would call me later, so I left."

I couldn't believe it. How could he be so callous? My emotions weren't stable, and I didn't trust myself not to do something stupid. I held onto the car door handle to anchor me. I was fighting the urge to run into the house and kill Jason.

"Thank you, Tiffany, for telling me the truth. I need to get my son home though," I said. Tiffany apologized again. We hugged, got into our cars and left. I cried all the way home. I got Tarec back into his bed without him ever waking up, but I was angry at myself for taking him out of bed to check on a loser like Jason. I had about two hours or so before I had to be up for the academy, but sleep eluded me.

I would love to say that I was smart and didn't take him back, but that would be a lie. My life was in a hectic state, and I couldn't deal with a breakup too. In the weeks that followed I tried to be more conscious of his whereabouts. I ended up catching him three more times with three different girls. All of them MSU undergrads.

With each episode of cheating, my mental state became more fragile. We were fighting constantly—sometimes it even got physical. I arrived at the academy for morning inspections most days with red puffy eyes. It became apparent to everyone around me that something was going on, but no one asked directly. I could tell that several of the instructors knew something because they began to treat me differently. Instructors who had spoken to me regularly now seemed to avoid speaking with me one-on-one. Instructors who were normally hard on recruits, pushing us to a breaking point, seemed to cut me a break. Not that I didn't have to work as hard, but they didn't single me out to be yelled at or made an example of. On more than one occasion instructors who had never spoken to me before pulled me aside and asked me if I was the one dating Jason. I didn't want to answer them, but I couldn't lie either. I answered yes and quickly exited the conversation.

Focusing on academy lectures, comprehending the abundance of information, and working through the physical exhaustion while dealing with my crumbling personal life almost became more than I could endure. I hated feeling like everyone was always looking at me; waiting for me to sink into a black hole of despair that I couldn't escape from. I kept my distance from everyone making the academy a very lonely time for me. On top of everything else, I missed Tarec. Graduation day couldn't come soon enough.

The rigorous schedule of the academy kept me from spending quality time with Tarec for days at a time. I sometimes worried that he would forget who I was. On a few rare occasions I would get to pick him up from his preschool. His little face would light up with joy and surprise and it reminded me how much I missed our time together. Over the months of training, it seemed I had utilized everyone I knew to help me take care of him. Even though my relationship with Jason was tenuous at best, his parents loved Tarec and they continued to help me care for him.

I will never forget Halloween. As most kids do, Tarec was getting increasingly excited about going trick-or-treating. I was so busy with the academy that I didn't have time to take him shopping for a costume and I wasn't sure I would get out in time to trick-or-treat with him. Jason's mother knew how much he loved *Toy Story*, so she handmade him a Buzz Lightyear costume. On Halloween, she picked him up from daycare and got him dressed and ready for an evening of trick-or-treating. I got out of the academy just in time to take him myself. I couldn't believe how amazing his costume was. I must have thanked her a hundred times.

This was also a time of relative peace with my ex-husband, and I was grateful for his assistance caring for Tarec. We had fought through a stressful divorce, but I had moved on with my life and he came to accept that our marriage was over for good. I would never forget all the awful things he had said and done to me, but I was determined to raise Tarec without forcing him to choose between us. I didn't want to become my mother and spend his whole life telling him how horrible his father was. I was generous with visitation and Mo was generous in helping take care of him when I had academy commitments.

Finally, graduation day arrived in November 2000. It was one of the proudest moments of my life. I had changed so much—body and mind. With my breakup officially over, I felt I had taken the first step away from my life as a victim. I accomplished something no one thought I could do. I will never forget the looks on the faces of my Mom, Dad, Carol, and Ryan as I walked across the stage. They had a sense of pride that burst forth through their eyes and smiles that I had never seen before. They didn't know it, but it bolstered my confidence and reassured me that I had made the right decision. They had no idea how fragile and unsure my past had made me and how much I needed their support.

5

A FALSE SHIELD

After graduating from the police academy, it was time to find a job. Unfortunately, the job market for law enforcement wasn't great in Michigan in 2000–2001. To make matters worse, there were really only three places that I wanted to work: Lansing, Pontiac, or Detroit. I wanted to be in a busy city where the action was. I don't think I had a death wish or anything, but I definitely craved the excitement and danger that came along with working in a bigger, busier city. Alas, none of the three departments were hiring.

Graduates of the police academy had one year to become a certified police officer, or their eligibility would expire. There was no way I was going to let my eligibility expire and be forced to go through the academy again, so I began to apply for jobs with any department that was hiring, which wasn't many. A month went by, and I began to become frustrated and angry. *Did I make a huge mistake?* I began to realize immediately that being a White woman was not going to help me in my job search. Many people talk about White privilege, but I certainly wasn't feeling it. I was shocked at how blatant some departments were in their desire not to hire women—Black or White.

The most egregious example was when I applied to Green Oak Township Police Department. It was a small department approximately an hour southeast of Lansing. Today, Green Oak is a township of only sixteen thousand people, but it was even smaller in 2001. I went there for an interview with the highest of hopes, but they were dashed within minutes when I was told at the start of the interview that Green Oak had never had a female police officer. It was then that the interviewer dropped the bomb.

"We don't have a female locker room here. Would you have a problem using the male locker room with the other officers?" I was shocked.

Thoughts of my son ran through my mind. I needed a job—any job—to support him.

"No problem at all. I'm not shy." What else could I say? Was this illegal? Of course.

The rest of the interview went well, but I knew as I walked to my car afterward that I would not get this job, nor would any other woman. A week later a male friend of mine was offered the job. Illegal or not, I couldn't prove discrimination and there was nothing I could do about it. I wasn't in a position to initiate that fight. Little did I know that this type of discrimination against women in law enforcement was not confined to small, rural cities.

A couple months after graduation I was able to get a part-time job at a small department about twenty minutes outside of Lansing. The city was a mere 2.5 square miles and had less than four thousand citizens. The city is most well-known for its many antique shops. The police department employed a chief of police and three full-time officers along with several part-time and reserve officers. Although the department had employed one female officer in the past, they currently had none. I knew the job would be boring, but I was desperate to secure my certification.

Though this was my first police job, I have nothing positive to say about my time there. There was no training program and nothing exciting ever happened, except for the time I got stung by a bee in the eyebrow during an arrest. By the time I walked the arrestee back to my patrol car, my eye was swollen shut.

I pulled over my first drunk driver in the middle of the day, and because I received no training, I had no idea where the jail was. Luckily, an Ingham County deputy wasn't too far away, and he showed up to help me. I worked for less than a year in that department and most of my time was spent driving around writing speeding tickets because there was nothing else to do. If I wasn't writing tickets, I would look for drunk drivers. Being the only female officer in town had its downside—everyone knew who I was. Within a few months I was branded the "bitch cop" who harassed all the locals. I was soon called into the chief's office and advised to "tone it down." I wanted to do what he asked, but I was so bored. During my time there, I would end up being called into the chief's office three times and given the same advisement.

The final straw came when I arrested the state championship-winning wrestling coach for drunk driving in the parking lot of the country club. It was a sunny afternoon when I observed a vehicle driving erratically. After activating the overhead lights, the vehicle turned into the country club parking lot. I approached the driver and noticed two things immediately: his eyes were bloodshot and glassy, and the smell of intoxicants was so strong that it must have been seeping out of every pore on his body. I asked the man to step out of the vehicle and as I patted him down for weapons several teenagers approached us.

"Are you OK, Coach Turner?"

"Do you need us to call someone?"

"You can't do this to Coach!"

The chorus of angry teenage voices overlapped as I tried to maintain control of the situation. I sternly told the kids that they needed to back up and leave me to do my job. I conducted a few sobriety tests, which the coach failed miserably. Coach Turner was handcuffed and transported to jail. Word spread quickly and the whole town was pissed. It wasn't long before I was called into the city manager's office and given a final warning. I was told in no uncertain terms that being the only female officer had shone a very bright light on me, and that if I didn't tone it down, a lot, I wouldn't be working there anymore. I redoubled my efforts to get to a bigger department.

By this time, late 2001, both Pontiac PD and Detroit PD were hiring. I applied to both and hoped one would call soon. Pontiac called first. I completed the extensive hiring process, bought a house in Lake Orion, and started work in February 2002. I was excited at the prospect of doing what I deemed "real" police work. No more smiling and waving. I was going to be chasing and arresting bad guys. But the best part was, after being away from my family for so long, I was excited to be moving back to the area where I'd grown up. Lake Orion was only about fifteen minutes from Pontiac and my new house was only five minutes from my mom and dad.

It was a difficult decision, but I decided not to move into my new house in Lake Orion right away. Tarec was in kindergarten, and I thought it would be cruel to move him before the school year was over. This gave me time to paint the new house and have new carpet installed before we moved in. Most of my days off were spent getting the house ready. With each trip I would try to bring a few more boxes from my townhouse in East Lansing. The downside of this decision was that I had a ninety-minute drive to and from work each day. When you added that drive time to my ten-hour workday it meant that I was exhausted all the time for the first few months.

Being tired was the least of my immediate concerns. My most pressing worry was for the safety of my son. When I told Mo that I got the job in Pontiac he was fuming. He bombarded me with insults and threats every time I saw or spoke to him. "You can't take my son away from me! How dare you move so far away. You just don't want me to be a part of my son's life. I'll see you in court. I'll take custody of him away from you. There's no way I'm allowing you to move him away." I needed his help to take care of our son in the evenings while I was at work, but I worried that the day would come when he refused to give him back to me or would disappear with him altogether.

The city of Pontiac is about thirty minutes northwest of Detroit. It's approximately twenty square miles and, in 2002, home to around seventy thousand people of all races and ethnicities. Over the years Pontiac became known for being home to the Pontiac Silverdome and to several General Motors automotive plants. During the 1970s, Pontiac's General Motors plants employed tens of thousands of hourly workers. The city's iron grip on the automotive market seemed assured. No one would foresee the decline of General Motors, along with Pontiac, the heart of the county, that was to come years later.

By the time I joined the Pontiac Police Department in 2002 the crime rate was high, and many referred to Pontiac as a "mini Detroit." The truth of the matter was that the high crime rate and diverse population was what drew me to working there. I also loved the fact that the police department was equally diverse. Pontiac PD employed many women and I thought that my days of being treated differently were over. That pipe dream would be dashed only a few short weeks into my tenure when I came face-to-face with the evil that Lieutenant Cornelius Haddock was masking from the world.

The first couple weeks working at Pontiac PD were spent in a conference room. As with most jobs there was an internal training period. If my memory is correct, there were six of us hired together in training: four men and two women. The internal training time was an orientation period where we became acquainted with Pontiac PD policies and procedures, introduced to report writing, and studied maps of the city and other miscellaneous information. However, most of our training would come from our field training officers when we got to the road.

Field training consisted of four phases. In the first phase the trainee is partnered with a field training officer (FTO) and is required to perform a minimal amount of work—10 percent or so. Most of the time is spent observing, listening, and learning. In phase two of training the officer is partnered with a different FTO and expected to do a larger portion of the work—up to 50 percent. In this phase the FTO is still actively teaching the trainee, allowing them to ask questions, but expecting the trainee to begin to understand what is expected. In phase three the trainee has a different FTO and does up to 90 percent of the work on their own. This is less of a time of learning and more of showing your understanding of the requirements of the job and that you are able to meet those expectations. The final phase rotates the trainee back to their phase one FTO where they are expected to perform 100 percent of the job. The FTO is outfitted in plain clothes and acts only as an observer. If the trainee needs assistance or has questions, they are expected to find another officer just as they would if they were working on their own.

I had just started my phase one training on the road about a week prior and it was my day off. My son was at his dad's house, and I was in Lake Orion working on my new house. I decided to take a break and stop into the police station to pick up some paperwork I had left in my locker. Lieutenant Haddock saw me and greeted me along with several officers I didn't know that were standing around the front desk talking. I was just beginning to learn the names of the command staff in the department, but I still didn't know the names of the majority of the officers. Lieutenant Haddock was the midnight shift supervisor, and I only knew him in passing because the afternoon and midnight shifts overlapped by a few hours. Lieutenant Haddock was African American, less than six-feet-tall and weighed at least 350 pounds. If you ever watched the 1990s sitcom *Family Matters*, Lieutenant Haddock looked just like the character, Carl Winslow. He towered over my diminutive five-foot-three, 125-pound body.

Lieutenant Haddock pulled me into a small room off to the right of the front desk under the guise of speaking with me. The room was used as nothing more than a walk-through to the evidence lockers and offices in the back. It was small, dark, and empty, other than a water dispenser. He pushed me into the corner of the room.

"Man, you look good," he whispered.

I froze. My brain stopped working. Lieutenant Haddock grabbed me by the arms and turned my body so that I was facing the wall. He pushed his large body against mine as he pulled off my jacket. The wall was cold against my cheek.

"You look so good in those jeans. All the guys love seeing you in them."

My brain suddenly kicked into action and a million thoughts raced through my head. *What the hell is happening? What am I going to do? I'm a nobody. He's a lieutenant. I'm brand new. Who would even believe me if I told them? Who would I even tell?* As he pushed himself against me, he buried his nose into my neck, burrowing through my hair. I could feel his warm breath against my skin.

"You smell so good," he whispered as he inhaled deeply.

Suddenly, I heard an officer walk into the room. Lieutenant Haddock quickly wrenched away from me and pretended to engage in conversation as if nothing had just happened. I grabbed my jacket and walked out of the room as quickly as I could without causing a scene. I drove home in a daze completely frazzled. I had no idea what I was going to do.

Going forward, I did my best to avoid Lieutenant Haddock with the hope that what happened was a one-time stupid decision on his part. One day I was in the station typing a warrant request. In the midst of typing I had let my guard down and wasn't attentive to my surroundings. Lieutenant Haddock came up behind me, placed his large hands on my shoulders, bent down close to my ear and whispered, "I'm going to get you transferred to my shift. We'll have lots of time together then." In the following weeks my attempts to avoid him were futile. He seemed to appear out of nowhere, and always finding ways to get me alone.

I knew I had to do something, but I was at a loss. I had so many emotions running through my head and no traffic sign to guide me in the right direction. I thought about talking to my training officer, but ultimately decided against it. Yes, he had more time on the job than me, but he was still just an officer. There wasn't going to be much he could do. There was no one outside the department that I could seek advice from either, so I spent my evenings at home trying to figure out what my options were. After much deliberation I decided to take a chance and talk to Sergeant Garibaldi. There was a female lieutenant on my shift, Lieutenant Keller, who I strongly considered going to, but there was something trustworthy about Sergeant Garibaldi.

For some reason I bonded with many of my male coworkers and supervisors, but with very few women. I have to admit that I have struggled my entire life to bond with women. I don't understand exactly why, but I struggle to trust women. I have found that my faith in women is low and find myself expecting them to betray me. The friendships I have had with women never lasted, but those that have stood the test of time have all been with men.

Sergeant Garibaldi was friendly, outgoing, and always joking around— even to new officers like me. Most sergeants weren't so nice to new people; in fact, they went out of their way to be harsh—all a part of the initiation into a paramilitary-like organization, I guess. Regardless, I was comfortable around Sergeant Garibaldi.

I pulled Sergeant Garibaldi aside and asked him if we could talk privately. He was very gracious and led me downstairs into the room attached to the shooting range. I tried to be professional and hold back the tears that were fighting to escape. I made him promise not to tell anyone what I was about to tell him. He was not happy, but he agreed.

Like a dam bursting, I tearfully told him what took place between me and Lieutenant Haddock. Sergeant Garibaldi listened intently while I divulged everything, revealing my shame and embarrassment. Sergeant Garibaldi reached out and hugged me as I cried. When I finally gained control, he pulled away and asked if I was OK. I nodded. There was no judgment or disgust, on his part, no anger in his eyes, only sympathy.

Sergeant Garibaldi strongly encouraged that I file a formal complaint against Lieutenant Haddock. I was adamantly against that. I told him that I was hoping that he could do two things for me: first, keep the lieutenant from transferring me to his shift. Second, during shift overlap hours, ensure I wouldn't ever be alone with Haddock. Sergeant Garibaldi promised that he would do everything he could to help me.

Sergeant Garibaldi was true to his word. He ran interference like an umpire at a never-ending baseball game. I was typing a warrant one day when Lieutenant Haddock approached me. The next thing I heard was Sergeant Garibaldi yelling at me to get into his office. From the tone of his voice, I was sure I was in trouble. I entered his office, and he slammed the door shut behind me. Too scared to even sit down, I saw that he was smiling. It was all a ruse to get me away from Lieutenant Haddock. I breathed a sigh of relief that I wasn't in trouble, sat down, and chatted with Sergeant Garibaldi for a few minutes. When I came out of his office Haddock was gone. Sergeant Garibaldi found many unique ways to intercept Lieutenant Haddock. Eventually, Lieutenant Haddock left me alone and moved on. My relationship with Sergeant Garibaldi was solidified. He became a protector who would look after me in the years to come and would remain my friend long after my career ended.

Many years later Lieutenant Haddock got himself into trouble in a similar situation with a civilian in a public place. His actions led to a formal investigation where I came forward and told my story. He was given the option to retire or be fired. He quietly retired and died a few years later. I did not attend his funeral, nor did I mourn his death.

I can distinctly remember times of driving back to East Lansing after work and ruminating about how devastated I was that the incident with Lieutenant Haddock occurred so early in my career. I had such high hopes that Pontiac PD would be different. Hope that I would overcome the obstacles that came with being a female in a male-dominated field. Hope that I would never again be victimized because I was a police officer. Naively, I believed that my job was a shield against the evils of the world, but the truth delivered a crushing blow. Unfortunately, Lieutenant Haddock wasn't the first time I'd been sexually assaulted. Long before Lieutenant Haddock there was Mike, who would come into my life when I was a young and vulnerable thirteen-year-old.

After being dropped on my father's doorstep when I was eleven, it wasn't long before I realized that life with him would not be any better than life with my mother and stepfather. My father was extremely physically abusive, an alcoholic, and a drug addict—everything my mother said he was. This combination concluded with my father never being able to keep a wife or girlfriend for long.

After Diana left my father, I often felt like I was his wife, not his daughter. Not only did I have to keep the house clean and cook the meals, but my father took me with him almost everywhere he went, including bars. Spending time in bars with my father would lead to one of the most devasting things to ever happen to me.

Most weekends were spent at a small local bar that most would refer to as "a hole in the wall." The bar was dark inside, a cloud of smoke always hanging in the air. Classic rock and roll played in the background: Bob Seger, Foreigner, Heart, Jefferson Airplane, Journey, and so on. My favorite song from that time period was "Don't Fear the Reaper" by Blue Öyster Cult. At the back of the bar were two small tables and in the far-right corner a Ms. Pac-Man video game, which was my sanctuary. I would play game after game as my father would sit at the bar, hit on women, laugh with the men, and drink for hours.

I would sit at that arcade game, out of sight and out of mind (just as I was expected to) and feed it quarters like an old lady at a slot machine. When I ran out of quarters, I quietly walked around the bar and took them from anyone who had change in front of them. I was such common sight there that everyone knew me, and no one cared that I took their quarters. Sometimes I would get so tired that I would fall asleep with my head on the machine. Eventually, the bar would close, and my father would somehow manage to drive home without killing us. To this day I'm not sure how we never got into an accident.

It was just a couple months later when my father met his next girlfriend at the bar. Caroline was a waitress who took a liking to my father's charming ways. A week after they met, I had been babysitting for a friend of the family. At 1:00 a.m. they dropped me off at home to a completely dark house. I found my father and Caroline in bed, TV on, laughing loudly. On the nightstand I saw a small square mirror with lines of white powder on it. I stood in the doorway and told them that I was home and going to bed.

My father was clearly high as a kite and yelled, "Good news! Caroline is moving in! We're getting married!" Caroline moved in a few days later and they were married shortly afterward. It was all so sudden to me. I couldn't believe it. The entire situation was odd. Not only was it sudden, but Caroline didn't seem like my father's type. Diana had been younger than my father and was beautiful. The mothers of my father's other children were also young and beautiful. Caroline, however, was several years older than my father and I didn't think she was attractive at all.

Life with my father and his new wife didn't change much. I began to feel like I was merely existing, not living. I measured time not in days and weeks, but in frequency of beatings. I remember trying to contact my mother numerous times, but she had apparently moved several times in quick succession, and I had no idea where to find her. Reality set in that this was my life.

My father and Caroline thought I was a troublemaker, though I never got in trouble in school or with the police. I was rarely trusted to be home alone, which meant I spent many late nights out at adult parties or at the bar, whether or not it was a school night.

When I was thirteen my father and Caroline took me with them for a big celebration at the bar. It was a school night, and I had a test to take the next day. By midnight, I was exhausted. I begged my father to take me home, but he refused. A friend of my father's, Mike (who was thirty years old), overheard our conversation and said he would be happy to take me home. His family had been friends with our family since he had been a child. My father finally relented and agreed to let him drive me home.

I felt grateful to be gone from the loud, smoky bar and I must have thanked Mike for getting me out of there ten times during the short drive home. I had always liked Mike. When he would come to the house to visit, he was always kind to me. Most of my fathers' friends ignored me, but Mike always spoke to me and asked me how school was going or what I had been up to. He was tall and towered over my tiny frame. He was athletic, had short brown hair, and blue eyes that reminded me of the clear blue water of the Caribbean islands. His smile lit up a room. As young girls often develop crushes, I thought he was handsome and charismatic.

When we pulled into the driveway the relaxed atmosphere inside the car changed dramatically. I tried to open the passenger door, but it was locked. I knew immediately that something was wrong. I reached up to unlock the door, but Mike grabbed my arm and turned me toward him.

"You don't have to leave so fast," Mike whispered as he leaned toward me. He then pushed my arms against the back of the seat and began kissing me. I could taste the unfamiliar flavor of beer mixed with cigarettes as his tongue continued to dart around inside my mouth. My heart was pounding so fast that I thought it might beat right out of my chest. I couldn't breathe. I tried to pull away from him, but he was twice my age and three times my size. I knew that I was helpless to stop whatever was going to happen next.

After more than thirty years of trying to forget that night, the details have, thankfully, become hazy. The kissing turned to groping and the groping turned to undressing. It wasn't long before Mike was on top of me. Eventually, I realized that fighting was fruitless and would only end in my being injured. I stopped struggling, laid motionless across the front seat, and tried to take my mind elsewhere as tears involuntarily rolled down my cheeks.

When it was over, Mike let me out of the car. I went inside the house and walked slowly into the bathroom, too stunned to realize how slow I was moving. *What just happened? How could Mike have done this to me?* Once in the shower, I cried tears of lost innocence as I tried to scrub the feeling of being dirty from my body. I crawled into bed, pulled the blankets over my head, and sobbed quietly until I fell asleep.

The next day I went to school and took my exam. I couldn't stop thinking about what happened just hours before. I began to wonder what my father would do if I told him. Unfortunately, my father was volatile, and I couldn't be sure. In the end, I decided to put the incident behind me, forget about it, and never tell a soul. That changed when Mike showed up at the house two weeks later.

It was a rare time when I was home alone. Caroline had run to the grocery store and my father was still at work. I was in the front yard hanging out with some neighborhood friends when Mike pulled into the driveway. My friends got up to leave as I tried to find a subtle way of telling them to stay, but they didn't realize why. Mike grabbed my arm and tried to get me to go in the house with him. I don't remember exactly what he was saying. My head was dizzy with fear. All I knew was that I had to get out of there. I jerked my arm away and ran. I didn't know where I was going, but I knew I had to run.

The next thing I knew, I was at the home of two close friends of my fathers, Juan and Serena. They had a son who was close in age to me, and I thought maybe they would be more likely to understand my fear.

I knocked on the door and was escorted inside. I was crying so hard that I could barely breathe. It seemed that all the emotions I had buried for two weeks had resurfaced with a vengeance. Serena held me tight while I continued to cry for what seemed like hours. Eventually, I was able to gain my composure and tell them exactly what had happened with Mike that dreadful night.

"Why haven't you told your father what happened?" Juan and Serena prodded.

"You know how my father is. I'm just afraid of what his reaction will be," I replied.

"Speaking as a father," Juan said confidently, "this is definitely something that he would want to know." It took some convincing, but I finally relented, and Juan and Serena drove me home.

By now, both Caroline and my father had long since been home and were wondering where their troublemaking daughter was. Juan and Serena escorted me into the house, my face red and eyes swollen from crying. My father yelled, "Where the fuck have you been?" Serena told me to go to my room while she and Juan spoke to my father. I complied without a word.

After a short time, I heard my father scream, "Get the fuck out of my house!" There was some brief muffled arguing and then I heard a door slam shut. My father burst into my bedroom with the fury of hell blazing in his eyes. In all the beatings that I had been subject to at the hands of my father, none scared me more than the one I was about to receive. I had gone outside the circle of our family, and nothing was considered a worse offense to my father than that. He grabbed me by my arm, jerked me off the bed, screamed that I was a whore, and that nothing would have happened if I hadn't thrown myself at Mike.

The truth is that I have blocked out, or mentally lost, the majority of this beating. I can remember flashes of screaming, punching, crying, but at some point, I blacked out. When I regained consciousness, I found myself battered, beaten, and bleeding on the living room floor. My father and Caroline had gone to bed, and I was left to tend to my own wounds. I quietly cleaned myself up and went to bed. I fell asleep with my aching head swirling with thoughts of what was wrong with me to make my father treat me the way that he did. *Why does my father hate me so much? Why would my father think that I threw myself at Mike? Why doesn't my father ever take my side or believe in me?*

I went to school the next day as if it were any other day. It was to be the last time I would see Juan or Serena, and the subject of what happened with Mike was never mentioned again. It was just one of many early lessons I learned about how much easier life would be if I locked away the memories of bad incidents and force myself to forget them. Over the years I would master the art of forgetting.

Today, in my late forties and a mother, I still cannot begin to fathom why my father behaved the way that he did. I would do absolutely anything to protect my son from harm. The very notion of blaming him for being victimized by another person doesn't make sense to me. No amount of counseling, therapy, or religious study has been able to bring any sort of understanding or clarity regarding my father's behavior. Being a mother, it has filled me with questions and resentment.

With Sergeant Garibaldi watching my back, I got to work trying to make my mark in Pontiac. Aside from the incident with Lieutenant Haddock, my first year at Pontiac PD was difficult, to say the least. It was full of ups and down, good times and bad, and the beginning of some surprising friendships. I take responsibility for my part in the difficulties that were to come, but I also know that all the blame wasn't mine.

My first field training officer was Officer Carlos Luna. There's no mistaking the fact that he was hard on me. Sometimes it felt like he was going out of his way to be tough on me, although I have no idea why. Honestly, for most of my training, I couldn't stand him. I thought he was a complete jerk. There's no major incident that I can point to but rather it was all the little things about him that drove me nuts. One time he screamed at me on the way to a call for turning at a red light where there was a sign that read "No turn on red." Another time we were driving lights and siren to a stabbing call when I mistook one street for another. Instead of verbally correcting my error and getting to the call, he made me pull over, get out my map of the city and figure out exactly where I was going, all the while screaming at me for not having the streets memorized yet. We ended up being the last officers on the scene. In the end it took me about a year to feel comfortable navigating the city without a map.

One incident that I will always remember with Officer Luna was my first dead body. It was a beautiful summer day and the temperature had been in the high eighties all week. Officer Luna and I were dispatched to a welfare check on Forest Road on the northwest side of the city. The man that lived in the house had not been seen for several days and his family and neighbors were worried.

Officer Luna and I arrived on scene moments later and spoke to the family who told us that the man had helped a friend cut down a tree several days ago and that he had been hit on the head by a large log. The man hadn't been feeling well so he went home and hadn't been seen or heard from since. Officer Luna and I walked around the house to see if anything looked out of place. When we walked onto the porch and looked in the window, we observed a white male slumped on the couch in front of the television. We banged on the glass, but he didn't respond. The man was not moving and didn't appear to be breathing.

Officer Luna kicked in the front door, and we stepped inside. We were both immediately knocked backward by the overwhelming odor. There are no words that can adequately describe the smell of a decomposing body: rotten eggs, feces, maggots, spoiled meat, an overflowing dumpster. Multiply the smell by one hundred and it would still pale in comparison. Ask anyone who has encountered a decomposing body and they will tell you that once you are exposed to that odor you will never forget or mistake it for anything else. There was no need to check for a pulse—it was clear that the man was deceased and had been for days. At that moment, I wanted nothing more than to go back outside and breathe some fresh air, but of course, there was work to do. While there were no immediate signs of foul play, we still had to survey the scene. I shut the front door to keep the family from coming inside and seeing their loved one in that condition.

The front door opened into the living room area. There was a television in the far left-hand corner and a couch directly in front of the door. Next to the couch was an end table with a half-empty glass of water sitting on it. The dead man was sitting upright on the couch, his back slightly slouched down, he was wearing boxer shorts and no shirt, a box of tissues sat next to him, and the television was on. It looked as if he had died peacefully while watching his favorite television show. The living room doorway opened into the kitchen and there was a stairway in the kitchen that led upstairs. We moved through the house checking the other rooms to ensure that there was nothing out of place or that would indicate a crime had occurred. Fortunately, it appeared to be a straightforward natural death.

Officer Luna then informed me that he was going outside to secure the house and make sure no family entered. He told me to stay in the house and write the report. Nowadays, all police reports are typed on a computer in the patrol car, but back then, reports were still handwritten. I looked at him with a mixture of anger and disgust.

"You've got to be kidding me!" I said.

"Nope, have fun rookie," he laughed as he walked out the door.

I sat in that house for over two hours trying not to vomit while I hand wrote the death report. I went home from work that night covered in the stench of death. I couldn't wait to get in the shower and scrub the odor from my pores. I would get to know the smell of death well in the coming years, but it never loses its potency or shock.

Death is something that happens to us all eventually; some die peacefully like at my first death scene and others violently. No death scene is pleasant to handle, but you learn to distance yourself from it. Every officer has their own way of dealing with death, but the most common way I have encountered is through humor. While that may sound cold or callous, it is, truthfully, how many officers are able to mentally cope. My coworkers and I would frequently try to find something to laugh about to distract us from the gore and/or heartbreak of what we were seeing.

For me the violent scenes were much easier than the hospice deaths. There's something about frail old people dying peacefully that I always struggled with. They were so still and pale with no signs of trauma to their bodies. I always felt like they might wake up suddenly and tell me to get away from them. Death is a part of the job, especially working in an urban city, and that's where I wanted to work, so I couldn't complain about it.

Between my phase one and phase four training with Officer Luna, I hired him to do some drywall work on my house in Lake Orion. He owned a general contracting business and did work on the side when he wasn't working as a police officer. As Officer Luna worked on my house, I began to see a completely different side to him. He was kind, funny, and compassionate. Our relationship changed dramatically in those months. Instead of seeing him as an asshole who lived to torment me on a daily basis, I began to see him as a friend. After my training period was over, Officer Luna and I decided to become regular partners.

We didn't work as partners every day, but a couple times a week when our schedules synced up. He had trained me, so we knew each other well, and could easily anticipate what the other would say and do. He no longer screamed and yelled at me during work. Instead, we laughed, joked, and confided in each other. Our friendship would continue to grow close, and he would become one of my dearest friends. When I think back to how much I despised him during training, it's a small miracle that we came out on the other side to become as close as we did.

Those early days in Pontiac also introduced to me to the most surprising person who would become a part of my life—Tina Ashton. She was a drug-addicted prostitute in Pontiac. I was introduced to her within my first few months on the job during a vice raid on a drug house. At that time there were no female officers in the vice unit, so whenever women were found inside a house during a raid, the vice officers would request a female officer from the road come to the house to search the women. Frequently, that task fell to me.

The first time I was sent to do the searches, I had no idea what to expect. As I pulled up to the dispatched address, I noticed that it was dilapidated, and if I hadn't known better, I would have thought it was abandoned. A large, cargo-type truck was parked a few houses down that I recognized as the one used by the vice unit. I walked into the sparsely furnished house. It looked like a tornado had blown through it. I don't know what the house looked like before the vice officers showed up, but it was an absolute mess now.

There were at least half a dozen officers wearing black tactical fatigues with the letters "POLICE" written across their shirts and ski masks covering their faces. They were removing everything from drawers and cabinets. There were a few men in handcuffs sitting in various places, each being "guarded" by a vice officer. One vice officer stood next to a table covered with money, drugs, scales, packaging materials, and guns. He was logging the illegal items found during the raid and then packaged and tagged them for evidence storage. One of the vice officers noticed me standing in the doorway and said, "Hey, the girls are over here."

I followed him into the house, down the dirty hallway, and into a bedroom where there were two women, handcuffed, standing in the room. Both women appeared to be in their twenties and in need of a shower. They were wearing dirty clothes, smelled of body odor, had smeared makeup, and drowsy eyes; both looked like they might fall asleep standing right where they were any minute. But the most noticeable thing about them was the track marks on their arms, which are easily recognizable—they can look like bruises, scratches, scabs, or puncture marks. They are frequently located on the arms but can be found anywhere on the body: legs, toes, neck, hands, even the genitals. These two women were clearly not new to heroin use.

"This is Big Tina and Little Tina," a masked vice officer said. "Make sure they don't have anything stashed on them anywhere." With that he left the room. I didn't know the women, but I did recognize that they were Baldwin Road prostitutes who I had seen frequently "strolling" for customers. I didn't have to ask who was who—there was a clear height difference between them.

"If you have anything on you it's easiest if you just tell me now so I don't have to go digging into your private areas," I said to them in my best "I'm not playing around" voice. Both of the women were high and clearly annoyed at the disruption. Little Tina didn't say much, but Big

Tina wanted to argue. Both claimed that they didn't have anything illegal on them, but for some reason, Big Tina didn't want to go along with the search. She kept moving and turning and trying to keep me from searching her, complaining and cursing at me the whole time. Eventually, I had enough and used all my weight to push Big Tina face-first against the wall.

"I'm done playing with you," I said quietly, but sternly. "I don't want to be here anymore than you do. Stop the bullshit or we do this the hard way." Big Tina didn't completely stop making things difficult, but enough that I was able to conduct a thorough search. Neither had anything on them, but similar scenarios would play out many times over the coming years with different results. However, one thing that stayed the same was that I didn't like either of the Tinas.

For one thing, both Tinas liked to use each other's names when they were stopped by police: Tina Marie Ashton and Tina Marie Keen. It was difficult to figure out definitively who was who and I confused their names for at least a year. Eventually, I figured it out and was able to call them out when they tried to use each other's identity. I also learned that Tina Ashton, Big Tina, was the one who always wanted to make things difficult. Over the years Big Tina and I would have many encounters. I would fight with her a handful of times, search her dozens of times, and despise her hundreds of times.

Through it all, there was something about Tina that pulled at my heartstrings. Like all the prostitutes I encountered, I felt a sadness for her. I didn't know what circumstances had brought Tina to this life, but it was certainly not something that anyone would want for themself. As the years passed, Tina and I softened toward one another. There were many times that I would find Tina high and behaving badly. At those encounters I really didn't like her, but overall, we found a balance. The physical altercations stopped, and we treated each other with a decorum of respect. On the rare occasion when I encountered Tina not high on drugs, I found that she could actually be polite, respectful, and a pleasure to talk to.

The first year on the job is probationary. When an officer is on probation the department can fire them at any time, for any reason. Getting through the first year is always the most important because after that the officer has the full weight of the union behind them should a disciplinary issue arise. The toughest part of that year for me was when I was written up and suspended four times. The first time was because of my first car chase. I was dispatched to a suspicious vehicle call. When I turned onto the street where the vehicle in question was, it pulled away quickly. I activated my overhead lights and sirens, but the vehicle continued to accelerate and turned down side streets in an attempt to evade me. Suddenly, I realized that I was in an actual car chase. I had previous training for this, but found it exciting, nonetheless.

It's difficult to explain why a car chase is exciting, but there is a specific moment when you realize that the vehicle you are chasing isn't going to stop, and you become euphoric. Adrenaline drowns your body as if you were standing under a waterfall. Your heart beats faster, your mind begins to race as you calculate your next move and try to anticipate the suspect's next move, you concentrate on where you are and communicate your fast-changing location to dispatch and other officers—everything seems to go in slow motion, and you become hyperfocused. Of course, there's also the little matter of keeping your vehicle under control as you maneuver around traffic, people, and other obstacles without causing an accident or injury. The chase continued and more patrol cars joined in. After about ten minutes nearly every officer on duty was actively involved.

During the chase, nearly every policy in the Pontiac PD's policy and procedures manual on pursuits was violated. I must have broken over half of them myself. We tried to box the car in. Some of us attempted to pass the suspect vehicle, which resulted in being hit by the suspect vehicle. Police cars were run off the road, and when the chase was called off by the sergeant, some officers continued pursuing—including me.

The suspect vehicle was heading toward the downtown area where the streets were full of weekend bar patrons. I tried to maneuver my patrol car around the suspect vehicle to get in front of him, but he jerked his wheel to the left and rammed the passenger side of my patrol vehicle. Upon impact I hit my head hit on the window. It was just about this time that Sergeant Garibaldi got on the radio and told all units to discontinue the chase. I'm not sure why I didn't hear that command. Maybe I was dazed from hitting my head, but I continued the pursuit. Within minutes the suspect vehicle turned westbound and left the downtown district. Someone got back on the radio and requested permission to resume the chase—it was granted.

As the vehicle continued westbound, we began to approach city limits. Another officer got on the radio and requested that dispatch contact the neighboring city of Waterford to advise them that we had a chase headed their way. Within minutes we entered Waterford, and several Waterford PD units also joined the pursuit. As the chase began to approach the western border of Waterford and White Lake, one of the Waterford officers laid stop sticks across the road in an attempt to end the chase. Unfortunately, the suspect saw the officer and made a last-minute right turn and headed northbound.

After that, the suspect turned his vehicle toward a large open field, jumped out of his car, and tried to run away. The chase had lasted over twenty minutes and spanned two cities. However, the suspect didn't stand a chance of getting away because there were too many officers involved in the chase. Officers stopped their vehicles at different places around the field and within moments the suspect was in a physical altercation with several of them. During the struggle, a Waterford officer was hit in the head by another officer and had to go to the hospital to get stitches. In the confusion no one was sure how the officer's injury had occurred.

I tried to get involved by handcuffing the driver, but there were many male officers on the scene, and they weren't going to let a female officer into the fight. I managed to work my way into the pile of bodies, but quickly felt myself being lifted up and set down outside of the pile. It was frustrating, of course, since it was my chase and my arrest, but it wouldn't be the last time that something like this happened. It was something that you learned to accept as a female officer.

While everyone involved in the chase was given a written discipline, I was suspended for ten hours unpaid. It was my chase, and I was deemed most responsible for the mistakes that were made. Someone had to pay for all the accidents and rule violations. I viewed it as part of the learning curve, and I deserved it.

A few months later I would be suspended again for calling a fellow female officer a bitch. I was dispatched with several other officers to a domestic complaint. The aggressor was a pregnant female. Domestic laws don't provide an exemption for pregnant women, and she had to be arrested. I placed her in handcuffs, and she immediately started screaming, cursing, and struggling with me. I finally got her in the back seat of my patrol vehicle, but she continued to act out and began kicking at the windows of my car as she hurled personal insults at me. Rather than take responsibility for her actions, she got angry at me for arresting her.

I was concerned about her safety, so I approached one of the other officers at the scene, Officer Sanders, and told her that the arrested female really didn't like me and that she was kicking at the windows of my car. I asked Officer Sanders if she would transport the female to the station instead. I thought it would be better for the woman so that she could calm down and not injure herself. I told Officer Sanders that I would meet her there and do all the paperwork for the arrest. Officer Sanders looked me dead in the eye and told me to do my own work. I was livid. I couldn't believe that she wouldn't be a team player and drive a two-mile transport for me. I said, "Thanks for your help, you fucking bitch," and walked back to my car.

The next day I was called into the sergeant's office and asked why I called Officer Sanders a bitch. I replied defiantly, "Because she was being a fucking bitch!" As part of "progressive discipline," I was suspended for twenty hours unpaid.

My next suspension came for arguing with a male officer on a shooting scene. I had recently begun to notice that every time I went to a call with an officer with more time on the job than me, even if it wasn't my assigned section of the city, they claimed seniority and made me take the report. I had started to get frustrated by it and wondered if they were truly claiming seniority or if they just felt that they could pick on me because I was a woman. Finally, I had decided that enough was enough. If seniority was the game, then I would play it too.

Officer Bean was dispatched to a shooting call in the White Castle restaurant parking lot, and I was dispatched from another area of the city as his backup unit. Officer Bean arrived on scene first; it was his section of the city, and he was a junior officer to me. Within minutes, Officer Bean began yelling at me that he had worked a double that day, was tired, and that I was taking the report whether or not I wanted to. After debating the point with him, I decided enough was enough. It would have been one thing if he had asked me to take it, but to demand it was the last straw for me. I told him that he was the junior officer, it was his section, and that it was his call so he was going to take the report. He continued yelling at me and then got in his patrol car and left me at the scene alone.

I wasn't surprised when I got called into the sergeant's office the next day. What did shock me though was that I was the one in trouble, not Officer Bean. I was told that it was unprofessional to argue on the scene and that I was suspended for forty hours unpaid. I accepted my first two suspensions fairly easily, but this one was ridiculous. How could Officer Bean not be in trouble for yelling at me on a scene? Worse, how could he not be in trouble for leaving me alone at the scene of a shooting?

My fourth suspension that year was the most difficult for me to accept. By this time, I had been dating a coworker, Officer Neil Dennis, for several months and everyone knew about our relationship. Neil was a training officer and had recently finished training a new guy, Officer Smythe. I was in the report writing room finishing up a report when Officer Smythe walked in and started up a conversation. I finished my report and got up to leave when he stopped me and asked me on a date. I laughed because I wasn't sure if it was a joke or not. I replied that he knew I was dating Neil and walked away. I didn't give it another thought after I left the room.

As the days passed, I had begun to hear rumors that Officer Smythe was telling everyone in the department that I was racist. Apparently, Officer Smythe assumed that I wouldn't go out with him because he was African American, not because I had a boyfriend. I was frustrated and angry. In police work you have to depend on your fellow officers to have your back; to be there for you in difficult situations. How could I trust anyone to be there for me or vice versa, if they thought I was racist?

I really wasn't sure how to handle the situation, so I fell back onto my tried-and-true solution to difficulty—I attempted to forget about it. Forgetting had been my natural reaction to difficulties for so many years that it was second nature to me. It became something I did almost unconsciously. Somehow, ignoring the situation only made things worse. My frustration continued to grow by the day. With my solution amounting to pure failure, I decided to change tactics. I tried to be nice, playful, and chatty with Officer Smythe.

One particular day, I walked into the line-up room, where everyone would meet before our shift began, for a briefing from the sergeant. While there were no assigned seats, it was routine for everyone to sit in the same seat day after day, year after year. On this day, I saw that Officer Smythe was sitting in my seat. Instead of yelling at him, I approached him, put my hands on his shoulders, smiled, and said in my most cheerful voice, "You're in my seat, silly."

Officer Smythe jumped up out of the chair and screamed at me to get my hands off of him, which was the beginning of a tirade that he would unleash upon me. Soon, we were screaming at the tops of our lungs at each other. I didn't understand why he had taken it to such an extreme, but I wasn't about to stand there and take his abuse. Then he said it: "Bitch, shut the fuck up or I'll shoot you and your man." *Did he actually just threaten to shoot me? And Neil?* Luckily, the sergeant heard the screaming and came to the line-up room to find out what was happening. Officer Smythe sat down and acted like nothing happened.

The next day I couldn't get what Officer Smythe said out of my head. I decided to speak with Captain Koller and tell him that I wanted to be administratively moved to another shift. I told him that Officer Smythe had threatened to shoot me and that I no longer felt safe either working with him or trusting him to back me up. Captain Koller took my information about the incident and sent it to Internal Affairs. After a short investigation, it was erroneously determined that I was the aggressor in the incident and that there was no evidence that Officer Smythe had actually threatened to shoot me. How could this happen, you might ask? Well, the only people in the room during the altercation were Officer Smythe's partner and Officer Sanders and her partner. When they were interviewed by Internal Affairs, they all lied. I was suspended for sixty hours unpaid and put on desk duty until I could pass a mental fitness for duty examination.

A few days later I was sent to a department-approved psychologist who would evaluate me. It's difficult to remember everything that was said in that meeting, but I do remember thinking as I was leaving that I couldn't believe the department used this particular psychologist for evaluations. It was so clear to me that he didn't believe that women should work in law enforcement. For most of the meeting he was condescending and rude. I remember him asking me why I was surprised that the situation had occurred between me and Officer Smythe. He seemed to imply that women should not only expect that type of treatment being in a male-dominated field, but that we should accept it. I didn't need to wait for news of the evaluation—I knew what the results were going to be

As expected, a few days later, I was told that I was deemed not fit for duty and that I would need to remain working the front desk until further notice. To say that I was angry would be a complete understatement. After a couple months working the desk, I couldn't take it anymore.

Chain of command be damned—I went directly to the chief of police and told him that I needed to talk to him. I told him that I felt the psychologist was biased and that my suspension was wrong. I demanded a polygraph test regarding the incident that had occurred with Officer Smythe and swore to him that I had told the truth and that Officer Smythe and the others had lied. I begged him to send me to a different psychologist for another evaluation. I'm not sure which part of what I said convinced him, but he agreed to send me to someone else. A few days later I was found fit for duty and allowed to return to work. My suspension was also reversed, and I was reimbursed for the sixty-hour suspension that I had already served.

Regardless of the reversals, it could not take away all that I had been put through in those months. I had been branded a liar, a troublemaker, and mentally unfit. The whole department knew, and I could feel officers judging me with every side-eyed glare I received. This was still too early in my career to understand the biases that were being perpetrated against me, but I see the situation more clearly today. The words *gaslighting* and *hysteria* come to mind. The truth of what occurred that day was completely dismissed in favor of a ridiculous story spun by a male officer. The persona that was thrust upon me was one of a mentally ill woman whose statements couldn't be believed rather than that of an angry woman who had been threatened and was seeking support and validation.

Eventually, the chief of police decided he had enough of me. He called a command staff meeting to discuss whether I should be terminated. I did not find out about the meeting until years later, but Sergeant Hess, Sergeant Garibaldi, and Lieutenant Keller all came to my defense and saved my job. After that first year was over, things began to get better for me. My coworkers and supervisors began to see that I had an outstanding work ethic and that I never lied, even when it would save me from trouble. I earned a reputation as a hard worker through my undercover work and my consistently high arrest and ticket stats. About a year later, Lieutenant Flint said to me, "If I had known when I was in Internal Affairs what I know about you now, I never would have suspended you." Better late than never, I guess.

Thinking about why that first year was so difficult, I have come up with several reasons. First and foremost, I don't think I really knew what being a cop meant or what policing really was. The truth is that there were no police officers in my family. In fact, my family was much more likely to be found on the other side of the bars. In my head, I wanted the excitement, the power, the courage, and the strength of Mel Gibson in *Lethal Weapon*. I didn't have the educational background to provide a basis in what the reality of policing was. Part of that reality is that policing isn't like the movies. Another part of reality is that being a female in a male-dominated, adrenaline-fueled field is not easy.

Frequently, I felt that the expectations of being a female police officer were much like when I was a child growing up in my father's house. It was better to be seen and not heard. My outspoken and in-your-face personality was neither wanted nor appreciated. My expectations for my fellow officers were equivalent to the expectations I placed upon myself. I must admit, I can't stand lazy people and there are times when I couldn't hold my tongue. Unfortunately, that's not how it works, not just in policing, but in all professions. On many occasions, I was reminded of this lesson the hard way, particularly shortly after being moved to the midnight shift.

Midnights were always a hard shift for me. After about 3:00 a.m. it just got too quiet. If I had any chance of staying awake, then I had to keep moving. Not just driving around but staying active. In fact, driving around aimlessly was a surefire way to put me to sleep. To combat this, I kept myself busy during the downtime by making traffic stops all night long. Apparently, this was not "standard protocol" for those that worked midnights. Those officers enjoyed the quiet and viewed my radio chatter as unwanted annoyance.

Toward the end of one shift, I was sitting at the front desk completing paperwork for my many traffic stops from that night. Officer Wolfe walked in the room, stood near the front desk, and complained to another officer how quiet and boring the night had been. I was immediately incensed.

"If you were so fucking bored last night maybe you could have stopped by and backed me on one of my many traffic stops," I sneered. No sooner had I finished the sentence when it happened.

"In my office, now!" screamed Sergeant Fuller.

As I stood up to walk to the sergeant's office, I noticed that Officer Wolfe was smirking. I glared at him as I walked away. I knew what was going to be said and I was already furious. As expected, Sergeant Fuller berated me for speaking to a senior officer as I had. Who did I think I was, show some respect, on and on it went. I tried to interject that he should be yelling at Officer Wolfe, but I was cut off and yelled at more. I sat silently through the remainder of his reprimand and walked out when it was over.

Did this happen because I was a newer officer or because I was a woman? I'll never know for sure, but I think it was a bit of both. As the years passed, I would come to learn that Officer Wolfe was the lazy piece of shit I thought he was and that a vast majority of the department thought so too. Complaints about Officer Wolfe came from many people over the years and I never heard anyone get yelled at or admonished for it in any way. In fact, when I spoke to Sergeant Hess about writing this book more than a decade later, he reminded me of the above incident with Officer Wolfe. He had heard my comment to Officer Wolfe that morning and my dressing down by Sergeant Fuller. He told me that he had respected my standing up to Officer Wolfe and that too many people had allowed Officer Wolfe to get away with laziness. Sergeant Hess was shocked when Sergeant Fuller came after me the way he did. This was when Sergeant Hess knew that he and I would be friends.

What I didn't realize then, but do now, is that everyone is different, and that difference is a good thing. Having a department full of officers like me would not be ideal, nor would having a department full of officers like Wolfe. The truth is that the world works best when there is balance. On a slow day officers like me will keep themselves busy. The problem occurs when a big call comes in. If everyone were keeping themselves busy, who would be available to take the call? My husband, Neil, is a perfect example. Neil is definitely not lazy, but he was never a big proponent of making traffic stops. He preferred to keep himself available to take calls that other officers might not be available for. And the truth is, if there was a shooting or stabbing, there was no one you wanted on scene more than him. As an officer, Neil has always been calm, cool, and collected and his demeanor puts everyone at ease and minimizes a chaotic atmosphere.

None of this is meant to excuse the outright laziness of an officer like Wolfe, but rather it's one of the many lessons I learned in the years since leaving police work and returning to school, a lesson that would have made my job infinitely easier had I known.

6

COCKROACHES AND
COMMENDATIONS

In my earliest days at Pontiac PD, I developed a unique friendship with one of my supervisors, Sergeant Hess. I can't say that I remember precisely how we ended up as friends, but I can tell you that we had an immediate bond, a connection on a mental level that few people are ever lucky enough to experience. The best way to describe our relationship is that we were like two halves of the same person. We understood each other perfectly. Our overwhelming passion for our chosen career and our desire to solve crimes, find suspects, and make arrests were unparalleled.

As much as we were alike, we were also very different. I am not OCD, but when it comes to work, I am very organized. I arrive early for everything, and few people can come close to my multitasking and report-writing skills. Writing is a skill I mastered while in high school and always enjoyed. The key to writing a good police report is to document every detail, from the moment you arrive on the scene of a call to the moment you finish writing the report, which many officers fail to do.

Sergeant Hess, on the other hand, is chaos in motion. He is consistently late. I don't think he has ever been on time for anything, ever. He's a terrible driver. He once drove the front end of a patrol car off the edge of a cliff. He never knows where anything is, like keys, wallet, cell phone, and is always searching for them. However, his instincts are uncanny, and no one can interrogate a suspect like he can. Put him in a room with anyone and he is sure to get a full confession. Call out a stolen car, and he's likely to find it within minutes.

My relationship with Sergeant Hess was just one of four important relationships that I developed during my first year at Pontiac PD, but they were all different. Sergeant Garibaldi was someone I could trust implicitly; someone I could laugh with and who I would come to see as more of a friend than supervisor. Officer Luna became my partner and best friend. We confided in one another about our personal lives and troubles we had both personally and professionally. There was absolutely nothing that I couldn't, or didn't, tell him. We spent time together in and outside of work. Over the years he became like a brother to me. Officer Dennis, of course, went on to become my husband. While Neil was my friend and confidant, he was someone I could always trust to support me. Neil never sugarcoated anything—he was forward and never hesitated to tell me the truth, even if it wasn't what I wanted to hear. The one thing we didn't share was my love and enthusiasm for police work. To me it was my life, but to Neil it was a job. And then there was Sergeant Hess. Sergeant Hess had some of the best traits from all three wrapped into one.

When I think about Sergeant Hess it feels as if he has been in my life forever, as if we were destined to be friends. Don't be mistaken, Sergeant Hess has been more than just my friend. He has been my mentor, my confidant, my biggest supporter, the person I sought out for advice, and the person I always wanted most to impress. I didn't confide my personal relationship problems to him, but that's not because I couldn't. Sergeant Hess and I shared a love of police work, and I didn't want to bury our enthusiasm for work with personal troubles. We kept each other excited and motivated in our jobs. At the same time his quirkiness always kept me laughing. Sadly, there were times over the years when I made it very difficult for him to continue to support me. Lucky for me he always managed to find a way.

With the undercover prostitution details going well, and my reputation with my fellow officers and command staff improving, other opportunities soon came my way. I wanted to believe that all the hard work I put into my job was the sole reason that those opportunities arose, but there were, undoubtedly, many who would say they came because of my friendship with Sergeant Hess.

By this time our close friendship was not a secret within the department. We often signed up for overtime details that we could work together, met for lunch at our favorite Mexican restaurant once a week, were always consulting and assisting one another on interesting cases, and frequently went to the prosecutor's office to seek out warrants for one another and handled each other's court cases. There were even times when one of us would come into work on our day off and ride around with the other.

We really enjoyed our time together and relished having someone just as enthusiastic to talk to about work. Neither of us had significant others who understood how we felt about work. Sergeant Hess's wife had less than zero interest in his work and wanted nothing to do with other officers or work events. Although Neil was a police officer too, it was just a job to him. He certainly didn't want to discuss cases outside of work.

One day I was enjoying a day off at home with my son when I received a phone call from Sergeant Hess. He told me that he had been authorized to put together a COMSTAT (short for computer statistics) unit. COMSTAT produced maps of each area in the city and pinpointed each crime that occurred. This technology allowed officers to determine which were the high crime areas, identify any patterns in the crimes being committed, and enable officers to tackle the problems of that area in a more effective manner.

I told Sergeant Hess how excited I was for him. He was my best friend and his success made me happy. After a few minutes, Sergeant Hess told me that he wasn't just calling to tell me about the unit; he was calling to ask me to be a part of it. I was speechless, for only a quick moment, and then I shouted, "Yes!" I didn't care what I was going to be doing, what the schedule would be, or who else was going to be in the unit. The only thing I cared about was that not only was I getting another opportunity at work, but I was getting to work with Sergeant Hess.

The first day of working on the unit was miserable and amazing. It was pouring rain, the type of rain that felt like it could drown you if you stood in it for more than a few seconds. Sergeant Hess was driving, which always worried me because, as I said before, he's a terrible driver. I was sitting in the passenger seat, a smile plastered to my face, full of anticipation of what the night would bring. I felt like I might explode, I was so full of joy. I didn't know exactly what we were going to be doing, but I didn't care.

As we drove around our designated area, Sergeant Hess explained more about what was expected of our little unit. There would be four officers, myself included, that would focus on the crime in a specified neighborhood. We were to analyze each case and decide how best to handle it. We were authorized to work plainclothes, surveillance, develop informants, flex our days and hours—whatever we thought it would take. We answered only to Sergeant Hess and, basically, as long as we were producing results, he would support us.

The neighborhood that we were focused on for our COMSTAT unit was called Indian Village. The city of Pontiac is named after a famous war chief of the Ottawa Indian tribe, Chief Pontiac.[1] As such, there are many street names and neighborhoods in Pontiac that were given American Indian names, such as Ottawa, Otsego, Miami, Chippewa, Cherokee, Algonquin, Navajo, and more. At the time, the Indian Village neighborhood was suffering from widespread crime, mostly stemming from drugs. Our mandate was to do whatever we needed to get the crime rates down.

With the details out of the way, we got down to business. Rain or no rain, we were going to make some noise. Sergeant Hess and I must have stopped nearly everyone in the neighborhood that day—at least it felt that way. The important thing about working a detail like this was to learn who belonged in the neighborhood and who didn't. The only way to do that was to stop and talk to people. If we could determine who were the buyers and who were the sellers, we could start to address both. Deterring people who didn't live in the area from being there was the first step to lowering crime rates.

The first ten hours were packed with traffic stops, stop and frisks, and misdemeanor investigations of all varieties. We made it our business to talk to and/or investigate nearly everyone who crossed our path. Walking down the middle of the street was a city ordinance violation and a misdemeanor. Sitting on a known drug corner was loitering and a misdemeanor. Cracked windshield was a civil infraction. No one was safe from our intrusions that night.

By the end of our shift, we were drenched. It was the type of wet that when you peeled your clothes off, they would drop to the floor with a heavy thud. The type of wet where cold chills permeated into your bones. Where even the hottest shower struggled to warm your insides. We walked into the station, dripping, and were met by Sergeant Friedman. He immediately said, "What the hell have you two been doing out there? Do you know how many citizen complaints I've gotten in the last few hours?" Sergeant Hess and I both laughed. I guess we had rattled some cages.

Having people in my life that I could depend on was fairly new to me. Being let down and abandoned was much more the norm. Some people like to say that a girl can always depend on her daddy, but that wasn't the case for me. In fact, no one let me down more than my father did. It didn't matter if it was something big or something small. The one thing I could count on was for my father to never be around whenever I needed him most.

To say my teenage years were restricted would be an understatement. My father didn't seem to trust me, even though I never did anything to destroy that trust. The one thing I *was* allowed to do was to go to the roller rink on most weekends. In those days everybody who was anybody hung out at the Baypointe Roller Rink. It was a place where I could escape the torture, sadness, and fear that pervaded my life. I was free to smile, laugh, socialize, and, for a few hours, forget the misery at home that devoured me like quicksand. Those times at the roller rink were probably one of the few things that kept me from going completely insane.

One typical Saturday night I was getting ready to go skating. I was meticulous about making sure each curl in my hair was perfect. My father was in the living room smoking a joint, which was typical. He yelled to me that he wanted to talk. I couldn't imagine what I had done now. In an instant, my day ran through my head. I had cleaned the bathroom, washed the dishes, vacuumed the floor, dusted the living room, cleaned my room. I had double-checked that each task was done to perfection. I hadn't left anything lying around. I had finished my homework. What could he want?

I meekly walked into the living room, secretly hoping that no matter what I had done, I could get the beating over with and still be able to go to the roller rink. My father started yelling at me (he never talked, always yelled) that I was not to get a ride home with anyone when skating was over. I was to wait there for him to pick me up, no matter what. I didn't understand where this lecture was coming from. I had never gotten a ride home from anyone else unless he had told me to because he couldn't pick me up for some reason. I always assumed that most of his ranting and raving was the result of drugs and alcohol and figured today was no different. I promised I would wait for him.

The roller rink could only be described in one way: a room full of raging teenage hormones. Puppy love, crushes, unrequited affection, friendship, heartbreak, anticipation could all be seen in full view when the DJ played a slow song. *Will he ask me to skate with him? Will she say yes if I ask her? I can't believe he's skating with her!* Girls rushing to the bathroom in tears. Boys sulking alone in the corner.

I spent the evening alternating between skating, eating nachos, requesting songs from the DJ, playing video games, and laughing with my friends. The Ms. Pac-Man machine was my favorite. All the trips to the bar with my dad had made me a force to be reckoned with on that machine. Few people could compete at my level. My friends were amazed that my name was always at the top of the high-score list. For those precious few hours, I didn't have a care in the world.

When midnight came around, all those carefree feelings went away. I felt reality sinking in as I took off my skates and returned them to the rental counter. I ran around quickly and said goodbye to my friends. I knew my dad would be outside and I didn't want to get yelled at for making him wait. I rushed outside and was slapped in the face by extreme cold. The temperature had dropped significantly since I arrived hours earlier and it had started snowing. The snowflakes were huge, and they were falling fast and hard. I pulled my coat tighter around me and looked for my father to no avail.

I wasn't dressed for this weather. I had on a lightweight coat, but no gloves or hat. I hadn't expected to be waiting outside for my ride. My father deemed me so untrustworthy that he was always there early to pick me up. I stood against the building and tried to shield myself from the weather as much as I could. My friends continued to exit the building, giving us another chance to say our goodbyes. Slowly, but surely, the building emptied.

One of the last people to leave was my friend Keri. Her father had been a good friend of my father's for years. Keri asked me if I wanted a ride home and I said thanks, but no thanks. My father would be there any minute. After Keri got into her father's car, they drove close to where I was standing. Her father told me to get in and he would drive me home. I again thanked them but said that my father would be arriving any minute.

Time continued to tick by. Eventually, the employees exited the building and one of them asked me if I needed a ride home. I thanked her but declined. After everyone drove away, I began to cry quietly. I didn't know what to do. I was afraid to walk home and risk my father arriving to find that I was gone, but I was so cold I couldn't stand there any longer. I looked at my watch—2:00 a.m. Finally, I made the decision to start walking.

I lived about two miles from the roller rink. I zipped my coat up as high as it would go, crossed my arms around my body, tucked my bare hands into the crook of my elbows to try to keep them warm, and began walking home. The snow continued to fall, and the wind was blowing to the east. Of course, I was walking west, and my face was being sandblasted by the wind and snow. I decided to put my head down and look at my feet as I walked. It wasn't much protection, but it was better than nothing.

It seemed like I was walking on a treadmill; never getting any closer to home. A million thoughts rushed through my head as I made my way through the numbing cold: fear, sadness, embarrassment, helplessness. While my mind raced, my body, completely numb from the cold, felt nothing. Eventually, I made it. I tried to uncross my arms to get my house keys out of my pocket but realized snow had piled up across them and froze my sleeves together. With a tug, I ripped my arms apart and the piled-up snow fell to the ground. I opened the door to find a dark and silent house, except for the sound of crackling and popping coming from the wood-burning stove.

With numb fingers I struggled to take off my coat and shoes. I tiptoed toward my father's bedroom and found that he and Caroline were fast asleep. I was immediately overcome with rage. My whole body began to shake as I realized I was fighting off the urge to kill him. I imagined myself jumping on the bed and choking him to death with my bare hands. The reality was that I was too small to accomplish such a task, which made me angrier. I couldn't believe that he had simply gone to bed and forgotten about me.

I walked to my room and changed into pajamas as I struggled to control my rage. I had hated my father, but I had never wanted to kill him the way I did at that moment. I walked into the living room and curled up on the floor directly in front of the wood burning stove. After a few minutes my fingers started to tingle as the warmth penetrated my numb fingers and the blood finally rushed back into them. Slowly but surely, the fire worked its magic. I went to bed, pulled the blankets over my head, and fell asleep.

Morning came entirely too soon. I was awakened by my father pulling the blankets off me and yelling. He accused me of getting a ride home when he specifically told me not to. I reassured him that I didn't get a ride home and decided to walk because he never showed up. He insisted I was lying and wanted to know who gave me a ride. I was resolute and too angry to back down. I screamed at him, "You fell asleep! You didn't pick me up! I could have gotten a ride home, but I didn't because you said you were coming to get me! I walked home in the middle of a snowstorm!" It was a rare moment of defiance—consequences be damned.

I pulled the blankets on top of me and rolled over so that my back was facing him. I braced myself for the battering that I was convinced was coming, but he did nothing. I think he knew he was wrong. I'm not saying he felt guilty, I'm not sure he was capable of feeling guilt, but he knew. A few days later I came down with pneumonia, which confirmed my story. My father never acknowledged what he had done. Never apologized. Never asked for forgiveness.

The COMSTAT unit was a dream come true. This was the type of work I was meant to do: identifying a problem, analyzing possible solutions, and implementing the best course of action. There was true freedom in this detail. We didn't have a set schedule, no one breathed down our necks, we didn't have to justify every little thing we wanted to do. Sergeant Hess was true to his word—we produced results and he supported us fully.

Each day working this detail was different, which meant we never got bored. A favorite day, the one that ended with a commendation, actually took place on one of my days off. I had gotten information from an informant about drugs being sold from the backyard of a house on Dwight Street. This was interesting to me because we had been aware of drug activity at that house, but due to increased presence in the area, all signs of dealing had ceased from that residence.

I decided to verify the information before bringing in other members of the unit. I took a cleaning bucket from my house and inside it placed a video camera, my police radio, and my gun. I drove to an apartment building directly behind the house in question. My informant was the manager of that building and had provided me with a key to an empty apartment on one of the upper floors.

When I entered the apartment I almost gagged. It was small, dirty, had peeling paint, spider webs everywhere, and cockroaches running around. I cannot stress enough how much I hate creepy-crawlies. I took a deep breath and reminded myself how important verifying this tip was.

I put my gun in its holster and placed it on my hip, set my police radio on the floor, and turned the ringer on my cell phone to vibrate. I flipped the bucket over, placed it in front of the window, and sat down on it. The view from the window gave me a perfect view into the backyard of the suspected drug house. I was ready to find out if the information I received was accurate.

It didn't take long before the action started. I turned on my video camera and placed it gently on the ledge of the windowsill, holding it for balance. I observed several young Black males, late teens to early twenties, walk into the backyard and post themselves at various areas. Soon, other people began to arrive one by one. I noticed that when someone new would arrive, one of the males would reach into a bush, behind a rock, under the porch, wherever they were posted, and retrieve something and give to the person. An exchange was taking place and I knew immediately that drugs were hidden in various places in the backyard.

My cell phone vibrated in my pocket, which startled me so much that I almost dropped the video camera out the window. I quickly regained my composure and set the video camera on top of the bucket and walked away from the window to quietly answer the phone.

"Hello," I whispered.

"Hey, what are you up to?" Sergeant Hess asked.

Whispering, I told him what I was doing. I didn't get very far when he interrupted me and said, "I'll be right there."

Minutes later Sergeant Hess walked into the apartment and stopped dead in his tracks. He was wearing blue jeans and a polo shirt. No gun, no uniform, no radio. Clearly, he wasn't on duty either. He looked around at the apartment with as much disgust as I had when I first entered.

I finished filling him in on the tip I had received and my attempt to find out if it was accurate, which I assured him it was. Sergeant Hess approached the window with me, and I put the video camera back on the ledge. At that moment a White woman rode her bike into the backyard. She appeared to be in her forties, had scraggly long blonde hair, and was wearing disheveled clothes. She approached one of the men and handed him money. The man then handed her something, motioning for her to put it in her mouth. She complied, got back on her bike, and rode away.

Sergeant Hess said he was going to get her and immediately ran out of the apartment. Approximately ten minutes later he came back to the apartment with a small rock of crack cocaine in clear plastic bag. He said he located the woman down the street, stopped her, forced her to open her mouth, and retrieved the crack. He also wrote her name and date of birth on his hand and told her that he would be contacting her soon with a warrant for her arrest.

I can only imagine what that woman must have been thinking. She was approached by a man saying he was the police, but had no badge, no gun, no radio, was driving his personal vehicle, and confiscated her drugs. I don't know why, but she never called the police to report it.

Sergeant Hess advised me that he was calling the vice unit to let them know what we witnessed. If they were able to come to the house and raid it, I could tell them exactly where the drugs were hidden. It took a couple hours to coordinate, but finally vice officers showed up. As soon as they entered the backyard, the young men selling the drugs ran in all different directions. It was utter chaos as officers began to chase them, each officer getting on the radio to relay their location to dispatch. With so many officers radioing in different foot chases it was all but impossible to maintain clarity as to where each officer was and what was happening. Eventually, all the drug dealers were captured and arrested, the drugs were confiscated, and my video tape was the star witness in court.

After sitting in a dirty, cockroach-infested apartment and then writing a long report, my day off turned into twelve hours of overtime. Later, Sergeant Hess was faced with the typical difficulties that always seemed to come with working with me. I had done great police work, but I had gone about it on my day off without telling anyone where I was or what I was doing. I have to admit that it wasn't exactly a good idea as far as officer safety was concerned.

Sergeant Hess resolved this dilemma by doing two things: he verbally reprimanded me for, essentially, doing something dumb and then rewarded my first-rate police work by submitting my bust for a meritorious service citation. Sergeant Hess always received flack when he showed his support for me. Other supervisors would question our friendship and what he saw in me that was special. The upper command of the department, who didn't know me personally, were still holding grudges against me and fought any attempt to give me positive recognition. Sergeant Hess never lied to me or tried to hide what was being said by other commanders in the department. It was one of the many things I respected about him. At lunch one day he told me the chief was denying the citation he submitted for my work in the drug bust. I wasn't surprised. This was the same chief who refused to give me the Officer of the Year award after I won it through a department-wide vote and the same chief who had wanted to fire me after my first year. To say he was unsupportive of my work is an understatement.

Although Sergeant Hess had to fight for me to receive it, the chief finally relented and agreed to award me with a lower citation. I was finally awarded a letter of commendation. It wasn't as high a commendation, but it was something. That was one of my proudest moments in law enforcement. Not only had I carried out superior police work, but Sergeant Hess thought enough of it to recognize me with an award. It was the first time I felt I had truly impressed him, which meant the world to me.

I continued to work on the COMSTAT unit for several months. They were filled with some of my best memories of police work. In those months I was able to learn a wide variety of skills such as properly conducting surveillance, developing informants, and how to cause a riot. Yes, that's right. I caused a small riot. It wasn't my intention, and I'm still pretty sure that it wasn't my fault, but nevertheless, it happened.

Since our unit consisted of four officers, we usually worked in pairs. Sergeant Hess was sometimes with us, but not always. On this day he happened to be working with us. I was partnered with Officer Anderson, a six-foot-two, 220-pound African American, from Pontiac. We had been partners for about a month by this time and got along well. Officer Anderson was a go-getter. It was great to have someone with the same enthusiasm to work with.

It was a beautiful August evening. Officer Anderson and I were driving around in a patrol car with our windows down, not doing or looking for anything in particular. "Do you hear that?" Officer Anderson asked me. I stopped the patrol car at the next stop sign and listened. I could hear very loud music playing. We didn't know where it was coming from, so we drove west in search of the source. The music got louder as we continued westbound, finally finding the source on Johnson Street near Liberty Street.

Sergeant Hess was assisting the other pair of officers in the unit for a traffic stop, so we were available to check out the loud music. At that time, the city of Pontiac had a noise ordinance that stated it was a violation for music to be heard more than fifty feet from a house or twenty-five feet from a vehicle. Since we had heard the music several blocks away, the people playing the music were clearly in violation.

The official police report of the incident reads as follows:

On 8-7-04 at approximately 2115 hours, Officers Anderson and I were on patrol in the area of Henderson and Cooley when we heard very loud music coming from the area of Johnson between Cooley and Liberty. Officer Anderson and I parked our vehicle on Cooley and walked over to North Johnson until we located the house where the music was coming from. The house we located the music coming from was 86 North Johnson.

Officer Anderson and I walked around to the back of the residence and immediately observed a large crowd, approximately 40–50 people, in the yard with many of them drinking alcoholic beverages. I walked over to a B/M [Black male] who was sitting in front of the stereo system. I told the man to turn the music off. The man turned the music down. I again asked him to turn the music off and he immediately complied. A B/F [Black female] standing approximately six feet away from me then said, "Who does that rude bitch think she is?" I asked her who she was, and she told me that she was the owner of the residence, later identified as Aaliyah Masters. I then told Aaliyah that she needed to get her ID for me. Aaliyah said fine and then started walking into the house. As Aaliyah was walking up the stairs she said, "See if I come back out." I had begun walking toward the door behind her to make sure that she did come back with her ID. As I approached the door, I heard a man's voice behind me tell her to shut the door and lock it. Just as I reached for the door, Aaliyah slammed it shut hitting my right hand with the door. I tried to open the door, but it was locked. I told Aaliyah to open the door, but she stood inside yelling something I couldn't understand at me from inside the house. I called to Officer Anderson and he came up to the door where I was.

While Officer Anderson was attempting to get Aaliyah to open the door, a B/M came up behind me from outside. The man, later identified as Carlton Masters, was yelling at me to leave his sister alone. I told Carlton several times to back up and go back outside. I then got on the radio and told Sergeant Hess that we needed backup now. Carlton continued to yell at me and was pointing and shaking his finger in my face. I again told Carlton to back up and he continued to refuse. I then told Carlton that was enough, and I grabbed his arm to place him under arrest for obstructing. Carlton jerked his arm away from me, backed out the door and slammed the screen door in my face. I opened the door and again grabbed Carlton's arm; again, Carlton jerked his arm away from me and pushed me backward. As I attempted to go toward Carlton again, a B/F who was holding a baby, later identified as Patricia Mazel, got between me and Carlton and started pushing me backward away from him. Because of the baby, I only pushed Mazel aside and out of my way. As I again attempted to take Carlton into custody, he again jerked away and pushed me backward. Mazel then got in between Carlton and me again and again started pushing me backward. At this point, Officer Anderson got between me and Carlton and Mazel. Officer Anderson walked Carlton to the back of the yard and attempted to talk to him. I began to walk toward them when Mazel again got in front of me and started pushing me again. During this entire incident, Carlton and Mazel were yelling ethnic slurs at me, the crowd of people was gathering around us yelling at us, and getting between us and the people we were trying to take into custody. In some cases, we were physically held back by the crowd.

Sergeant Hess and Officer Cabana then arrived on scene and assisted with breaking up the crowd. Officer Anderson was then able to take Carlton out to the patrol vehicle parked in front of the residence. I then briefed Sergeant Hess about what had happened. Several other officers then arrived on scene to assist with crowd control. Sergeant Hess told Officer Anderson and Officer Cabana to go with me into the back yard and locate the females that had been involved in the earlier altercation with me.

Officer Anderson, Officer Cabana, and I went into the residence and located Mazel. I advised the officers that this was the female that had been holding the baby and we attempted to take her into custody. Mazel started yelling at us and told us that we were not handcuffing her. Officer Cabana and I reached out to grab Mazel and she jerked away and took off running through the house. Officer Cabana and I ran after Mazel as she ran up the stairs of the house. I was stopped by an unidentified B/M who grabbed a hold of me and held me back and told me to leave her (Mazel) alone. I pushed him aside and ran up the stairs where Officer Cabana was calling to me. Officer Cabana advised me that Mazel had locked herself into the bathroom. Another man came upstairs and told Mazel to come out. Mazel opened the door and Officer Cabana and I again attempted to take her into custody. Mazel pushed away from us and ran down the stairs where there was a large crowd of people waiting. Officer Cabana again attempted to take Mazel into custody on the stairs, but Mazel jerked away and pushed Officer Cabana away from her. Officer Anderson then came into the house and told Mazel to come outside with him. Mazel replied that she would go with Officer Anderson, but that she wasn't "going with those two white bitches."

I then identified Aaliyah to Sergeant Hess as the female homeowner who had slammed the door on my hand and refused to come outside and provide ID. By that time, Aaliyah had changed her clothes (admitted), but was still identified. Aaliyah was advised that she was to be placed under arrest as well. Aaliyah stated that she wanted to get her shoes and her purse. Officer Cabana walked upstairs with Aaliyah while she got her things and then she was walked out to the patrol vehicle.

Officer Anderson and I walked out to the patrol vehicle that Carlton was in to transport him to PPD. As I walked to the passenger side of the vehicle, Carlton came over to the passenger side window, pointed at me and started making threats at me. I was unable to hear everything that Carlton said due to the loud noise of the crowd that was still gathered outside, but I did hear Carlton say that he was going to "get me." While Officer Anderson and I were enroute to the PPD, Carlton was yelling ethnic slurs at me calling me the "White Devil" and that he was "going to pray and something was going to happen to me."

Once at the PPD, Carlton refused to let any white officers book him. Carlton made several ethnic slurs to white officers and cadets that attempted to complete the booking process. Carlton also refused to let officers fingerprint him. During the booking process, Carlton said that Officer Anderson was "going to rot in Hell for siding with the White Devil." Aaliyah and Mazel were also initially very uncooperative with Cadet Kinder, but eventually Mazel allowed Cadet Kinder to fingerprint her and Aaliyah allowed Officer Cabana to fingerprint her.

Due to having my hand hit when Aaliyah shut the door and multiple incidents of jerking and pushing, I had a great deal of soreness in my right wrist. I went to POH (Pontiac Osteopathic Hospital) to have my wrist checked and was seen by Doctor Buck. Doctor Buck determined that I had a sprained wrist, prescribed pain medicine, and released me from the hospital with care instructions. I was off work for one day.

It should be noted that by the time officers were leaving the scene to transport the three arrested subjects to the PPD, there was approximately 10–15 officers on scene and there was still a large crowd of people yelling at officers to calm and disperse the crowd.

Will be seeking State Law Warrants through the Prosecutor's Office.

Regardless of all the crazy things I've seen and done in my police career, nothing frustrated me more than when people would introduce race into the equation. Laws aren't enforced based on race or ethnicity, but on their wording. Am I claiming that there's never been a racist police officer? No. But can anyone say that about their chosen profession? No. There are bad apples everywhere. But police officers don't write the laws and rarely get to decide who to enforce them on. This was especially true during the COMSTAT detail.

What I have come to understand is that these situations aren't really about whether or not I was racist, but how the people I interacted with viewed me. Maybe I could have done more to try to assuage their concerns about my intentions, but at the time I felt like I was just doing my job. I admit that I never considered how the people at the party might have experienced our intrusion. I thought only about the job I was assigned to do and what the laws of the city were. This is not to say that I believe blame rests solely with me, only that a little more patience and consideration on both sides may have made a difference in the outcome.

At the time, I thought that we were practicing community policing. Up to that point in my career it was the only model of policing that I had ever heard of, and it was commonly spoken of by department supervisors and at City Hall meetings. With this in mind, it shouldn't be surprising that I didn't know at the time exactly what community policing entailed. I wouldn't find out until many years later that what we were actually practicing was a broken windows policing model with an added strict enforcement/ zero-tolerance policy.

Broken windows policing was first introduced to the public in 1982 in *The Atlantic* by academics James Wilson and George Kelling. Their theory states that "at the community level, disorder and crime are usually inextricably linked, in a kind of developmental sequence."[2] Wilson and Kelling believe that crime rates would increase as the level of disorder increased. Basically, if it appears a community tolerates increasing levels of disorder, then people will develop more of a sense of freedom to do whatever they want.[3]

Wilson and Kelling described how citizens felt safer in their neighborhoods when officers were more visible and interacted with them. After firsthand observations of policing in Newark, New Jersey, Wilson and Kelling wrote that people fell into two groups: regulars and strangers.[4] Strangers are the problem and that's exactly what we were trying to identify and deal with in our COMCAST detail.

Our COMSTAT unit acted on every infraction regardless of how seemingly small or insignificant. By acting on all small infractions, we believed that disorderly criminal behavior would be less likely. We surmised that strict enforcement would allow law-abiding residents to feel safer and make the strangers and criminals realize that their chances of getting caught and arrested would be higher. At the time, I thought we were working hard for the community. I believed with all my heart that what we were doing was right and making a difference for the better in the lives of the good citizens who wanted to live in a safe neighborhood.

Today, broken windows policing is very controversial, but in the early 2000s when we were practicing it, it wasn't. In fact, the State of New York didn't stop practicing broken windows policing until the middle of the 2010s. Many people contend that broken windows policing is a way to target minorities and the cause of the ruinous relationship between the police and community. Even though broken windows policing was practiced in New York and dramatically reduced crime rates, there are many that still condemn it. Race never influenced my policing decisions, but I can only speak for my actions, not the actions of others.

By the end of our time in Indian Village we had virtually eliminated all calls for service from that area. Instead of nonstop calls coming in like they were when we began the detail, we would go an entire day without a single call. The citizens living there were happy and many attended City Council meetings raving about our work in cleaning up the neighborhood. The unit was deemed successful, and we were shut down. It was time to go back to road patrol. I was disappointed, but my career was on a perfect upward trend.

Today, looking back at that time with my newly learned academic knowledge of policing policies, I see my time in the COMSTAT unit a bit differently. I can now see both the positives and the negatives of broken windows policing. We achieved our end goals of lowering the crime rate, made the citizens feel safer, and drove out the criminal element. On the flipside, it's clear that at least some of the Black citizens, such as those at the house party, felt that we were targeting them because of their race. In college I learned that zero-tolerance policing causes officers to create a line that forces everyone to be placed on the good side or the evil side, which really made me think.[5] *Did I do that? Did I place the citizens in my community on the evil side? Did I actually divide my community more than I helped it? Did I get so wrapped up in "helping" the community that I forgot to judge everyone fairly?* The truth is, I don't know, but I think about it a lot these days. Some memories make me smile because I know I saved someone or made a positive difference in their life. Other memories make me cringe because I know there were times when I could have been kinder, more compassionate, less judgmental.

Additionally, in hindsight, I'm not sure how much we actually "solved" the crime problem. Did we really arrest all the criminals, or did we just chase them to a new area where they would continue their activities? It's frustrating to look back and wonder if I was really doing the good police work that I thought I was doing at the time.

Graduation from police academy, November 2000

Pontiac Police Department, 2004 Used with permission of David Weiner

Neil & Ann Marie wedding, September 2005

Sitting on the Great Pyramid of Egypt, August 2006

Standing next to the Great Sphinx of Giza, August 2006

Locker room selfie, 2017

Patrol car selfie, 2017

Tina Marie Ashton, R.I.P. Used with permission of Amy Ashton Stewart

7

THE GOOD, THE BAD, AND WORSE

While my career seemed to be going well, what I didn't know was that the world as I knew it was about to be turned upside down. Things had changed drastically in Pontiac by 2005, and, in fact, in the state of Michigan as a whole. It was the beginning of the financial crisis, and it was going to hit the City of Pontiac especially hard. At the police department we had begun to hear rumblings about financial problems and began to see big changes all around us.

It was finally released to the public that year that the City of Pontiac had a large budget deficit. Depending on who was giving the information, the deficit was estimated to be anywhere between $20 and $60 million. Many people debate how this deficit occurred: corruption, poor management, frivolous spending? The truth is that it was probably a little bit of everything, but none of that mattered in the grand scheme of things. The city was in dire straits and major changes were on the horizon.

In 2006, Louis Schimmel, who would go on to become one of a series of three emergency managers in Pontiac, wrote an article called, "The City of Pontiac: A 'Going' Concern."[1] Schimmel details many of the causes of Pontiac's financial crisis, such as the loss of tax revenue from General Motors, poor accounting, budgeting, and asset management.

As word began to spread that layoffs were imminent, the department did two things that infuriated the officers: first, they changed the policy severely restricting how earned time off could be used, and second, they brought in unpaid and untrained reserve officers to replace unionized officers. Both of these practices were against the union contract. The officers decided to fight back in the only way they felt they could—they organized a "blue flu." The day was selected and most everyone agreed to call in sick.

The idea was to show the city and the citizens what life would look like without sufficient police manpower.

I never got a chance to call in sick. My regular shift was 5:00 p.m. to 3:00 a.m. By the time 3:00 a.m. rolled around the sick calls had already started to come in for the day shift and I was ordered to work overtime. The rule was supposed to be that you got to go home after a maximum of sixteen hours, but I was unlucky enough to arrest a juvenile and was required to go to the juvenile court that same day. By the time I got out of juvenile court it was 4:30 p.m. and I could barely keep my eyes open. I called work and told them I was going on twenty-four hours, apologized, and said I wasn't coming in.

By this time the "blue flu" was in full effect, and the command staff all the way up to captains, were on the road taking calls. I was yelled at for calling in sick even though I tried to explain, again, that I was working on nearly twenty-four hours without sleep. I finally decided I didn't care how angry they were. I went home, turned my phone off, and went to sleep.

The consequences of the "blue flu" were swift. Those officers that were still on probation were fired or laid off several weeks earlier than planned. Even though I had worked twenty-four hours straight, technically not a participant in the "blue flu," I was also laid off earlier than mandated.

The immediate repercussions of the financial crisis included over seventy employees laid off, over one hundred positions eliminated, the city's golf course and cemetery sold, all the community centers closed, taxes raised, and nearly every department in the city eventually subcontracted out to a private company. As a result, Pontiac's citizens would have to wait eight to ten hours for police response. The police union would do its part to help by agreeing to no raises for the remainder of our time working in Pontiac in an attempt to assist with the budget crisis, but in the end, it was all for naught.

One entity within the city that refused to make any concessions was the fire department. While it seemed that everyone in Pontiac was trying to save the city from destruction, the fire department chose to enforce its union contract to the letter by continuing to hire. It was not uncommon to see eight to ten firemen at one of the five city's fire stations outside playing basketball or having a barbeque. It was a slap in the face to the officers sacrificing everything to keep the city intact and to the citizens who were waiting hours for help and throwing their tax dollars away to keep the fire department intact.

While this would be upsetting to most, even in the most optimal conditions, for those of us that were privy to "insider" information, it was wildly frustrating. There were numbers of stories about how the city's money was being misused. I have no proof of any of them, but there is evidence that some, if not all, were true. One story surrounds the mayor. Supposedly, he had been elected to office while living paycheck to paycheck; some who knew him well even claimed he was a heavy gambler. However, when he left office at the height of Pontiac's financial crisis, he was able to purchase a large plot of land and relocate out of state.

Another story pertains to a sergeant who was in charge of scheduling all overtime and special work details and accused of embezzling money from the department. It was rumored that she was taking vacation days, and then before payroll the end of the pay period, she would change the vacation days to workdays. This allowed her to be paid when she wasn't there along with continuing to accumulate vacation time that could be used later. It was speculated that she did this for many years. Two detectives who had been newly promoted to sergeants had become suspicious and began to investigate. When the chief of police was notified by the sergeants about the investigation, the sergeants were ordered to stop. One agreed and one refused. The sergeant who refused was demoted to detective and, not long after, fired. The reason why the chief squashed the investigation isn't clear. Again, I only have rumors to explain why, but speculation was that he was protecting the sergeant because she did a lot of work for him.

There was another rumor that some employees in City Hall had been providing "no-show" jobs to family and friends—reminiscent of the old New York mafia practice within labor unions. A no-show job is where someone is paid for a "position" but never does any work or even show up. Again, I have no evidence that this was taking place; however, one of the early steps to curb fraud during the financial crisis was employee audits. I clearly remember going to pick up a paycheck from the City Hall treasurer's office in person to verify who I was and my position. Rumors swirled about "employees" that were unable to pick up their paychecks because they were living out of state or deceased.

These incidences exemplify the chaos that enshrouded Pontiac starting in 2005. Suddenly, the stress of the job wasn't all about what happened on the road, but rather if we would we even have jobs.

I understood seniority and that employees were laid off based on who had the least amount of time on the job; however, it didn't make it any easier to accept. I had been doing exceptional work and my accomplishments were garnering attention with the command staff, city leaders, and citizens alike. Nevertheless, I received my notice of layoff in July 2005. How could this be happening to me? Shock quickly turned to anger and then to fear. I was a single mother. How would I support my son? Make my house payment? My car payment? The economy was terrible. It was going to be very difficult to find a job at another police department. Layoffs were going on everywhere; very few departments were hiring.

By this time Neil and I had been dating for about three years. We had discussed getting married, but had never made concrete plans. Now that I was laid off and losing medical insurance, Neil decided that maybe it was time. Luckily, Neil had been working at the police department six years longer than I had, and his seniority saved him from layoff. The loss of my income would result in some changes in how we spent our money, but it wouldn't be impossible to survive on one income temporarily.

Wedding planning started immediately. The first decision we made was not to have a big wedding and invite only family members. We knew that many of our friends and coworkers might be mad and hurt, but this was our wedding and our decision.

We went shopping and found a beautiful engagement ring. Next, we had to choose a wedding venue. We decided to ask my mom and dad if we could have the ceremony in their backyard by the lake and they agreed.

Our next stop was the courthouse to see a judge at the 50th District Court. Neil and I had both had numerous criminal trials in front of this judge over the years and we respected her immensely, so we decided to ask her to officiate our ceremony. We were told by the court administrator that judges could perform ceremonies only at the courthouse, on certain days and at certain times. Neil and I were disappointed, but since we were there, we went to see her anyway. She was gracious and honored that we wanted her to officiate. She immediately agreed and stated that she would be happy to come to whatever location we chose.

My partner, and one of my closest friends, Officer Carlos Luna, was the only person I wanted as my attendant on my special day. I knew it was unconventional, but I asked Carlos to be my man of honor and Neil asked his childhood best friend, Scott, to be his best man. I had several options for who I wanted to walk me down the aisle, but I really wanted our children to be involved in the wedding. At the time, Tarec was nine years old and Neil's son was just six months younger. After speaking to the boys, we decided that they would walk me down the aisle together, making it a true family affair.

The coming weeks were full of wedding preparations. There were dress and tuxedo fittings, hiring a caterer, renting chairs and canopies, shoe shopping, and much more. I had learned to make jewelry years before, so I made my own necklace, earrings, and bracelet from white pearls and

Swarovski crystals. I bought artificial flowers and made my bouquet, along with boutonnières for the men. My mom and Katy made a wedding trellis covered in tulle, flowers, and other decorations for the yard and aisle. My mom's friend made us a beautiful three-tiered cake. We topped it with a crystal Cinderella carriage and castle. Katy even agreed to be our photographer for the day. Everything was coming together quickly and easily.

A week or so before the wedding, I got big news. Someone at work had retired and I was being recalled. I was to report back to work in just a few days. Neil and I decided to go ahead with the wedding, but I had to request a vacation day to get married. I went to the captain, swore him to secrecy, and told him what was happening. Luckily, he agreed to give me the day off.

On September 25, 2005, the wedding went off without a hitch. This wedding felt so different from my first one. I didn't cry beforehand, worry about whether I was making a mistake, or call anyone to ask if I should call it off. I felt strong and secure in my relationship and knew that Neil was a wonderful father to my son. Over the years, I had worried about what would happen to Tarec if I were ever killed on the job. Not anymore. I knew that Neil would fight until the end of time to make sure that Tarec stayed with him and that he would always be well cared for.

I returned to work the next day with a smile on my face and a pep in my step. A few people noticed that Neil and I were wearing wedding rings and word spread throughout the department like wildfire. We explained that it had been a small family affair. I officially changed my last name and hit the streets. I was back and more excited than ever to get to work.

As much as I loved my job there was no doubt that it was incredibly stressful—especially after coming off a layoff. I wanted to jump back in and pick up where I left off, but my coworkers had other plans. It seemed everyone around me was doing the bare minimum amount of work. The more I worked, the more some of my coworkers criticized me. People were angry that the city was in financial trouble, angry that there were no raises, and angry that our manpower levels were drastically slashed. I guess people felt that we shouldn't be busting our asses for a city that didn't appreciate us. I felt differently. In my mind, it wasn't the city that I was working for, it was the citizens. It wasn't their fault that city officials had financially run the city into the ground. I was grateful to have been called back from layoff and I still cared about the city and its citizens. Regardless of how much my coworkers yelled at me or refused to back me on calls, I kept giving 100 percent of myself to the job.

After Neil and I got married we immediately put my house up for sale. My son and I officially moved in with Neil but didn't move all of our things into his house. We moved some clothes, but that was about it. We still went to my house and stayed there from time to time as we continued to do small renovation projects on the house. We spent Christmas at Neil's house, but a few days after, I received a call from a perspective buyer who wanted to view the house. We made an appointment, and I met him there the next day.

We arrived at the same time and approached the front door together. I unlocked the door, swung it open, and stopped dead in my tracks. The ceiling was collapsed in many areas, the carpet completely flooded, there was mold on everything, a cloud of steam hung in the upper half of the room, and water was shooting full blast from the bathtub wall. The man pushed me aside, ran through the house, out the back door, and turned off the water from the main. I stood at the front door in shock and started to cry.

Everywhere I looked I saw destroyed memories. My son's favorite childhood book that I had read him thousands of times was drenched and covered in mold. The one-of-a-kind artwork hanging on my bedroom wall that had been made for me years ago by an artist friend was now discolored and moldy. Baby pictures hanging on the walls throughout the house warped, ruined in their frames, on the floor, sitting in a pool of water that was once a plush carpet.

"Well, it looks like you have some phone calls to make," the man said. "Call your insurance company and let them know what's happened. After you figure out what they are going to do, call me. I'm still interested in buying your house—even in this condition." I couldn't really comprehend what he was saying at that moment. I was just too stunned.

It turned out that the hot water handle in the bathtub had broken off due to years of rust, and water had been shooting out of it for the last few days that I had been gone. The steam from the hot water filled the house causing all the damage. It was a long process, but the insurance company agreed to pay me a large sum of money for repairs and to replace the contents.

I called the prospective buyer and told him, "The insurance company has agreed to give me money for the house repair and for the contents. I will put all of the money they give me for the repairs directly onto the principal. I'll sell you the house for the exact amount remaining on the mortgage. I don't need a profit. I just want to sell the house." He agreed, and the house was sold as is.

After selling the house, I used the insurance money that covered my home's contents to replace items that had been ruined, but because Neil and I were now living together, there were many items that I didn't need to replace, leaving me with thousands of dollars leftover. This was one of those rare opportunities that presented itself that may never come again, so I decided to use some of my insurance money and take a dream trip to Egypt. Neither Neil nor Tarec had any interest in going, so I decided to go by myself.

The day before I booked my trip, I told Sergeant Thomas about it at work. He told me that his wife, Gina, would love to go on a trip like that. I had met her a couple times at various police events, but I certainly didn't know her well. The idea of traveling alone wasn't all that exciting to me, so I told him that Gina was welcome to come along if she wanted to. Later that night I got the call that Gina wanted to go. She met me at the travel agency the next day and we booked our trip for August 2006.

The upcoming months of anticipation were going to be achingly difficult, but I distracted myself with work, getting to know Gina better, and conducting all the research I could on Egypt. Gina and I decided we were going to make sure that when we got to Egypt, we knew what questions to ask and what places were must-sees. We wanted to make sure we didn't miss out on anything. In the meantime, it was work, work, work.

The next opportunity at work came as a complete surprise. I was approached by Detective McAuley and asked if I would be interested in working another undercover assignment. Detective McAuley told me that he had been working with investigators from the Target Corporation on an operation involving the sale of stolen baby formula. I can imagine what you're thinking right now—baby formula? I thought the same thing.

Apparently, people were stealing cans of baby formula that retailed from twenty-five to thirty dollars per can and selling them to local party stores for five dollars per can. The party stores would then sell them for full price. Detective McAuley had an informant that provided him with the specific information on what was happening. Detective McAuley then reached out to Target loss prevention investigators who confirmed to him that the theft of baby formula was a huge problem for them. A partnership was formed with Target and the informant offered Detective McAuley an introduction to some of the party stores involved in the illegal sales. Unfortunately, several refused to work with him.

I had a lot of respect for Detective McAuley and considered him a friend, but if I were selling stolen goods, I wouldn't have worked with him either. Detective McAuley was a military police captain in the Army

Reserve. He was tall, well built, and spoke with unquestionable authority. I couldn't imagine him trying to pass as a homeless drug addict thief.

My past work had garnered me positive reviews and Detective McAuley offered me the opportunity to take his place. I excitedly accepted. I was even happier to find out that Sergeant Hess was working on the detail. Once again, the rumors started up that he was the only reason I was offered the detail.

Working as a prostitute for several years had prepared me for how to dress for undercover work. I donned my old high school tennis shoes, my faded blue jeans, and a worn-out t-shirt. I greased up my hair with wax and messed up my day-old makeup—it was a routine I knew well. My alter ego, Rosie Jacobs, was back. By this time, Rosie had become a part of who I was, and I could bring her out readily.

I would say being Rosie was like acting, but it wasn't. To me, Rosie was who I could have become had things turned out differently. I had grown up surrounded by drugs and alcohol and had been physically, mentally, and sexually abused. These experiences were a recipe for disaster, and I could have easily become the prostitute or drug-addicted criminal that Rosie was. Becoming Rosie, for me, was a matter of channeling the surroundings and people of my childhood—the person that I had spent my whole life trying not to become. While I would say that I was ultimately successful in not becoming Rosie, there were still times when I let my pain and anger lead me down paths of destruction.

I had been living back with my mother and stepfather again for approximately two months after being released from an inpatient psychiatric facility when my stepfather had open heart surgery. After decades of smoking, drinking, and drug use, his aorta finally gave out and needed to be replaced. After coming home from the hospital, everyone walked on tip toes not to disturb him during his recovery. Only days later, I woke up feeling horrible. I was having terrible stomach pains and vomiting blood. My mother said that I couldn't be in the house sick when my stepfather was recovering and in danger of catching whatever I had. She told me I needed to move out immediately. Any chance for my mother to kick me out she took. This was just another excuse for her to throw me away.

I didn't know where to go. I couldn't go back to my father. I was terrified of what he would do to me. I called the only person I could think of, Carol. She was the lady that I had babysat for in the trailer park when I was eleven years old. I tearfully told her what was happening, and she said that I was more than welcome to move in with her and the kids. I grabbed a bag and haphazardly threw my few belongings inside. I was getting good at packing quickly.

Carol showed up around an hour later. My mother quickly signed a piece of paper giving guardianship over to Carol and we were on our way. Carol still lived in the trailer park, which was about thirty minutes away. As we drove, the sadness of the situation faded as the prospect of seeing my old friends took over. It felt like this was the first step toward erasing the horror of the last three years of my life.

It was great to see Carol's kids again. Taylor and Jeremiah had been such a big part of my life as their babysitter, and I never got to say goodbye to them when I was forcibly moved away. Taylor and I had to share a room with bunk beds, but I didn't care. I was just happy to be there. I settled in quickly, but unfortunately, my illness hadn't gone away. Although it seemed to come and go, the stomach pain hadn't completely subsided.

I ended up at St. Joe's Hospital in Pontiac. A quick x-ray confirmed the doctor's diagnosis: my appendix was rupturing. Apparently, the pain and vomiting of blood over the last couple days were signs of appendicitis. The doctors informed us that I needed emergency surgery to remove my appendix. There was some minor paperwork to work out between Carol and the hospital since she had only been given temporary guardianship of me, and it was quickly handled.

After about a week I was feeling good enough to leave the house. My first stop was to see my former best girlfriends, Chelsie and Whitney. Chelsie lived the closest, so I went to her house first. I knocked on the door and Chelsie opened it, freezing in shock. After a split second she screamed like only a teenage girl can and embraced me. I told her the short version of events that had brought me back to the old neighborhood. The details didn't really matter to her. The important thing was that I was back.

Chelsie called Whitney and told her to come over right away. Whitney lived on the other side of the trailer park, maybe ten streets away. When Whitney walked into Chelsie's house and saw me there was another round of teenage girl screaming. We embraced long and hard as pure joy filled the room. To an outsider the next few hours would have sounded like pure pandemonium. There was so much to discuss: heartbreaks, relationship gossip, and parental drama.

"You won't believe who Scott is dating!" Chelsie stated.

"And Jim! Oh my gosh, he's been dating Marie!" Whitney interrupted.

"Wesley just sleeps with everyone!" Chelsie said in her best disgusted tone.

"I met the cutest guy ever, but we broke up last month," Whitney bemoaned.

"My mom is working nights now, so I can sneak out no problem," Chelsie exclaimed proudly.

The remainder of the summer flew by in a haze of parties, drinking, cigarettes, marijuana, and sex. Times had definitely changed. No longer were our days spent playing kick ball, hide-and-seek, or practicing gymnastics. We were teenagers now and none of us had particularly strict parents. There was always a parent somewhere in the trailer park that had to go to work, so that's where the party was.

With all the alcohol I consumed and the marijuana I smoked the remainder of the summer seemed to fly by. Some events, however, are unforgettable, like the three-day drinking binge where my friends and I continuously moved from one house to another without ever going home. Sitting at one of the playgrounds in the trailer park smoking marijuana with my friends all day. Learning to drive a stick shift on my fifteenth birthday with a wine cooler between my legs. But the most vivid memory was the night that ended in a car chase with police.

My friends and I were partying at a neighborhood house when five of us left to go buy more alcohol. We piled into a car and headed to a party store on Baldwin Road in Pontiac that was known to sell to minors. The driver, Sam, who was nineteen years old, entered the store and came out with a case of beer, a six-pack of wine coolers, and a fifth of vodka.

We had been drinking for hours, but that didn't stop us from continuing. I opened a wine cooler, Sam opened a beer, and the other three passed the vodka bottle between them. The mood in the car was one of carefree jubilance. We were laughing and joking and not paying attention to our surroundings.

We had gone only a couple of miles when police lights appeared behind us. The inside of the vehicle exploded in mayhem. *Oh my God, it's the police! We're all going to jail! Drive faster! Lose the cops! My parents will kill me!* Everyone was yelling, but Sam somehow kept his cool.

Sam slammed the gas pedal to the floor and continued to make quick, evasive turns down side streets. He turned onto a small street with parked cars lining the right side and quickly pulled over and parked between two cars. We all ducked down on the floor and hid. No one spoke. No one moved. I don't think any of us even breathed.

I don't know how long we stayed there, motionless, on the side of the road, but eventually we cautiously pulled out and drove northbound out of the city. Once we were out of Pontiac the shock of the situation began to wear off. Within a few miles we were all whooping it up again. While we believed that we had gotten away safely, each of us still went home afterward and spent the remainder of the night hoping the police didn't knock on our doors.

Something had changed in me by this time. I can't pinpoint when it happened or what caused it, but I became a different person. I had spent my whole life trying to be the perfect child. I struggled to get all A's in school, to be the fastest runner, the best reader, to be pretty and well-dressed despite my family's lack of wealth. Most importantly, I had struggled to be liked, but I no longer cared about any of those things. I reveled in anarchy.

The next phase of my life can probably be attributed to a colliding of circumstances. I had changed dramatically, and Carol was not strict with me. While I had become a big sister to Taylor and Jeremiah, Carol treated me more like a little sister than a daughter. That freedom fueled my wild streak.

Carol really only had one rule when it came to me: total honesty. If I was going to a party to drink, I was required to tell her where I was going. If the party moved and I relocated, I had to call and let her know. Sometimes Carol would show up at the parties just to confirm that I was where I said I was going to be. Often, she would arrive with a bottle of alcohol and have a drink or two with me and my friends.

Carol was still working the midnight shift, so she would always get home in the morning when I was getting ready for school. Many days, Carol and I would lock the door to the bathroom and smoke a joint together while I curled my hair and put on my makeup. Then off to school I would go, relaxed and unconcerned about anything.

Many days I ended up in the woods behind the school rather than in a classroom. There was a large forest behind Brandon High School that had a well-worn path made by students like me over the years. If a person followed the path far enough into the woods, they would come to a firepit with several large fallen trees arranged around it. It was a perfect place to waste the day away smoking and drinking. All too often that's exactly what I did.

School didn't just become secondary to me—it became completely unimportant. Luckily, school had always come easy for me, and I never had to put much effort into getting good grades. As long as I showed up for class occasionally and took the tests, I managed to maintain a passing average. I'm not sure how long I thought I could continue behaving the way I was, but it was all about to come to a very dramatic and precipitous end.

It was just another day at school—at least I had actually gone that day. One of my teachers was out and we had a substitute. Two of my girlfriends and I made up an excuse to work on a project in the hallway outside of the classroom door and the substitute teacher agreed. A short time later the three of us went into the girls' bathroom down the hall to smoke a cigarette. When the substitute noticed that we were gone, she sent another student to the bathroom to check if we were there.

The student that the teacher sent was a pretty blonde cheerleader named Tiffany. Of course, Tiffany found us in the bathroom smoking and immediately returned to the classroom and ratted us out. All three of us got detention. For the next couple of weeks the resentment against Tiffany intensified with each passing day. Soon, everyone in my friend group was telling me that I needed to teach Tiffany a lesson and beat her up. Not a day, not an hour, went by without someone antagonizing me and questioning when I was going to get it done.

Finally, I had all I could take. I couldn't stand the pressure. We were all in class—Tiffany sitting near the front, my friends and I sitting near the back. The teacher was playing a movie and it provided the perfect opportunity for the attack. I was going to get out of my seat early and stand near the door when the bell rang. That way I could leave the classroom before Tiffany entered the hallway. My friends, along with other classmates that knew what was happening, would stand in the doorway blocking the teacher from exiting and breaking up the fight.

A few minutes before class ended, I walked up to the front of the class and stood near the door. I glared at Tiffany. My eyes spewed pure hatred at her. Tiffany looked at me only once. I looked her in the eyes and silently mouthed the words, "You're dead." I saw fear in her eyes, but I can only imagine what must have been going through her mind.

The bell rang. I stood in the hallway and waited for Tiffany to exit. I felt like I was standing outside my body watching the event as it occurred, not participating in it. My friends had been pumping me up for so long that all I can remember is feeling seething anger.

As soon as I saw Tiffany's face, I grabbed her by the hair and began to repeatedly punch her. She tried to get away from me, so I pushed her against the lockers on the other side of the hallway and slammed her head over and over with a locker door. Somehow, Tiffany managed to escape and ran down the hall. I chased after her, tackled her, straddled her body, and pummeled her face with both my fists.

I don't know how long the fight went on, but finally, our teacher was able to get out of the classroom and break up the fight with the help of another teacher. Tiffany was taken to the office via one stairway, and I was taken to the office via another. As the teacher walked me down to the office other students cheered me on, high-fived me, and patted me on the back. I felt like a hero. I had taught Tiffany a valuable lesson about being a snitch. Next time she was faced with this situation, I thought, she would think twice.

When I arrived in the principal's office, I experienced one of the most shocking moments of my life. I saw Tiffany across the room, bleeding profusely from her face, dark bruises already forming as her taut skin swelled. For a moment I wondered what happened to her during the walk to the office. Surely I didn't inflict that damage on her. Reality soon washed over me as I began to realize that in my violent, angry, out-of-control frenzy, I had hurt Tiffany—a lot. It was as if I had woken up from a dream and could suddenly think clearly. All I could think of was how horrible a person I was. *Had I really just viciously assaulted this girl just because she told on my friends and me for smoking? What kind of person was I? Is this the kind of thing that will happen every time I get angry and lose control?* These questions and more would haunt me in the days to come. For now, I had the police to deal with.

I was questioned by the police, a report was filed, I was suspended. Carol was called to pick me up. She was furious with me. Up until now my crazy behavior had been tolerated, but this was a step too far even for Carol. She decided that the best way to teach me a lesson was to assign me a ridiculous number of chores to do during my suspension so that I couldn't enjoy my time off. Of course, I was also grounded and couldn't go anywhere or hang out with my friends. I washed walls, cleaned bathrooms, did yard work, dusted every inch of the house, mopped every floor by hand—there seemed to be a never ending list of new tortures.

It wasn't long after this when Carol and I received notification that Tiffany's parents were suing me for medical bills due to assault and battery. I was scared to death; Carol was livid. The court proceedings are a blur to me now. My mind was so racked with fear that it was hard to comprehend much of what was happening. In the end, the judge decided that I had to reimburse the copays for Tiffany's treatment, which wasn't a lot, but he didn't stop there. The judge found out that all of this had occurred while I was not living with a relative. He made it clear that must be remedied immediately. *Where would I go now?*

Now that I had resurrected my Rosie persona and was given a new undercover detail, I started to get excited. I was sent into the first store with the snitch, wired with a recording device, and introduced to the owner.

There's a special skill required to keep your hands from shaking and your voice from cracking when you're so nervous that your heart is beating out of your chest. Homeless drug addicts don't get nervous—I couldn't either.

The first store owner looked to be a Middle Eastern man in his fifties. He looked at me with a mix of suspicion and contempt. It was clear that he wasn't happy about the snitch bringing in a new person. I decided the best way to stay calm was to act like I didn't care what happened. I had the product and if he wanted it, then he was going to have to work with me. I could always take my product elsewhere.

Apparently, my casual attitude worked. I struck a deal with him. My first store was secured. Over the next two weeks I was sent into several more stores, securing deals with most of them. I went into the various stores periodically, usually once a week, and sold them baby formula. Over several months the store owners became more comfortable with me.

My cover story wasn't developed all at once—it came together slowly but surely. I couldn't seem too eager or trusting of them. I told the store owners that I routinely stole from the Target store in Waterford and Mervyn's store in Pontiac. As they developed more trust in me, several began to ask me to steal items for them other than baby formula. The items were provided to me by our Target investigators and sold to the stores for pennies on the dollar. I continued to develop a relationship with the store owners and their trust in me increased with each transaction.

I decided it was time to push my luck. "Why don't you make me a list of everything you want. It's hard to remember sometimes," I said to one store owner. Some store owners got out a piece of paper and did exactly that. I couldn't believe the evidentiary gold mine that had been handed to me. The list contained specific brands of shoes, shirts, and jeans, along with sizes and colors. Not only did I have the store owners on audio, but I now had them requesting that I steal items for them in their own handwriting. After several months of increasing sales, the case was presented to the prosecutor's office, and they decided that we had enough evidence to authorize writing the warrants and making the arrests.

A large group of officers, detectives, and undercover units were assembled. We all met at the police department and were broken into smaller groups. Each group would be sent to a different store, and at a designated time each group would simultaneously enter their assigned store and execute search and arrest warrants. I stayed outside and watched the action with a huge smile on my face. The raids went off without a hitch. Another successful assignment in the books.

8

PAWN SHOPS AND PYRAMIDS

I always took great pride in my work but working undercover brought a new sense of accomplishment. I reveled in the praise I received and no longer doubted my ability to tackle any opportunity presented to me. My coworkers saw me in a different light and commanders recognized my potential. I was seen as a talented, hard-working police officer with a great deal of integrity. The days of being viewed as a troublemaker were over.

During the baby formula detail I had become good friends with the head investigator from Target, John. Over time he would become one of my biggest supporters and friend. The budget crisis in the City of Pontiac continued to get worse, turning my life upside down once again. I would need as many allies like John as I could get.

In late spring of 2006, I was approached for another undercover detail working with the investigators from Target. Detective McAuley had developed information that a pawn shop in Pontiac was illegally purchasing stolen merchandise and selling it through an eBay account. Pawn shops are legally required to track all purchased merchandise by checking the seller's identification as well as fingerprinting them. That information is then required to be forwarded to the police department. This particular pawn shop was believed to be following these procedures only sporadically.

I was tasked with reviving Rosie by going into the pawn shop to sell an item without having to show identification or get fingerprinted. As successful as I had been in the past, I was worried that I was going to fail this time. I have no explanation for why I felt this way, but I was determined to shake it off and give my best effort.

The overall plan was to document and photograph the serial numbers of several electronic items and then sell them to the pawn shop. The eBay account belonging to the owners of the pawn shop would then be monitored for the items to appear. The items would immediately be purchased by the Target investigators. This process would allow us to track the full circle of the items and prove that the pawn shop was selling stolen goods and failing to legally document their sales.

Detective McAuley, being a captain in the Army Reserve, had access to the military armory in Pontiac, which we used as the staging area for our detail. Detective McAuley, Sergeant Hess, Sergeant Tapp, the Target investigators, and I would meet at the armory and discuss the day's plan. After the details were worked out, I would be wired with a microphone and driven a couple blocks away from the pawn shop and walk the rest of the way. Rosie was a homeless drug addict; she couldn't be seen driving a car or being driven anywhere.

I walked in the pawn shop with a new, unopened GPS unit from Target. I probably should have thought about what I was going to say when I got inside, but I didn't. I never wanted to sound scripted. I stood just inside the doorway, GPS in hand, and looked around.

The pawn shop was large and cluttered. There were items stacked from floor to ceiling covering every inch of the space. There were bicycles, tables, vases, jewelry, stereos, speakers, and so much more. In the very back-left corner, I observed a small booth-like room with glass windows. Along the wall on the right was a large room with bulletproof glass. I could see an employee behind the glass and stacks of merchandise behind him. A White man, in his mid-sixties, stood in front of the window speaking to the employee behind the glass. When he saw me, he began to walk over.

It turns out he was the store's owner. He wore a smarmy smile and looked at me like I was on the menu in a restaurant. He looked me over from top to bottom. I didn't know what my strategy would be when I walked in, but I decided to use his sliminess to my advantage. I gave him my best drug addict sob story.

"I'm not from this area. I was brought here by a boyfriend, and he just left. I'm from a little town up north—Lewiston. Have you heard of it?" He shook his head. "I have no family and no one to help me. Since my boyfriend left, I've been sleeping in an abandoned house. I need money. I just can't keep doing the things I've been forced to do." I let my voice trail off to a whisper as I looked down feigning humiliation. I hoped to gain his sympathy by intimating that I had been forced into prostitution in order to survive.

I could see his face soften. The man pulled me closer and put his arm around me. "This is a rough city, baby. You need to be careful," he said as he squeezed me closer and smiled that creepy smile again. I was repulsed by the disgusting way he was trying to take advantage of a girl in trouble, but I kept up the naïve routine. My small-town girl turned drug addict prostitute ploy worked. "All right, I'll take your GPS," he said. "Come with me."

He walked over to the small booth-like room. He walked inside, closed the door, and asked me for my ID. I forced myself to get teary-eyed. I looked down and let a single tear fall. "I don't have any ID. My boyfriend took everything I had. What am I going to do now?" I cried. The man looked at me silently for a moment and then said, "It's OK. I'm here for you." Before I knew it, I had cash in hand and had avoided being IDed and fingerprinted.

I walked the couple blocks back to the drop-off point bursting with pride. I knew that I had just taken the first step toward accomplishing another successful undercover detail. I got back into the waiting car with Detective McAuley, and we drove back to the armory. We had a debriefing in which we discussed what had occurred and what our next steps were going to be. We all went home feeling like we were well on our way to shutting down that pawn shop.

I went back to the pawn shop regularly, once or twice a week. I continued to play my naïve homeless act. As the relationship with the store owner became closer and more comfortable, I told him that I had gotten a job at Target in its electronics department.

"With my job I can easily take just about anything, especially electronics. What will get me the most money?" I asked. To my surprise, the store owner ignored the fact that I told him I was stealing the merchandise and gave me a rundown of which electronic items were the easiest and most profitable to sell. In addition to all the other evidence we had, I now had him on audio acknowledging that I was selling him stolen items and him telling me exactly what to steal. Later, there would be no denying in court that he didn't know the items I was selling him were stolen. It was another evidentiary milestone.

In the weeks to come I would sell the pawn shop GPS units, handheld video games systems, cameras, and more. I even took a full-size Dyson vacuum into the pawn shop to sell. "How did you get that out of the store?" he exclaimed. "I just walked out with it," I said with a smile.

Unfortunately, bad luck was about to hit me again. In the middle of the pawn shop detail, I was notified that more layoffs would be coming. I was officially laid off for the second time in July 2006—less than one year after being brought back from the first layoff. I was given the news that I would no longer be allowed to participate in the pawn shop detail and that someone else would have to take over. I was crushed. The Target investigator, John, called me at home shortly afterward.

"We are really happy with your work. We decided that we aren't willing to work with anyone else. We'll be notifying Detective McAuley that it's either you or we're done," John said.

"John, I'm so flattered with your faith in me, but the work is the most important thing, not me," I replied. John wasn't going to be swayed. He called Detective McAuley, Sergeant Hess, and Sergeant Tapp and told them that if I wasn't going to continue working the detail then Target would discontinue its partnership with them.

After failing to change John's mind, a new solution was suggested. I was not privy to who came up with the idea, but it was decided that I would continue to work the detail, although not as a police officer. I would be paid $100 out of the vice unit forfeiture fund for each sale I made as an undercover informant. This was great for everyone. For me, it wasn't about the money. It was about finishing what I started and seeing my hard work followed through to completion. One hundred dollars here and there wasn't going to pay my bills, but it would give me a little spending money. The operation continued for several more weeks before the prosecutor's office decided that enough evidence had been gathered and warrants could be issued.

Similar to the baby formula detail, several groups of uniformed officers, detectives, and undercover officers were assembled and broken into groups. One group would raid the pawn shop and other groups would go to the owner's residence and storage areas. The search warrant raids were initiated simultaneously and were a complete success.

I had been proud of the success I had achieved in past details, but there was something special about this one. I wasn't just selected for it. My participation had been fought for. Not only that, Target discontinued working additional details when they determined that I would not be recalled from layoff. It felt good to be valued. For most of my life I had felt like it didn't really matter if I lived or died.

When I was fourteen my father received a call from my older maternal half-brother. He had been living with our maternal grandparents for years but had gotten himself in trouble and been thrown out of their house. Even though he had no biological connection to my father, they had become friends. My assumption is that my half-brother maintained a relationship with my father because he always had drugs and was willing to share them.

My half-brother asked my father if he could move in for a while. My father told him that he was sorry, but he didn't have the room. Apparently, my half-brother decided to try to make an extra room. He told my father that he heard that I was pregnant and hiding it from him.

I was not pregnant. I didn't have a boyfriend and I certainly wasn't having sex with anyone. My father hung up the phone, jerked me off the couch by my arm, and started screaming, "You fucking whore! I'll make sure that baby is dead!" My father launched into beating me. He punched and kicked me in the stomach repeatedly, even after I fell to the floor. Eventually, as frequently happened, I blacked out. I woke up later, angry and in pain.

Two days later I couldn't stop thinking about how much I hated my life. No matter what I did, no matter who I asked for help, I couldn't seem to stop the beatings. I had reached my breaking point.

I woke up the next morning and decided I was done. It was early, but my father had already left for work. Caroline was asleep and wouldn't be up for hours. I went into the kitchen and opened my father's pill drawer. Most people have a junk drawer; we had a drug drawer. I took out a large bottle of aspirin, got a big glass of water, and started swallowing. I began swallowing them by the handful and could taste the bitter chalkiness on my tongue as they struggled to go down.

I was only about fifty aspirins in when my stomach began to reject the pills. I could feel my stomach cramping as if there was a vise around my torso. I began to involuntarily heave as my body tried to force the pills back out from where they came. I continued on through sheer determination. Nothing was going to stop me from accomplishing my mission. Somehow, I continued to swallow the aspirin until there was nothing left in the bottle. I then grabbed some random pills out of the drawer and swallowed those too.

I laid down on my bed and prayed it would be over soon. My stomach alternated between churning violently to feeling like it might spontaneously explode. I couldn't seem to control my breathing and it continued to increase to the point of hyperventilation. I was sweating, and I couldn't see straight. I was heaving uncontrollably, but I kept telling myself that if I vomited, it was all for nothing. I would still be stuck in this hell I called my life.

I managed to hold the pills down for about thirty minutes until my ability to control the situation no longer worked. I staggered to the bathroom and threw up so violently that it felt like I might actually vomit up my internal organs. It seemed to go on forever. I could, again, taste the bitterness of the aspirin, which made me vomit even harder. When it finally ended, I sat on the floor next to the toilet and cried. I had failed. I couldn't even manage to kill myself properly.

I went to the phone and called Sue. I told her that I needed her to come over quickly. She arrived at my house just minutes later. One look at me and she knew something was very wrong.

"Oh my God! What's wrong with you?" Sue exclaimed.

"I couldn't do it anymore, Sue. I swallowed all the pills I could get my hands on, but I threw them up. I failed. If my father finds out what I did he'll kill me," I cried. "I need your help, Sue. Can you just help me get ready for school and get to the bus stop?" I asked.

"You can't go to school like this," Sue said. "Let me call my mom. You know she could help you."

"Please, Sue. You know she will want to call my father or take me to the doctor. I can't let my father find out. I threw up the pills. I'll be fine. I just need to get to school." I cried harder, and she finally conceded.

I remember feeling like my legs didn't want to work. I struggled not to pass out. The urge to vomit was ever-present. Somehow, Sue got me dressed and we left for the bus stop, but I don't remember getting there or on the bus. I don't remember arriving at school. The next thing I do remember is waking up in St. Joe's Hospital the next day.

I have some fuzzy memories, but I don't know if they are really memories or just dreams: ambulance sirens, a tube being shoved down my throat, hearing people talking in my hospital room saying, "It's touch and go. There's no guarantee she'll make it."

I had no idea what was going to happen next, but the one thing I did know was that I was alone. I didn't wake up to find my father or my mother sitting next to my bed. In fact, I don't remember either of them coming to the hospital at all. I lay in my hospital bed and admonished myself repeatedly for failing in my task. My thoughts became completely obsessed with a single thought—how I would succeed next time.

After recovering from my suicide attempt, it was decided, I'm not sure by who, that I was not to be returned to my father, but instead to be admitted to a treatment center. The facility, the Fox Center, was next to St. Joe's Hospital. My father's wife, Caroline, dropped some clothes off in a bag for me. The Fox Center offered inpatient and outpatient therapy for both adults and children. I was sent to a wing that was inpatient and locked down.

I walked through the locked doors to find myself in an L-shaped unit: boys on one side, girls on the other, dining area in the middle. I still wasn't feeling all that great and now I had a whole new wave of emotions coming over me. I was scared to be in this new place, but relieved not to have to go home to my father. Embarrassed because I was sure everyone knew I had tried to kill myself, but angry that I was being locked away. There were staff and kids walking around freely throughout the unit. I don't know what I expected to see: Everyone locked in a room with bars on the doors like a jail cell?

I was shown to my room and given time to put my clothes away. Next, I was given a quick rundown on how things operated and then was left alone. There would be group therapy, individual and family therapy sessions, scheduled meals, scheduled school time, shower time, and free time to socialize or watch TV. Calls and visitors were initially restricted until the privileges had been earned. Boys and girls could socialize but could never be found in each other's rooms.

I quickly found out that there were kids of all ages, from every demographic, and with every kind of problem there. Janette was there for anorexia. June because she couldn't seem to stay out of legal trouble. Phoebe was a heavy drug user. Jim was there for stealing a car.

When you go to a place like the Fox Center, there is one question that you have to ask yourself right away: am I going to cooperate and accept the help, or am I going to rebel and fight the process the entire time? I decided to fight. The longer I was there the angrier I got. I felt like I was being punished instead of my father. He had been so horrible, so abusive, and no one seemed to care.

I had been at the Fox Center for about a week when I was told that I might have to be released. It seemed that my father had still not shown up to sign authorization for my admittance. He had left that responsibility to Caroline, and while they accepted that temporarily, he was still required to show up and sign the papers as my legal parent. Apparently, the idea of having me back home was so abhorrent to him that he finally showed up. After signing the papers, I was told that I would be given visitation time with my father. I declined but was soon informed that it wasn't optional.

My father was brought into the girls' side of the unit to a sitting area kitty-corner to my room. The room had two couches. My father sat down on one end of a couch, and I sat on the other. The same old trembling came over my body. I looked into his grayish-blue eyes and saw nothing but pure hatred. I knew I was safe with staff members everywhere, but I was terrified of my father, nonetheless.

Subtlety was never my father's strong suit, and he failed miserably now. He tried to tell me how embarrassed and angry he was at me as his voice became louder and louder. It seemed to amplify and echo through the enclosed unit. It didn't take long before several staff members were staring in our direction. I started to cry, half out of fear and half out of embarrassment. When the staff turned their eyes away, my father grabbed me by the arm and jerked me into my room and shut the door. He threw me against the wall and started screaming at me. I tried to stay calm. I knew someone would hear him and come to the room and save me. Things escalated quickly and the next thing I knew my father was punching and hitting me in rapid-fire succession. I'm sure it was only seconds later that the staff busted in, but it felt like time had stood still. My father was removed from the unit. My humiliation was complete.

Family therapy started soon after. I resisted and begged the staff not to make me go, but I was forced to. Therapy with my father was a joke. I insisted I had attempted suicide because I had been an abused child; my father insisted that he had never hit me and that I was just a spoiled brat. We were both stubborn and neither of us was going to budge from our positions. I tried to bring up his assault on me during his first visit to the unit, but he even denied that. I always believed my father was a compulsive liar, and he was proving that theory true again. The problem was that either the therapist believed him or just refused to confront him about his behavior. Either way, my anger continued to build, and my resentment toward the facility deepened.

It didn't take long before the therapist figured out that there was no fixing the relationship between my father and me. Somehow, the therapist managed to contact my mother and she and my stepfather were brought in for counseling instead. It seemed that the new plan was to try to fix that damaged relationship and prepare to transition me back to them upon my release. This, too, was going to be a challenge.

By this time I was as angry a child as one could imagine. I hated the world and everyone in it. I didn't want to go along with any program, in fact, I wanted to do the exact opposite of anything I was told to do. From here on out I was done being the good girl who tried to make everyone happy. It hadn't worked for me up to this point, so I saw no reason to continue. I had been helpless to control anything that had happened to me for so many years. Finally, I was in control. No one would force me to forgive anyone. No one would force me to accept help. No one would force me not to be angry.

Life at the Fox Center was not what one would expect. Most people would think that it would be horrible to be locked up in what essentially amounted to a mental facility, but not me. I was with a group of people who understood how much it sucked to be a teenager. People who understood what it was like to be abused and angry at the whole world. And, best of all, I wasn't living with daily abuse.

I stuck with my plan and bucked the system. I decided that I was going to use this time to socialize with my new friends and enjoy the carefree life of not being abused anymore. I refused to participate in any form of meaningful therapy. I was constantly breaking rules: going on the boy's side, smoking smuggled cigarettes in the shower, having angry outbursts, refusing to do chores, being disruptive during school time, and so on.

Deep down I wasn't a bad kid; I was just angry—so angry. At the time, I couldn't express that anger, but it was there. Some days I felt like it was so powerful that it would consume me from the inside out and I might just explode into a ball of fire.

Days turned into weeks and weeks turned into months. Slowly but surely, all my new friends were being released and sent home. Phoebe had become my best friend and my partner in crime. Although smoking was not allowed on the unit, cigarettes and lighters were frequently smuggled into the facility by kids that were granted home visits. Those cigarettes frequently found their way to Phoebe and me. It was nearly impossible to smoke without being caught, so we would get into a scalding hot shower with lots of steam in hopes that the steam would camouflage the smoke. I'm not sure if the steam didn't conceal the smoke as we hoped, or if we were ratted out by other patients, but we always got caught. The good thing in my mind was that punishment never involved physical abuse.

When Phoebe was released, I fell apart. I didn't know how to cope with the sadness and anger I felt in being without her. Without the ability to manage my emotions, I began to act out in even more egregious ways. I was openly hostile to both staff and patients. I hated everyone and I let them know it.

One outburst led to me being physically restrained in a straitjacket and shot full of the antipsychotic Haldol. It felt like thick glue being injected into my butt. I was then locked in a padded room for hours to calm down. I can honestly say that I never wanted to repeat that experience again. I realized it was time to reevaluate what I was doing.

While there were plenty of kids still at the Fox Center with me, it just wasn't the same anymore. I didn't want to be there. I didn't want to be friends with anyone. I wondered what was wrong with me that I wasn't able to be released too. I finally spoke with one of my counselors about it and she told me bluntly that I needed to get with the program. She explained that they were working hard to help me, but that I had to stop fighting it. After years of asking for assistance and never getting it, here it was, finally being offered, and I thumbed my nose at it. It was time.

My life at the Fox Center changed dramatically after that. I did chores around the facility, I completed my schoolwork, I volunteered to help with anything I could. I became an active participant in my treatment, including therapy sessions with my mother and stepfather. It felt strange to have family therapy with them. I could tell that my stepfather didn't really want to be there, but my mother seemed to miss me desperately. This was troubling because I felt so deeply conflicted about her. I had always yearned for a close relationship with my mother yet despised her for her lack of protection.

Soon, a field trip to a park came up and I wanted desperately to go. I figured it was a long shot with my history of being a troublemaker, but I maintained hope. Finally, I was informed that I would be allowed to join the group. I was excited and proud of myself as I realized that changing my attitude had worked. It was on that field trip that I would find out that the next phase of my life was to begin. I was being released the next day to my mother.

Now that I was laid off from the police department again, I had some decisions to make. I had booked my trip to Egypt and was set to leave the following month. If I was responsible and cancelled it, I would be upsetting Gina, as well as ruining my chance to do the number one item on my bucket list. If I didn't cancel the trip, I felt like it would be fiscally selfish to my husband and son.

There was also the question of finding a new job. If I started job hunting immediately, I could be required to test or interview during the time I would be in Egypt. If I waited until I returned from the trip there was a good chance that I would miss out on several job opportunities that would be taken by my coworkers who had also been laid off. In the back of my mind, I was sure that the city would work things out somehow and I would be called back to work again soon. Ultimately, I decided that I had the money and the time; therefore, I was going to follow through with my trip.

The day finally arrived when Gina and I were leaving. Sergeant Thomas and Neil drove us to the airport. We said our goodbyes, made our way through airport security, and headed for the bar to have a drink. We were giggling and talking like teenagers going on spring break. People around us probably thought we were drunk.

As excited as I was, I wasn't looking forward to the flight. I had only flown on short flights twice prior to this trip. As we boarded the plane my excitement turned to fear. Sitting in my seat by the window, tightly buckled in, I could feel my breathing accelerate as I fought to stop from hyperventilating. Gina loved flying and her giddiness continued unabated. The flight took off at 7:00 p.m. and it didn't take long before Gina fell asleep.

Approximately eight hours later, we landed in Paris for a four-hour layover. Gina and I had been debating for weeks the merits of leaving the airport for a quick trip to the see the Eiffel Tower. Of course, both of our husbands had declared that we were not to leave the airport and risk missing our connecting flight. We understood why but weren't happy. It was around this time that there had been numerous terrorist attacks around the world and getting through customs could sometimes take longer than usual. Our husbands made it clear that they would not be happy if we called them to say that we had missed our flight.

We got off the plane, walked to the gate for our next leg of the trip, and plopped down into our chairs. We sat slumped down, armed crossed, sulking like children in a time out. Only moments later, I jumped up and said, "Fuck this! Let's go!" Gina smiled, and we ran for the airport exit.

Once outside we observed a line of taxis. We approached the first one we came to and asked the driver, "Do you speak English?" The driver, a man in his midforties, clean cut with brown hair and sparkling green eyes, replied that he did.

"We only have a four-hour layover, but we really want to see the Eiffel Tower," I said.

He smiled. "Get in. Let's go."

We jumped in the taxi and held on tight. At the time, I didn't know if he was a terrible driver, trying to kill us, or if everyone drove like that, but he was driving very fast and weaving in and out of traffic as if it didn't exist. I began to wonder if we were going to make it to Egypt at all.

The time continued to tick by, and Gina and I began to get nervous. After thirty minutes, I asked the driver, "How far is the Eiffel Tower from the airport?"

"About forty-five minutes," he replied casually.

Gina and I looked at each other wide-eyed and panicked. How would we explain to our husbands that we completely ignored their directive and missed our connecting flight in Paris? We decided that there wasn't much we could do at that point, so we sat back and enjoyed the view. Our driver then decided to change plans.

"You can't come to Paris and only go to the Eiffel Tower. There's so much more to see," he said. Gina and I were concerned, but we weren't in control of the situation anymore. We decided to trust our driver and believe that he would get us back to the airport in time to make our connection. We had no idea that we were about to go on a whirlwind tour of Paris' highlights.

Our first stop was the Champs-Elysées. Our driver stopped in the middle of the road, had us get out of the car, and took our picture standing in front of the Arc de Triomphe. We then got photos of the Louvre, Notre Dame, the Luxor Obelisk (from Egypt), the L'Académie Nationale de Musique, the house where Voltaire lived, the Assemblée Nationale, the Pont de l'Alma tunnel where Princess Diana died, and finally, the Eiffel Tower.

We made it back to the airport, unbelievably, with thirty minutes to spare. The taxi driver charged us $250 for the trip. Gina and I knew that we were ripped-off but didn't care. We paid him, ran into the airport, and hoped that we didn't get stuck in customs. Luckily, we breezed through, ran to the gate, and plopped back down in our original seats. I took a deep breath of satisfaction, exhaled slowly, and looked over at Gina. We both started laughing. Next stop—Cairo, Egypt.

The flight to Cairo took a little less than five hours. By the time we landed it was evening and beginning to get dark outside. The Cairo airport was an assault on my senses. It was packed full of people speaking Arabic, the unusual smells of cardamom, clove, and saffron-infused coffee confused my olfactory system, and the modern architecture with palm trees and flowers inside the airport were a wonder to gaze upon. Gina and I made our way to baggage claim and retrieved our luggage. A representative of our tour company, holding a sign with our names on it, was there to meet us.

The instant we exited the airport we ran into a brick wall of heat. I've experienced heat before, but this felt like being inside a sauna fully dressed. August temperatures in Cairo, Egypt, average around one hundred degrees and there was no doubt that it was at least that hot. The temperature was overpowering on my now exhausted body. Up to this point I had been running on pure adrenaline after being unable to sleep on the plane. I was hoping that my excitement at finally being in Egypt would be enough to carry me through. If I had any hopes of falling asleep during a relaxing drive to the hotel, I was sorely mistaken.

Driving in Egypt is like nothing you can imagine. I thought the taxi driver in Paris was bad, but this was another level. Egypt does not have traffic lights, stop signs, or any other type of traffic control. The roads have lane markers, but no one uses them. A four-lane road will easily accommodate seven cars or more in Egypt. If a car wants to merge onto a road, the driver just honks their horn and moves into the lane. I was wide awake now and wondering if we were going to make it to the hotel alive.

I was shocked and relieved when we finally arrived at the hotel safely. We were quickly checked in and escorted to our room by armed security. Maybe I was too tired to realize that it was weird to have armed escorts, but I didn't give it a second thought. As a police officer, I was used to being around guns. I felt safe having them near me.

By the time we got to our room and put our luggage down it was 11:00 p.m. It had been nearly twenty-four hours since I had last slept. The adrenaline was wearing off and my body was close to collapse. I put my pajamas on and was about to climb into bed when I noticed double doors on the other side of my room. Curiosity got the best of me, and I opened them. To my surprise, they led to a balcony that overlooked the beautifully manicured grounds of the hotel and, in the distance, the Great Pyramid of Giza. It was completely illuminated by lights. I stood on the balcony, unable to speak, unable to move, barely able to breath, and tears streaming from my eyes. I had dreamt of this moment since I was a child, and here I was, gazing upon a monument that was more than four thousand years old. I sat down and stared. I couldn't take my eyes off it. It felt like the pyramid had put me in a trance. A few minutes later Gina joined me on the balcony. We sat in silence soaking up the experience.

Suddenly, the room's telephone began to ring, but we were so wrapped up in the pyramid that we ignored it. Moments later there was a loud, hard banging on our room door. Gina and I were startled out of our daze and ran to the door. When we opened it, we were met by the two security guards that had led us to our room earlier. This time their AK-47s were clearly visible and they were ready for any trouble they might encounter. They explained that they were in charge of our safety, and when we didn't answer our telephone, they became concerned. Again, maybe we should have been alarmed by this, but we weren't. Instead of worry, we felt secure knowing that there were people keeping such a close eye on us. With the serenity of the moment broken, we closed the balcony doors and fell into an exhaustive asleep.

I woke up only a few hours later and tip-toed back out to the balcony. It was still dark, but I could see in the distance that the sun would soon be rising. I sat down and watched the sun rise over the Great Pyramid. It illuminated the hotel grounds, which I now realized were absolutely gorgeous. It was comprised of granite as far as the eye could see. The sidewalks, stairs, walking paths, tables, and statues were all made of different colored granite.

All of it glistened and sparkled as the sun reflected off the tiny crystals imbedded in the rock.

There were manicured palm trees and delicate flowers in every color of the rainbow. A large pool filled with shimmering crystal-clear water was the centerpiece. Just to the right of the pool area was an oversized chess game. Each piece was artfully sculpted and stood approximately two feet high. Everywhere I looked there was nothing that didn't take my breath away.

Our first stop of the day was the Great Pyramid. Seeing it in the distance was one thing, but up close was a whole different experience. It's impossible to describe the magnitude of the it. It's amazing to think that it was built thousands of years ago by people with absolutely no technological advances or special equipment. We spent about an hour walking around the pyramid complex and taking pictures. My favorite is one Gina took of me sitting on an enormous block of ancient stone.

Next, we drove a short distance to the Sphinx, the world's largest and oldest statue. Prior to the trip, I researched all there was to know about the Great Pyramid and the Sphinx. It was surreal to see them in person. I began to think about the history surrounding the Sphinx. I was standing in the place where a young boy, who would later become Pharaoh Thutmose IV, found the Sphinx buried in sand up to its neck around 1400 BC. Standing where Napoleon Bonaparte stood with his soldiers when they fought in Egypt in the late 1700s.

I still couldn't wrap my brain around the fact that I was actually in Egypt. The week flew by in a blur of monuments and historical sites: the 4,700-year-old Step Pyramid of Djoser, which is believed to be the first attempt at building an Egyptian pyramid; the Valley of the Kings where I viewed King Tut lying in his original sarcophagus; the Valley of the Queens; the temple of Hatshepsut, who was one of only a few female pharaohs and where remnants of original paintings can still be seen on the walls and ceilings; and the Cairo Museum where mummies of ancient pharaohs are kept in temperature-controlled glass boxes. It's an indescribable feeling to see the red hair, eyelashes, and fingernails still visible on the mummy of Ramesses the Great who ruled Egypt from 1279–1213 BC. Each sight was more mind-blowing than the next. It's impossible to say which was my favorite. Every moment was the realization of years of my hopes and dreams.

On the eighth day of our trip everything changed. It began with a tour of the Karnak Temple Complex, which is well over two hundred acres and located near Luxor and once a part of the famed city of Thebes.

Throughout history, each Egyptian pharaoh added something to Karnak to mark their time as ruler. I had been looking forward to seeing it.

It was another hot day—over 110 degrees. Our tour guide took us around a small part of the complex and pointed out areas that he thought were important and then gave us the next couple hours to explore on our own. Most of our group walked to the shaded refreshment area rather than continue to explore in the heat. I, however, was not going to squander this opportunity.

I spent the next two hours exploring every inch of the complex that I could get to. There was so much to see, and I was determined to absorb and memorialize each piece of history in my brain. Later that day, by the time we got back to our room, I had a pounding headache, felt light-headed, and was nauseous. I laid down in my bed and ended up staying there for the next two days. My symptoms continued to get worse by the hour. I had debilitating cramps, a high fever, I couldn't think clearly, and alternated between conscious and unconscious. I had no idea what was wrong with me, but for the second time in my life, I was pretty sure that I was going to die.

Gina was an excellent nursemaid during my illness and checked on me between excursions. She brought me water and dry toast periodically, but I couldn't keep anything down. Our tour guide kept bringing me pills, but to this day, I have no idea what those pills were. I would later find out that I had gotten heatstroke during my exploration of Karnak. I probably should have been admitted to a hospital and am lucky to have lived through the experience. Looking back, I realize that I should have made hydration a priority.

By the third day, I was finally able to get out of bed. I still felt dreadful, but I was determined not to miss any more of the trip. The last couple days were a bit of a disappointment because I was still weak, but I tried to do my best to soak up every bit of history I could.

When I look back on my trip to Egypt, I don't think about the fact that I almost died there. I remember the history, the culture, the monuments, the temples, the food, and the memories. I treasure that my friendship with Gina was solidified and that we will always have that shared experience to bond over. I think about the fact that in a life of tragedy and sadness I was granted a thirteen-day respite that made a lifelong dream come true.

9

THE URBAN CURSE

The return home from my trip to Egypt was bittersweet. I had crossed off the number one item on my bucket list but was unemployed and had zero job prospects. Although the recession of 2008 hadn't arrived yet, the economy in Michigan was not good. It seemed that every police department in my area was laying people off. If I was lucky enough to find an opening, I would arrive to the testing site to find two to three hundred people all vying for the same spot.

After a couple months of constant searching, to no avail, I could tell that the substantial cut in our household income was taking a toll on Neil. He and I had always avoided debt. We didn't carry balances on our credit cards, we never bought a new car until the other one was paid off, and we didn't go out to eat or go shopping unless we had the cash on hand to pay for it. My inability to find a job was forcing us to cut out all extraneous spending that previously we never had to give a second thought to. I could see that not working was going to have a serious effect on our marriage if something didn't change quickly.

I was consumed with guilt and sadness on a daily basis as our financial situation blanketed Neil with stress. My identity had been wrapped up in my career for so long that I didn't know who I was anymore. It seemed that all the great work I had accomplished was for nothing. Almost no one was hiring police officers. The couple rare openings that did come up ended in more heartbreak.

The most frustrating part of trying to find a new job was the treatment I received from departments regarding my experience. When I looked at my resume, I saw an officer who had worked a variety of special details with a wide range of skills that any department would be lucky to have. What other departments saw was very different.

Finally, an opening for a police officer in Grand Blanc Township, forty minutes north of where I lived, opened up. Grand Blanc Township wasn't as busy a department as Pontiac, but it did border with the city of Flint, so there was potential to do some work. I applied for the job and took a written test for them a few weeks later. I scored among the top and was asked to come in for an interview, which was conducted by a lieutenant in the department. Again, I scored among the top candidates. The last step before being hired was an interview with the chief of police.

I was excited and convinced myself that this last interview was only going to be a formality and that I would soon be working for GBTPD. The interview was going well with no indication of problems. That all changed when the chief decided to stop wasting his time and tell me the truth. "I need to be honest with you," he said. "We have hired officers from urban departments before and it has never worked out well. I decided last time we had an issue that I would never hire another officer from an urban area."

What was I supposed to say to that? Was he really telling me that my excellent test and interview scores along with all my experience and hard work was negated solely by the department that I had previously worked for? Worse, by past employees that screwed up? I imagine that the look on my face was one of confusion and anger. The chief went on to tell me about several Flint officers that had been hired in the past and how each of them had been fired due to misconduct or criminal behavior. I tried to explain that I wasn't like those officers, but he wasn't interested. "I'm sorry, but we're done here," he said.

About a month later I found that GBTPD had advertised that they were hiring for police officers again. I reapplied, retested, reinterviewed, and ended up in front of the chief again. Unfortunately, he had not changed his mind. He reiterated his stance on hiring officers from urban departments and the interview ended—even more quickly than the first time. It seemed that this was not a departmental policy, but rather a policy of the chief. What else would explain being continually moved through the process only to be turned away by the chief?

Shortly after this I found out that Oakland Community College was hiring a police officer. Working at a community college wasn't exactly my dream job, but I had to put my family's needs first and there were multiple campuses, including one as close at ten minutes from my house. I applied and was brought in for an interview with a sergeant a couple weeks later. We discussed my experience and all the undercover work I had taken part in. I thought he was impressed, but it turned out to be the opposite.

"There's no doubt that you have some impressive experience," he started, "however, this is a community college. I don't think this is the job for you. You'll be bored here. Sorry."

I tried to tell him that he was wrong and that I wanted this job. I lied and said, "I've done all the big stuff. I'm ready to slow down. I don't need to be chasing and fighting people every day."

"Thanks for coming in, but I just don't think this is the place for you. Good luck," he said as he stood up and held out his right hand. I shook it, flashed a fake smile, held back my tears, and walked out to my car. Once I was back in my car, I had a good, hard cry. I dreaded going home and telling Neil that once again I didn't get the job.

As a child I struggled with feelings of worthlessness. Nothing I ever did was good enough and I was frequently beaten for no reason. However, as a police officer, I was used to encountering enormous levels of stress. I was generally unflappable in the face of pressure and adversity. Managing multiple problems and finding solutions was effortless for me. Times of personal difficulties were different, though, and it wasn't uncommon to find myself overwhelmed by familiar feelings of helplessness.

My earliest memories of violence are when I was four years old. I can remember my older brother holding me down on the floor. Because he was an overweight kid, and I was so undersized, there was nothing I could do but struggle fruitlessly. My brother would sit on my stomach and punch me repeatedly as I kicked and squirmed. Then he would put his hand over my mouth and try to pull my pants down. I would bite his hand, scream, and kick my legs as hard as I could. I assumed he was afraid my scream would draw the attention of my mother, so he would get up and let me go. I would run away from him as fast as I could.

During this time my family lived in a trailer. As best as I can remember it was a one-bedroom trailer with two bunkbeds for my brother and I. They were not in a bedroom, but rather in a small opening like a storage area. A sheet hung from the ceiling to conceal the bunkbeds from view. I can remember times when my mother and stepfather would be outside with friends and my brother would pull me behind the sheet "to play." I don't remember the details or recall anything particular that occurred behind that sheet, but I do remember the feeling of being dirty and uncomfortable.

Years later, when I was around eight, and we lived in an apartment. Across the hall was a brother and sister a couple years older than my brother. One day I walked in from outside and heard my brother talking to them about practicing sexual acts with me. I distinctly remember how embarrassed, disgusted, and ashamed I was. I screamed at him, "Shut up, you disgusting pig! Don't tell people gross stuff like that!" I ran into my bedroom and cried. While it's true that I've blocked out the memories of anything physical, the emotional feelings that overcame me during that time were debilitating.

One afternoon, when I was ten, my parents went shopping, leaving my brother and I at home. As soon as they left my brother went into my parent's room and retrieved an X-rated movie. He put the video into the VCR and told me to sit down and watch the movie with him. I felt sick and became overwhelmed by a fear that I can't explain. I quickly ran out of the house. I didn't know where I was going, but I knew I didn't want to be there with my brother.

I don't know why I never told my mother about these incidents. Was it because I thought she already knew and didn't care? Was it because I felt too dirty and ashamed? Was it because my mother had become someone that I knew I couldn't depend on? I have no answers. What I do know is that I wasn't my brother's only victim. I have since learned that he molested several other members of my family, male and female.

The longer I was unemployed, the higher the stress level climbed between Neil and me. It became clear that my marriage may be in trouble if I didn't get a job soon. I couldn't believe everything I had gone through to become a police officer and now I was being forced out of the field. I had to put my family first, so as much as it pained me, I decided it was time to expand my job search outside of law enforcement.

Prior to entering a career in law enforcement, I had worked in an office setting. It had been many years, but I hoped that someone would take a chance on me. I began applying for various office jobs. I started with management positions, but as time passed, I lowered my expectations and applied for secretarial and assistant positions.

Finally, I got a full-time job as an office manager. The pay wasn't great, less than half of what I had been making as a police officer, but it was better than nothing. I hoped that being back to work would help lessen the financial stress on Neil and calm some of the disputes at home.

It felt great to be out of the house and working again. I still missed police work, but at least I was no longer sitting around the house feeling like a financial burden. The one good thing about my new job was that I had many responsibilities, which kept me busy every day. I have always worked best under pressure and a fast pace. It wasn't police work, but I reveled in the challenge, nonetheless.

Unfortunately, this job wasn't going to be enough to resolve our financial shortfalls. For the next two and a half years I would simultaneously work at least two jobs, and sometimes three, but still never managed to earn the amount of money I had at Pontiac PD.

One of those jobs was as a police officer at Holly Police Department, about thirty minutes north of Waterford. It was a small town similar to my first job. The village of Holly is approximately three square miles with a population of around six thousand people. The department employed a full-time chief, lieutenant, two sergeants, seven officers, and numerous part-time officers. I worked there on a part-time basis for two years and hated every single minute of every shift.

One of the worst examples of the poor treatment I endured was when the chief called me into his office and asked me to do my best to locate a wanted suspect. The man had held his wife and children hostage, assaulted them repeatedly, including with a taser. The incident had even caused the schools to go on lockdown. I won't reveal the specifics of how I located him because of the circumstances, but within hours I found out he had checked himself into a mental facility to hide. I advised the chief as he was leaving for the day that I had found the suspect. He praised me for the fast work and told me to take another officer with me the next day to arrest him.

The lieutenant hated that the chief had hired several laid-off Pontiac police officers and took his dislike out on them. After the chief went home, the lieutenant called me into his office and instead of praising my excellent investigating skills, he berated me. He finished by ordering me to go pick up the suspect the next morning by myself. I was furious. Sergeant Stern, who was retired from Pontiac, told me to disregard the lieutenant and take Officer Garza with me. That type of inconsistent and unfair leadership was constant and frustrating. It was an incident similar to this that caused me to finally call it quits after two years in Holly.

After three years of juggling jobs, trying to find a full-time police job without success, and praying every day to get recalled to Pontiac PD, I was at my mental breaking point. It was fall of 2009 when Neil came home from work and told me that Pontiac was looking to hire a full-time dispatcher. I didn't want to be a dispatcher again, but it would mean making more money than all my jobs combined and going back to the city and friends that I loved. As officers retired from Pontiac PD, the department recalled several officers from layoff over the years, and I was getting close to being recalled too. I thought by being there as a dispatcher it might make it more likely that I would get recalled sooner—at least it couldn't hurt.

I started work in dispatch in December 2009. Neil was immediately less stressed out now that my income would be closer to what it had been three years prior, and I felt closer to being my old self again. The police officers were happy to have me back, but similar to when I worked for Ingham County dispatch, the other dispatchers were not happy to have me there knowing that I would leave as soon as I was recalled back to patrol.

The setup and operations of Pontiac's dispatch center was very different from Ingham's, but I was familiar with how Pontiac operated so it made for a smooth transition. I wouldn't be relegated to the LEIN console this time. Where Ingham County's dispatch center was in a building in downtown Lansing away from all the officers that it dispatched for, Pontiac's center was on the second floor of the police department. Officers would come in and out frequently and make requests in person. The location also allowed me to visit with my friends during my breaks or help out officers when they needed me.

I knew the LEIN station so well from prior dispatching and from using it for years in my patrol car, training took minimal time. As a police officer the call screen in our patrol cars was the same as the police dispatchers' screen, so there wasn't much new to learn besides how to send out the calls to the officers and how to clear them when they were done. Fire dispatching, however, was another matter. I had no experience whatsoever with the fire department. Their lingo was different, their policies were different, their preferences were different—it was a lot to learn. I definitely took more time to learn that station than any other.

Being back in Pontiac was good for me in many ways. I was making more money, seeing my friends again every day, and I got to feel more like a police officer again. I spent a lot of time going on ride-alongs with my friends, which was more like working as partners. I always assisted with calls and wrote the reports. It took some of the sting out of not actually being a police officer. Sometimes, I didn't even have to be on a ride-along to help—the need came to me. There were several times when I was at work in dispatch when I was called down to assist officers with one thing or another. The most memorable of those times was when I was called to assist Neil with neglected children.

I was working overtime on midnights when Neil came into dispatch and asked me if I had any food with me. Of course, I did. I always tried to keep some food in my locker for times when I was unexpectedly held over for another shift.

"Is the food for you? You wouldn't like anything I have," I said laughing.

"No, it's for some kids downstairs. Their mother hasn't fed them all day."

I asked one of the other dispatchers to cover my station and I went to my locker to see what I had. Neil told me that the kids were seven months and two years old. Luckily, I had soup, crackers, and a yogurt in the refrigerator. I warmed up the soup and took everything downstairs where the mother and children were sitting in the lobby waiting room.

When I walked into the dark waiting room, I saw an African American woman who looked very young, maybe twenty, sitting in a chair watching TV. There was a baby in a car seat on top of the table crying. The two-year-old was sitting in a chair with her head on the table. It was clear that she was not only tired, but that she didn't feel well. She was coughing, sneezing, and had a runny nose. The mother looked ragged and tired. She seemed to be completely unaware of the baby crying next to her. Neil and I realized quickly that she had some type of mental deficiency.

I introduced myself and told her that I had some food for her and the kids. I gave the mother and the two-year-old a bowl of soup, a package of crackers, and yogurt to feed the baby. She looked up at me while I spoke but seemed to be looking right through me. There was no change of expression on her face, no smile, no real acknowledgment of my presence. It was like she was there physically, but not mentally. She nodded her head, and I went back upstairs to work.

Neil walked back upstairs with me, and I asked him what the hell was going on with them. He explained that the woman lived in a homeless shelter in Detroit and had met a man from Pontiac on the social media app, MocoSpace. The man drove down to Detroit early that morning to pick her up and took her to an abandoned house on the southwest side of Pontiac that he claimed to own. The house had no water, no heat, and no furniture.

Once inside the house the man convinced her to have sex with him and then he left her there with the kids saying that she could stay there as long as she wanted. The mother had stayed in the house alone all day before neighbors noticed her and the kids wandering around the abandoned house and the baby crying incessantly. The neighbors finally called 911 around midnight.

Initially, the mother asked Neil for a ride back to Detroit. After hearing the woman's story, Neil recognized that she was not the first person to be victimized by that man. There had been numerous reports previously filed of troubled women who had met him online and that he had sexually assaulted them. Neil drove her and the kids back to the station to file a report for criminal sexual conduct and to contact Children's Protective Services. Neil's biggest concern was that she had been in the house all day with the kids with no food. Neil said the house was not only dirty, but that the floor was covered with used condoms, needles, and other drug paraphernalia.

About two hours later it was my scheduled lunch break. I went downstairs to ask Neil how the kids were doing, and he told me that the mother still had not fed the kids the food I brought them. We decided that he was going to distract her by taking her into another room to ask more questions while I stayed with the kids to feed them. We walked into the still dark waiting room. The baby was still crying, the two-year-old was still sitting with her head on the table, and mom was still watching TV, but the mother had bought some chips and cookies out of the vending machine and had eaten them. The empty bags were sitting on the table. I could feel my anger boiling up as I looked over at Neil. He knew he better get that mother out of there before my anger erupted on her.

After Neil and the mother left the room, I bent down next to the little girl and asked what her name was. She whispered softly, "Shayanna."

"Are you hungry, Shayanna?" She shook her head side to side. "When the last time you ate?"

"I don't remember," she replied so softly that I could barely hear her.

My heart broke for this beautiful little girl with chestnut-brown eyes that penetrated all the way to my soul. I told Shayanna that I brought her soup and that I would really like her to eat some. She smiled and nodded her head. I pushed the bowl of soup in front of her and she started eating immediately. It was time to turn my attention to the baby, Jazmin. I picked Jazmin up, changed her well overdue diaper, and set her back down in her car seat. I opened the yogurt and began to feed her. She finally stopped crying, eating the entire cup of yogurt in just minutes. I then picked her back up and rocked her to sleep in my arms.

When Neil brought the kids' mother back into the room Shayanna had finished the soup and Jazmin was sleeping. I could tell that Shayanna was still hungry, so I quickly drove to McDonald's to get her some more food. Later, Neil came upstairs to tell me how angry he was that the food I bought for Shayanna was eaten by her mother. I was angry and annoyed. I told Neil that I wanted to take the kids home with us. He agreed, but we both knew we couldn't, which was a common frustration in police work.

I went home from work miserable and discouraged. These kids were the reason I became a cop. They were exactly the type of kids I wanted to help. It felt like I was looking into a crystal ball seeing how awful the lives of these two beautiful little girls were going to be. Of course, there was no way of me actually knowing that was going to happen, but the possibility tormented me.

My mother wasn't someone I could confide in or turn to in times of need. One example is when I woke up in a pool of blood after I turned eleven. My mother never had "the talk" with me, so the only information I received about menstruation came from reading the book *Are You There God? It's Me, Margaret* by Judy Blume. Unfortunately, it did not prepare me for the reality when my period arrived.

One morning I woke up to my stomach cramping. Still half asleep, I rolled onto my side and pulled my knees up and wrapped my arms around my legs under the blankets. Maybe I just had to go to the bathroom, I thought. After a minute or two I woke up enough to realize that I was wet. Had I peed the bed? I released my legs and flung the blankets off. I looked down and saw blood covering my sheets. Immediately, I wondered if I was dying. What else could explain that much blood? I began to check my feet, legs, and arms for signs of injury, but there was none.

"MOM!" I screamed.

"What?" she replied.

"Come quick!" I yelled frantically. My mother didn't rush, and a few minutes later she finally walked into my room to find me sitting on my bloody sheets crying.

"What happened?" she asked.

"I don't know," I cried. "I just woke up."

"Let's go," she said nonchalantly as she pointed down the hall toward the bathroom. Why wasn't she freaking out? I got up, still crying, and ran to the bathroom. My mother turned on the shower and told me to get in. I climbed into the shower, still sobbing, still confused.

"Stop crying. You're fine. You just got your period," my mother said sternly. I got out of the shower and my mother handed me a small box of sanitary pads. "Put one of these in your underwear. It will go away in a few days," she said matter-of-factly. "And wash your sheets," she said as she walked out of the bathroom.

I removed a pad from the box and examined it. I pulled the plastic strip off the back and pushed the sticky side into my underwear. *Do I keep this here all day? Based on my sheets I'll need a new one every hour. Do I flush them down the toilet? Is this supposed to feel like wearing a diaper? Will everyone be able to see this thing through my clothes?* There were so many questions and so few answers. I resorted to reading the directions on the box, which answered some of my questions. I felt terrible and somehow embarrassed. I got dressed, went to my room, and put my sheets into the washer. Then I returned to my room and spent the day in bed reading.

The momentous occasion of my becoming a woman was not brought up again until I ran out of pads. I found a moment when my mother was alone and told her that I was out of them. Her reply? "Walk up to the party store and buy some." I was mortified and still reeling from what was happening. Now she wanted me to walk into the neighborhood party store, where I would probably run into friends, and purchase pads. There was no way that was happening. Instead, I turned to Carol. When things at home got especially difficult it was nice to have an adult to confide in and seek advice from. This was one of those times. I walked to Carol's trailer, and thankfully, she was home.

"Do you have a minute to talk?" I asked meekly.

"Of course," she replied. I told her all about getting my period, how my mother hadn't explained anything to me, and how she told me to go to the party store for pads. Carol shook her head and said, "Have a seat." She spent the next hour or so telling me all about how the female body worked and what exactly was happening when I had my period. Not only that, she asked me how I felt about wearing the pads, which of course I said felt like wearing a diaper. Carol explained to me the difference between pads and tampons, showed me how to use them, and made sure that I always had what I needed. Looking back now, I wonder why my mother didn't take that opportunity to bond with me. Is there anything that can bring a mother and daughter closer than explaining what's happening when a daughter becomes a woman?

I waited up for Neil to get home from work so I could hear what happened to the kids. Neil had contacted CPS, but initially, they refused to respond. CPS told him that the mother and kids were from Wayne County and, therefore, not their problem. Fortunately, Neil refused to back down and contacted the supervisor of the CPS worker. A CPS worker arrived at the police department angry that Neil had "bothered her" with another county's problem. Neil explained to the worker that the mother and kids were victimized in this county and that the mental status of the mother made her unable or unwilling to care for her kids. If they were transported back to Detroit, they would disappear without receiving any help. Neil's shift was coming to an end, but before he went home the worker assured him that she was working on getting housing for the mother and kids. Neil was called on the way home and told that the worker waited for him to leave and then told the sergeant on duty that there was nothing she could do. She drove the mother and kids back to a Detroit homeless shelter. Ultimately, this news left me feeling even worse than when I left work that evening.

This incident is just another example of the frustration of being a police officer trying to work with the system that seemed to work against us. If officers were to do nothing in this situation and something bad happened to the kids, then officers could be held liable. However, when we try to get something done, help someone in need, we get turned down. It's always the calls involving children that cause an officer to lose sleep at night and continue to ruminate over them for years.

I have seen the dead bodies of many adults and it becomes hard to remember the specifics of them all. The calls involving children, however, are never forgotten. The children, whether neglected, abused, or killed, still visit me in my dreams. There has to be a better system than the one we currently have. Too many children fall through the cracks. Too many parents are given the benefit of the doubt. Too many people avert their eyes from the torment children are experiencing behind closed doors.

Working in the dispatch center wasn't perfect, but it was still better than the alternatives. I continued to wait, hoping and praying that I would get recalled from layoff and resume working the street as a police officer. Unfortunately, after approximately a year and a half, the financial problems of the city had continued to get worse. Not only was I not going to get recalled from layoff, but another fifteen officers were laid off.

Soon after the additional layoffs took effect, negotiations for the County Sheriff's Office to take over the police department became more substantial. It quickly became evident that nothing was going to stop the takeover. This was especially frustrating when the proposed contract with the county was over $3 million more than the current budget for the police officers. Regardless, Emergency Manager Schimmel made the decision that going to the county would be the best option. On July 31, 2011, the Pontiac Police Department ceased to exist and patrol of the city was turned over to the county. It was a horrible blow to everyone. For me it was the realization that once again I was not in control my own destiny. It felt like everything I worked so hard to achieve had been taken away once and for all.

The worst part of the transition to the county was that I was not allowed to apply for a position as a deputy with the rest of the officers because of my laid-off status. Once again, I was forced to apply to their dispatch center and hope to be transferred later. Being a part of Pontiac's dispatch had been tolerable because I was still able to go out with the officers and be a part of police work. Being a dispatcher for the county would be completely different. The county was a much larger department, my friends would be spread across a variety of jurisdictions that the county patrolled, and dispatchers worked out of a building completely separated from deputies.

10

THE INMATE LOVER RETURNS
TO BALDWIN ROAD

My first day in dispatch for the county was on July 31, 2011. There isn't much to say: I hated my job, I hated my coworkers, I hated my supervisors, and I felt incredibly alone. Still reeling from the realization that my opportunity to be recalled as a Pontiac police officer was gone and that I would no longer see my friends every day, I struggled to put on a brave face in my new surroundings. All the years spent building up my reputation in Pontiac with my fellow officers, supervisors, and citizens was over. In addition, the pension that had been promised to me years before was gone and the county offered only a 401(k). I couldn't believe I was starting over in my late thirties. A person expects their career to be stable by this time, but here I was, swirling in a tornado of career chaos.

No one at the county was particularly excited about absorbing employees from the Pontiac Police Department, so the reception I received was chilly to say the least. Maybe it's just typical jurisdictional competitiveness, maybe it went deeper. What I do know is that the county thought Pontiac was full of corrupt officers and Pontiac thought the county was full of lazy, incompetent deputies. The hostilities were exacerbated during the transition when the president of the County Deputies Association asked the Pontiac police union president how many of its officers were going to fail the drug test (FYI: none did). I will not assume that he or anyone else at the county was racist, but I will say that the makeup of officers at Pontiac was substantially more diverse than the county. I have always wondered if the assumption of drug use by Pontiac officers had racial overtones or were all Pontiac officers being branded as drug users simply because they worked in an urban city? Maybe it was both.

The hatred didn't just apply to those that worked the road, it was also in dispatch and the jail. As with every other dispatch job I had in the past, my coworkers were angry and offended that I had been hired with the intention to leave as soon as possible. Dispatch was always short staffed, so hiring someone who wasn't planning on staying seemed wrong to them. I told myself every day that it was just a matter of time, and I would be gone. I didn't worry about making friends, instead I focused on just getting through each long day.

Approximately nine months later I was transferred to the jail to work as a corrections deputy. I was completely torn. I didn't want to work in the jail. In Pontiac, jail deputies had always been thought of as lesser than, not real cops. Real cops arrested criminals, not babysit them. I was a real cop and didn't want to debase myself by going to work in the jail. At the time, it felt like another step backward in my career, but I knew that in my new reality it was the next step to getting back to working the road.

The worst part of transferring to the jail was that I had to complete a twelve-week Corrections Academy and then another round of training in the jail. I was almost forty years old and the last thing I wanted to do was go through another academy that would beat up on my aging body. The Corrections Academy became a true reality check on how horrible working for the county would be.

The Corrections Academy was similar to the police academy, but not nearly as physically hardcore. Most days were spent in a classroom learning about corrections laws and policies and how to effectively interact with inmates. For someone with law enforcement experience there was a great deal of redundant training: report writing, shooting proficiency, less-than-lethal weapon training, defensive tactics, and more. In all honesty I barely paid attention, never studied, and still aced all the tests. I ended up finishing first in my class.

As in dispatch, I stayed to myself. While many of my academy classmates went to lunch together, I sat in the classroom alone reading a book and eating. When they went out drinking after work, I went home. I didn't have the energy or inclination to go out of my way to befriend anyone at the county. Many of my classmates were younger, most didn't have policing experience, and I felt the chances of us having much in common was slim. Maybe it was a mistake, but the county hadn't been good to me up to that point, and I wasn't willing to open myself up to more pain. Instead, I yearned for my Pontiac friends.

On the last day of a week-long training in ground fighting the instructors decided to fill time at the end of the day by playing a round-robin style game. Each of us took turns laying on the floor where every member of the class put you in a restraint position and you had to get out. Tragedy struck when it was my turn to restrain the largest guy in the class. He was at least 6'4" and approaching three hundred pounds. I got on the ground and straddled his waist with my feet tucked under him. He was supposed to "buck" me off over his head, but I had gripped him too tightly with my feet. Instead, he rolled over so that he was on top of me, causing my foot to become wedged under him. An audible pop emanated from my foot. He didn't know what exactly he had done, but immediately jumped off me and began apologizing.

I quickly realized that I couldn't put any weight on my foot. I removed my boot and found that my foot was swelling quickly. One of the instructors drove me to the hospital where testing revealed that I sprained my foot in several places and torn several ligaments. Thankfully, nothing was broken. I was put in a soft cast/brace, given crutches, and told not to walk on it for eight weeks. I went back to the academy the next day with my crutches and in substantial pain because I couldn't take prescribed narcotic pain pills while working.

Later that day Lieutenant Young pulled me aside to speak to me about my injury. He asked me what happened and how long I would be on crutches. Afterward he informed me that he would probably send me back to dispatch. I was crushed. I couldn't believe that I had been injured, not only on the job, but because the instructors wanted to play a stupid, needless game after the training was over, and worse, that I would be punished for it. I knew that there was no way I could go back to dispatch, so the next day I showed up in class without my cast or crutches. I wrapped my foot tightly in a bandage, loosened by boot to fit my swollen foot, and spent the next couple months trying to hide my limp. Needless to say, it took much longer for the injury to heal. I was still limping when I finished the Corrections Academy and began my training in the jail.

I completed the training a few months later without difficulty and was finally allowed to work on my own. I was assigned to the jail annex where mostly women are housed. The county jail is very large and consists of a combination of old and new buildings. The old parts of the jail are no longer up to current building standards and could no longer be legally built, but have been "grandfathered" in. The new parts comply with current building standards, yet ironically are not safer from a security standpoint. For example, inmates are easier to control in the older parts because inmates have less space and privacy and the sightlines for deputies have fewer blind spots. The newer style "pod" system gives inmates more freedom to roam, more privacy, and more blind spots where victimization is easier. This is why the county will probably never build a new jail—the old section provides a safer environment for inmates and deputies.

The main jail consisted of a variety of areas where inmates were brought into the jail, processed, and housed. The one unusual area was called K-block where the most severely mentally ill male inmates were housed. The block was constructed much like Bentham's panopticon, which is a circular design that allows for constant surveillance of prisoners, but instead of a circle there were twenty-five cells arranged in a horseshoe formation. In the middle was a room enclosed by one-way view windows where deputies monitored the inmates twenty-four hours a day. The cells in this area had no bars, but instead had glass windows and suicide-proof blankets. The inmates were often clothed in paper hospital gowns rather than fabric clothing and not allowed items that could be used to injure themselves or others. These inmates were allowed out of their cells only one hour a day in which they could walk around or take a shower. K-block was built out of necessity due in large part to the mass closures of Michigan's mental hospitals. Suddenly, the county jail, like jails all across the United States, became the default option for many seriously mentally ill inmates that were now being arrested instead of being treated in the appropriate facilities. For the safety of the mentally ill inmates, the general population inmates, and the deputies, a special housing area became a necessity.

The newer part of the jail was called the Annex. The Annex consisted of two floors each with four inmate areas called pods. The big difference between the blocks and the pods was that inmates on the blocks were in their cells nearly all the time. Inmates housed in pods were allowed to roam around with their cells unlocked for a majority of the day.

As with the blocks, one deputy supervised the sixty-four inmates housed in each pod.

Over time, I worked in each of the areas in the jail, both male and female, but finally ended up working the majority of my time in 1H. Once I was stabilized into working a specific pod, work life became much easier and more enjoyable. I was able to learn the names of the inmates, I knew who was friendly with who, who were the troublemakers, and which cell each inmate belonged in. The best part of my job was truly getting to know the inmates. I spoke to them frequently learning about their crimes, their upbringing, their children, and how they ended up in jail. I had spent my career putting people in jail and knew very little about most of them. This was a chance to learn more about the "other side" of my job.

No one was more surprised than me to find myself relating to the women in my pod. Not only that, but I began caring about them. I understood the traumas many of them experienced in their childhoods. I understood their stories of youth rebellion that led them to a life of crime. I understood why many of them turned to drugs to dull their pain. One day it hit me—*I was one of them*. The only difference between us was that I wasn't caught for most of my crimes, and I got lucky when some wonderful people came into my life and helped guide me in a different direction.

I actually came to enjoy my time at work. Some days I would spend hours talking to the women in my pod. I counseled them on their drug use, listened to their struggles, and gave them advice on how to turn their lives around. I began to feel protective of them and they of me. I called them "my girls" and 1H became "my pod." Other deputies deferred to me when it came to making decisions regarding the pod—changing inmate cells, receiving new inmates, discipline, and so on.

All of this is not to say that I was a pushover—I wasn't. I developed a strict regime in my pod. I woke the girls up by 8:00 a.m. and did cell inspections at 10:00 a.m. There was one jail sergeant, a former military man named Sergeant Jackson, who would come around and do cell inspections between 10:30–11:00 a.m. and any violations would result in punishment for the inmates. Most of the deputies hated dealing with him because he would come into the pod, get the inmates worked up, hand out cell lockdowns for the most minor of offenses, and leave the pod in chaos for the deputies to deal with. With my system the girls would have two hours to clean and make their beds before his arrival. I would have already inspected their cells. I would have all the inmates out of their cells and sitting on the couches in absolute silence when Sergeant Jackson walked into the pod. It didn't take long for Sergeant Jackson to realize that I had my pod organized and my girls in line, so he stopped doing cell inspections. Instead, he came into my pod, asked if all was well, if I had already done inspections, and then left. This relieved stress for both me and the inmates.

There were also times when I had to really crack down on the girls. One such case involved showering. Being in jail tends to make some people, male and female, lazy about personal hygiene. If I came into the pod in the morning and smelled body odor, then I declared it "National Wash Your Ass Day." I would wake the girls up and tell them everyone must take a shower and check in with me immediately afterward. I would check the names off my list and make sure they actually took a shower. All showers had to be done by noon and anyone not in compliance would be locked down in their cell until they agreed to bathe. It may sound silly, but most of the girls would thank me. No one wants to live with or around someone who stinks of body odor.

I had strict rules about behavior too. I required the girls to be kind to one another—at the very least to be tolerant and respectful. I instituted a "welcome group" that would help all new incoming inmates into the pod learn the rules and routines and what was expected of them. We hung signs around the pod with positive messages. The signs proclaimed: "Be kind. You don't know what someone is going through" "Giving feels better than taking," and "You are enough." It only took a couple weeks before I came into the pod and found that all of the signs were removed. The girls told me that the other deputies complained, and the supervisor removed them. Why they were so upset about the signs I will never understand.

The girls were encouraged to come to me when they were having problems with another inmate. Rather than end in a physical fight, I would pull the girls aside, discuss the problem, and seek a resolution. If it felt like things were going off the rails as far as pod discipline, I would lock down everyone in their cells and ask who wanted to come out and clean. Volunteers would deep clean the pod: walls, bars, doors, handles, floors, chairs, windows, bathrooms, and so forth. I always made sure the cleaning lasted the entire shift.

There were plenty of fun times in the pod too. The girls would sit on the couches, and I would ask them questions in a game of trivia. If they answered correctly, I would throw Jolly Ranchers at them. Sometimes we had comedy shows where the girls would take turns doing stand-up comedy routines. We had talent shows where they would sing or read poetry. If there were times when the girls had to be locked down for one reason or another (other than discipline), I would play music from my iPod for them. I bought a DVD player for the pod and would reward good behavior by bringing in movies to watch. Around the holidays we would watch seasonal movies. At Christmas, I advised them which girls didn't have money being deposited in their commissary account. The other girls would then buy extra commissary items and make gift packages for those that received nothing.

You may or may not agree with how I managed my pod, but I have sound reasoning behind it. Many deputies would start their shift by releasing the inmates from their cells and then closing their office door. One deputy told me that she used to go into her office, put her feet on the desk, and watch movies on her computer. If inmates bothered her or got too loud, she would lock down the whole pod again. My way was not the only way, nor was I perfect, but I feel like part of rehabilitation should be helping to show the inmates that they can be better. I don't see how you can do that if you are locked in your office ignoring and avoiding the inmates.

This may also sound odd, but I felt like maybe I was making a difference in their lives. I expected the inmates to respect me, and I showed them respect in return. I began every morning by waking them up with a "Good morning, ladies" over the intercom. While other deputies' inmates were loud, rambunctious, and sneaky, my pod had few incidents of disciplinary problems. Any problems I did have were dealt with immediately and strictly, reminding the other inmates that I was not to be toyed with. The girls knew that they could trust me, but they also learned boundaries. I couldn't be manipulated or walked on, but I could be relied on for advice and help. I was teaching them kindness, generosity, personal responsibility, and discipline—all things that many of the girls had never been taught or experienced. All of this ended up negatively affecting my career and my relationship with coworkers.

It didn't take long before my coworkers declared me an "inmate lover." There was no worse insult in the jail. I was harassed, insulted, and looked down upon by many of my coworkers. Some deputies talked behind my back while others called me an inmate lover right to my face. Heated arguments weren't uncommon between some coworkers and me. One argument ended with me telling another deputy that whether she agreed with me or not, I could guarantee that the inmates wouldn't lift a finger to help her if she fell down the stairs; in fact, they'd probably be more likely to push her down them and walk away. I, however, never had to worry about that. Not only did my inmates like and trust me, but any inmate considering hurting me would face the wrath of the other inmates. In hindsight, it was wrong of me to say that to her. While it was true, it was still wrong and her treatment of me shouldn't have caused me to sink to her level.

Deputies wouldn't go out of their way even when I asked for help. The simplest request, such as for an inmate to be moved or getting more supplies for my pod, was always questioned. Everything was made more difficult for me. That's not to say that I didn't develop any friendships. Over time I did become close to a few people, but I felt bad for them because our friendship often brought them the stress of being in the middle—being my friend and being forced to listen to others insult me. I was angry and frustrated by the "inmate lover" moniker, but I wasn't going to let that change my tactics.

Unlike my coworkers, I never felt that it was my responsibility to punish the inmates. Punishment came from the court system. My job was making sure they were safe and secure, not reminding them on a daily basis that they were less than human. However, I found that most of my coworkers didn't understand, or agree, with my assessment. Instead, they felt that they were an arm of the court meant to further punish the inmates. It was a fundamental disagreement that wasn't going to be resolved. My sergeants, however, thought highly of me. Very few problems came out of my pod, and they loved that. My solution to the problem was to keep my coworkers out of my pod as much as possible. I stopped taking lunch breaks and worked as much overtime as I could so I could be in my pod for sixteen hours a day. The girls were grateful, and I felt good about the work I was doing.

In December 2012, less than a year into my time working in the jail, I needed spinal fusion surgery. After years of wearing a heavy gun belt, fighting with people, and other back-breaking behaviors, my spine finally gave out. I had been in constant pain and receiving numerous medical treatments for years, but they were no longer helping. The disk between my S1-L5 vertebrae was completely gone and it was bone on bone. The L5-L4 disk was also damaged, but my doctor thought we might get a few more years out of it.

I broke the news to the girls in 1H that I was going to be off work for several months. Many were upset and said they didn't know how they were going to get through their time without me. They worried that all of the practices that I had instituted would be discarded. I felt bad, but there was nothing I could do. I told them I would get back as soon as possible. On my last day of work the girls presented me with a homemade "book" that was filled with drawings, poems, and letters. Each girl thanked me for everything I had done and wished me well on my surgery. The following are excerpts from the notes written in the book:

> I just wanted to take a minute and thank you for your generosity and for caring so much about each and every one of us. This is a very depressing place to have to be, which makes a lot of us feel like we are nobody, but you make us feel like somebody. Even though we made a mistake, we aren't bad people. Of all the times I've been in and out of here, I have never met a deputy like you! You're awesome and I appreciate you. You give me peace and happiness when you are here. I love your positive energy!

> Thanks for listening to all my worries and troubles. I appreciate you and everything that you do.

> I just want to say thank you for being someone I can talk to if I have a problem. Thank you for having patience cause some people do not.

Not many deputies are as kind and tolerant like you. You have definitely inspired me and have given me some self-esteem back in my life. I truly thank you for helping me.

I just want you to know how much I appreciate you being the stand up [*sic*] kind of woman and officer that you truly are. I appreciate your no-nonsense kind of attitude and your good nature. What I really admire in you is that regardless to the fact that we are inmates that have committed a crime, we are still human beings and women and you treat us accordingly. That means more to me than you could ever imagine.

You personally make a huge difference for the inmates as well as your co-workers by always having a positive attitude and a fun sense of humor. But, more importantly, a sense of fairness and respect for others. You truly do go out of your way to accommodate others. Thank you for all that you do and working so hard here in H pod!! You are the most realest, genuine, caring, nicest dep I've ever come across in my years of coming to jail. H-pod may be crazy, but I'm glad to be one of your girls. One thing you said that will stick with me is the only difference between us is the uniform we wear. Thank you for the time you take out to talk to us and get to know us. There's no other dep like you. I really respect you. Thank you for being you!

I must say you are by far the most caring, sweet, and beautiful inside and out dep that I've ever met. You truly care about every single woman in this pod no matter what they might be in here for. Please don't ever let someone else tell you any different or that you should change. I feel extremely blessed to have met you and be a part of your pod. Thank you so much for just being you every day. I'm sure it's not easy walking in this jail every damn day with a beautiful smile on your face. I know none of us want to be here but I'm sure I speak for everyone when I say every day I see you I can't lose the smile off my face. We all just adore you.

I just want you to know how much I appreciate you and all the things you do for us girls here in H-pod. You're such an amazing woman with such a big heart. You always have our backs. You treat us like people where most treat us like just criminals. When we need to talk you never turn us away. When we're sad you're always there for us to lean on. It's almost like you're the mom most of us have never had because you're always trying to push us to do better.

To this day I treasure that book and keep it secured in a box in my closet. It's a constant reminder of the difference I made in the lives of those women.

I ended up being off work for less than five months. As expected, everything in my pod changed while I was gone. Not only had all of the routines I put into place been abandoned, but most of the inmates in my pod were different. I had to start from scratch and reinstitute rules and routines, and more importantly, I had to renew building trust with the girls. Initially, there were lots of punishment days, lockdown cleaning days, National Wash Your Ass Days, and so on. Many of the girls challenged me in order to see how I would react to their behavior and figure out what my boundaries were.

One of the biggest challenges I faced was a racial rebellion. There is always an inmate social hierarchy among the inmates in a jail. Prior to my surgery, I had worked hard to stop, or at least minimize, that hierarchy. While I was off work recovering, all of that fell by the wayside. Shortly after I returned, I ended up giving a twenty-four-hour cell lockdown for a Black woman named Lashell, the leader of the pod during my absence, who refused to clean her room, failed her cell inspection, and verbally and physically challenged me by getting an inch from my face and screaming at me. After her lockdown she immediately began a campaign to have me removed from working in the pod.

When inmates file a complaint its written on what's called a "kite." It's then turned in to the Annex supervisor. A few days after the incident with Lashell I was called into the supervisor's office, a Black women named Jackie. She threw down a handful of kites on the desk in front of me.

"Do you want to explain this?"

"What is it?" I inquired. Jackie pushed the kites toward me. I picked them up and quickly glanced through a few of them. The ones I read accused me, in one way or another, with being a racist and mistreating the Black inmates. I was furious. I knew that it was completely untrue. I threw the kites back down on the desk.

"If you want me to explain to you why these inmates would send out these kites, I'm happy to. They don't like discipline. If you want me to explain why I'm a racist, then we're done here. I'm not a racist and I won't justify these bullshit accusations." With that, I stood up, walked out, and went to work in my pod. I never heard another word about the kites from Jackie or any of the jail sergeants. I think the inmates were shocked to see me back in the pod, but I stayed silent about the matter and moved on as if nothing happened.

A couple months later the racial issue came full circle. A twenty-year-old Black girl, Tamika, in my pod was nine months pregnant and cellmates with Lashell. I came into work one day with Tamika complaining of stomach pain. The clinic staff checked her and determined that she wasn't yet in labor and didn't need to be transported to the hospital. I joked with her all day that she better not make me deliver that baby in the pod. When my shift ended I was grateful that she hadn't gone into labor.

The next day I was off, but decided to come in to work overtime. I was assigned to the hospital that shift because Tamika was in labor. At the hospital I found Tamika in the end stages of labor, one of her feet shackled to the bed, a male deputy standing outside her door. I immediately sent the deputy home, unshackled Tamika's foot, stood next to her, held her hand, and encouraged her while she pushed her baby girl out. The baby came within minutes of my arrival, and she was placed into Tamika's arms. Tamika looked lovingly at her baby girl for several minutes and then held her out to me.

"Do you want to hold her?"

"I would love to hold her," I replied. The smile on my face couldn't have been bigger. It had been many years since I had held a newborn baby. More importantly, it felt good that Tamika trusted me to hold her baby.

"Miss Dennis?" Tamika said in a whispered voice.

I turned and smiled at Tamika questioningly while still holding the baby.

"I'm sorry," Tamika said. I saw a tear rolling down her cheek. "I was one of the people that sent a kite out saying you were a racist. That was wrong. You have been so kind to me, and I'll never forget how you helped me through this delivery."

"Tamika don't even think about it. None of that matters right now. You just brought this beautiful baby girl into the world!"

As much as I loved holding her, I knew that Tamika's time with her baby was limited so I handed the infant back to her. A few hours later the end of my shift was approaching, and I knew that my relief deputy would be arriving soon. I told Tamika that I had to shackle her foot back to the bed and she said she understood. Then I did something I knew I probably shouldn't have. I used my cell phone to take a picture of Tamika holding her baby. I knew that her baby would be taken from her, and she would be returned to jail to serve the remainder of her sentence. I thought that time might be easier for her if she had a photo to look at.

The next day I went straight to one of the jail's sergeants and told him what I did. I asked his permission to print a copy of the photo for Tamika.

I told him that if it wasn't OK, I apologize and would delete the photo immediately. He said he understood why I did it and that it was fine. It only took two days for the rumor mill among my coworkers to circulate what I had done. The "inmate lover" moniker resumed with renewed vigor. It was frustrating, but I didn't care. I knew that what I had done was right and compassionate.

It was during this time working in the jail that I came in contact again with several of the Pontiac prostitutes that I had known over the years—including Big Tina and Little Tina. As usual, Little Tina drove me nuts. Even clean, sober, and medicated she was annoying and manipulative. Big Tina, however, showed me a very different side to her. She and I would spend hours talking about her life, her drug use, how she ended up where she was, and the many regrets that she had. During our talent shows in the jail I found out that Big Tina could sing. She had a beautiful voice that could stop you in your tracks. The first time I heard her I couldn't believe it. Her singing was powerful yet gentle and with a confidence that I had never seen in her before.

The one thing that always struck me about Big Tina was that she wasn't proud of the things she had done and who she had become. Over the years, I had gotten to know many of the prostitutes in Pontiac and none of them seemed to feel any remorse or sadness for where they had ended up. One of my other favorites was "Blowjob Julie." Julie had a horrible childhood and both she and her younger sister had ended up as drug-addicted prostitutes after the death of their parents. She always talked positively of her life and how much fun she had. She bragged about how good she was at her job, hence the nickname. Even after becoming one of the victims of a serial rapist, Julie still felt no desire to change her life. The only remorse she ever expressed was the overdose death of her sister—her last living relative. But even so, Julie continued being a prostitute.

Big Tina was an anomaly with respect to her regrets. She talked about thoughts she had about her children, victimizing people she loved, and constantly feeling like she was letting everyone down. I had become jaded over the years and forgot that a shitty childhood, committing crimes, and being unable to control your base instincts didn't mean that you wanted to be that person. I certainly wished I could have changed who I was over the years. Why was it so hard to believe that Big Tina and the other girls might have the same desires?

Another inmate that heavily impacted my thinking was a woman named Jessica. She was also a drug-addicted prostitute who seemed to come and go from the jail on a fairly regular basis—a "frequent flyer." I think her jail visits helped keep her alive because she didn't use drugs when incarcerated. After a particularly lengthy span of time without seeing Jessica, she finally reappeared. After she was transferred back to 1H, I found out that she had been caught in a sex-trafficking ring and held against her will in Flint, Michigan. Jessica told me that her captors had kept her so drugged up she couldn't keep track of the time or day of the week. She was imprisoned in a basement where men were brought to have sex with her over and over throughout the day. Jessica was finally rescued when police raided the house for suspicion of drug activity there. Prostitute or not, drug addict or not, no one deserved to go through that. I felt horrible for her. Worse yet, rather than treat Jessica like the victim that she was, she was arrested on an outstanding misdemeanor warrant and brought to jail where she went through severe drug withdrawals. Where's the compassion in that?

The other issue that weighed heavily on me was the treatment of the mentally ill inmates. It was amazing to me to learn how many inmates were on psychotropic medications. At any given time more than half of my pod were medicated. It broke my heart to see that they were medicated but not receiving proper psychological treatment. They usually had a very brief meeting with a doctor and then given whatever psychotropic medications the jail distributed. When released from jail, they weren't given any medications to take with them. When a mentally ill person stops their medications abruptly, they may experience anywhere from mild withdrawal symptoms to a full relapse into psychosis. Many inmates use street drugs to help with withdrawal, but of course they don't work the same as prescribed medication, which leads to further destructive behavior.

The longer I worked in the jail the more obvious it became that I didn't belong there. I enjoyed my work with the girls and hoped that maybe my words and advice might positively influence at least a few of them and spur them to make some real changes. However, the gap between my coworkers and me continued to grow. I grew weary of the constant harassment I received for being an "inmate lover." No matter how many times I tried to explain to people that it wasn't my job to punish the inmates and that by being kind to them made my job infinitely easier, the message never got through.

The time I spent in the jail still frustrates me to this day. I will never claim to have all the answers and maybe the way I interacted with the inmates was not the best choice, but there has to be a better way than how it's being done now. No one would ever accuse me of being soft on crime, quite the opposite actually, but if we want to break the cycle of criminal behavior, then we have to begin somewhere. Why not begin by showing compassion and offering advice? I'm certainly not a trained therapist, social worker, or guidance counselor, but I am a human being with feelings and sometimes the inmates just need someone to *see* and *hear* them. I know what it's like to feel invisible to the world, to feel like you're screaming in a crowded room, but no one hears you. Sometimes I saw my own pain in the eyes of my girls, and it felt good to watch that pain dissipate as they told me their story and knew that I was truly listening. I don't know why other deputies wouldn't or couldn't do this, but I knew that I was never going to be able to change things alone.

Eventually, I couldn't do it anymore. As much as I enjoyed working with the inmates, I hated working with the other deputies. I was mentally and emotionally drained. I watched my girls come and go, return repeatedly, and worse yet, heard about many of their overdose deaths from other inmates. I finally decided to make a change. I had completed the required testing to transfer to the road and was on the promotional list, but until then there was only one other place to go. I applied to leave the jail and transfer to the circuit court detail where officers guard inmates in the courtrooms or handle security at the courthouse entrances.

Circuit court ended up being an incredibly boring assignment. There was minimal inmate contact, long stretches of standing, even longer stretches of sitting in the court office with other deputies waiting for something to do, and walking inmates back and forth through an underground tunnel between the court and the jail. There is a saying about the courts: "Hurry up and wait." For someone who enjoyed staying busy and having personal interaction it was mind-numbingly monotonous. Sometimes I would get assigned to an interesting trial, but more often than not, cases ended in plea deals.

One trial that I was briefly assigned to was a child molestation case. The victim had been a three-year-old girl who had been molested by her stepfather. The day that I was in the courtroom the prosecution showed a video of the victim being interviewed by social workers detailing what happened to her. The little girl revealed that the stepfather had made her "swallow the cream" and that she had thrown it up afterward on the couch. The mother testified that the man had used the same phrase with her when he wanted a blowjob, so when her daughter told her what happened, she knew immediately what he had done to her daughter. I had taken many sexual assault and molestation reports over the years but listening to this trial made me physically ill. I sat behind the defendant and watched tears run down the faces of some jurors as I struggled to hold back my own.

When the trial wrapped up for the day it was my job to put the defendant in shackles and escort him back down to the basement holding cells. During the elevator ride down, he began to talk about how that "stupid cunt" of a wife had lied and how that "little bitch" was making up stories about him. He went on and on insulting the little girl and talking about how he hoped that they would both "burn in hell" for what they had put him through. With each word out of his mouth I could feel my anger rising. I realized that my left hand had balled up into a fist and my right hand was resting on my gun. For a moment I thought about how good it would feel to grab him by the back of the head and slam it repeatedly against the elevator wall. On the streets this would have been termed "street justice." I had never done anything like that, and I wouldn't now either, but people like him didn't deserve to breathe the same air as the rest of us. As quickly as those thoughts entered my mind they were gone. I reminded myself that I was not judge, jury, or executioner. My job was to take him from the courtroom to the cell, nothing more. The next day I did not volunteer for that courtroom assignment.

Working in the courthouse could be very busy or very boring. Every day was different and depended on the number of trials that were going on, the number of arraignments, plea deals being entered, drug court days, and so on. If you wanted to be lazy and do nothing, then you sat in the deputy office and didn't volunteer for anything. Rare were the days when it was so busy that everyone was assigned to something. The last thing I wanted to do was sit in the office and socialize, so I tried to keep myself busy and volunteered for assignments as frequently as I could. When there was nothing to do, I would walk the building. Starting in the basement I would walk around the entire floor, up the stairs, around the first floor, up the stairs, and so on. Up and down and around and around. It was equally tedious, but at least I was moving.

In order to get back to road patrol I had to take a written exam and have an in-person interview along with dozens of other deputies. The first time I took this test was just six months after I transferred to the jail. Unfortunately, the test results were rumored to be manipulated by command staff and the first list expired before it got to me. While the written exam results couldn't be changed, the oral interview scores could be manipulated. It was frequently said that the final combined scores were *arranged* to put deputies in the order that upper command would like them to be. The list stayed active for one year and then the test expired and had to be repeated.

This may sound like I'm just complaining about the process, but the reality is that the county conducts its testing without any external monitoring that could easily be done to eliminate questions of impropriety. Most departments bring in other law enforcement command staff from surrounding departments to ensure that the interview process is fair. For example, during my time working for the Pontiac police all promotional interviews included three external jurisdictional commanders. In addition, a representative from our police union would sit in on the interviews to assure the fairness of the process and the scores. The county offered none of these protections, which allowed for possible manipulation rather than being based on fair and accurate scoring. Upper command promotions were even worse. There was no testing or interview—submit a resume and the sheriff picks whoever they want for an open position.

The first time I tested I scored in the teens and the list expired with me sitting at number one. I took the test again the next year and finished a few spots lower, which was wildly frustrating because they don't change the interview questions from year to year. This means that I was much more prepared for the second test than the first. It seemed to me that my reputation for being an "inmate lover" may have attributed to my scores being manipulated downward. Regardless, there were a high number of retirements that year and I was finally promoted back to the road.

Even with all my prior experience I had to complete field training again. It turned out not to be a big deal since my first and last month of training were with my former FTO and partner, Carlos Luna: two fun months of reconnecting with my old friend. The second and third months were with deputies that respected my experience, and we worked as partners, not as trainer and trainee.

When I finished my training, I worried about where I would be assigned. The county had contracts to patrol twelve different jurisdictions— mostly rural areas. I requested to be assigned to Pontiac and was grateful that my request was granted. It felt like going home. I was back with my people—friends, business owners, criminals, and citizens I had known for years. Unfortunately, by this time many of my former Pontiac colleagues had left the Pontiac substation for other areas of the county. It felt good to be back on the road, but I soon found out that everything had changed.

Working for the Pontiac police was nothing like working for the county. Pontiac command officers respected hard work and proactive policing. They expected you to make decisions for yourself and to handle your own business. County command was very different. To say that they micromanaged their officers would be an understatement. Deputies were expected to ask permission before doing anything and to ask a sergeant before making decisions—something frustrating and hard to adjust to. Honestly, I'm not sure I ever did.

I quickly learned that being a woman at the county was also a negative. Pontiac police had many female officers, detectives, and command staff. In fact, at the time the county took over the department, Pontiac's chief of police was a woman. Women at the county, however, were rare and tolerated, not embraced. At the time of the takeover, the county only had one woman above the rank of sergeant. It felt like women were expected to do their jobs quietly and not be outspoken, ambitious, or knowledgeable. When it came to discipline it seemed there were different standards for men and women. I observed that female deputies were routinely punished more severely than male deputies, including higher rates of termination or forced resignations.

The county didn't know about the extra assignments I had participated in when I was with the Pontiac police. There were similar special assignments, such as narcotics enforcement, auto theft, and fugitive apprehension, but they were county-wide and seemed to be reserved for deputies that had connections to leaders within the department. Within the Pontiac substation there was only a Detective Bureau and a small four-man unit called DPU (the Directed Patrol Unit) that was similar to the COMSTAT unit I had participated in years prior. Again, both units seemed reserved for those deputies viewed as special or who had a personal relationship with a powerful decision maker. Most importantly, you had to be male. Eventually, a female deputy was assigned to the Detective Bureau, but that took several years. Several years later, a female deputy was briefly assigned to the DPU unit as well, but she was removed and replaced with a male deputy less than a year after her appointment. At the time of this writing, the DPU unit has doubled in size and still includes no female deputies.

Unlike most of my coworkers, I was lucky enough to be assigned to the same section of the city to work every day. Being moved around from section to section on a daily basis drove me nuts. Maybe it comes from so many years of instability as a child, but I need stability and consistency in my life to feel comfortable. My luck came by the way of Sergeant Garibaldi who had been assigned to Pontiac. We both worked the afternoon shift. After spending the last few years away from all my former Pontiac coworkers and surrounded by county employees, it was a welcome relief to be working under Sergeant Garibaldi again. I didn't have to worry about proving myself to him. He knew me better than almost anyone and trusted me. We often took our breaks together and met up for dinner, which offered rare moments of being able to vent our complaints to one another because we trusted each other implicitly.

In addition, Sergeant Hess worked in Pontiac on day shift. When I signed up for overtime, which was a couple times a week, I tried to do it so that we could work together. It felt great to spend time again with two of my favorite people. Of course, my luck didn't hold out and Sergeant Garibaldi didn't stay long. Eventually, he was promoted to another position and left Pontiac. It was a very sad day for me.

Patrol of Pontiac was divided into five sections: section one covered the northwest side of the city, section two covered the northeast, section three covered the southwest, section four covered the southeast, and section five covered the downtown district. I preferred section one for many reasons, but mostly because it was the busiest. It also encompassed the Baldwin corridor, which was where I previously worked my undercover prostitution details and where the prostitutes still conducted their business. Section three was where I formerly worked the COMSTAT detail, so working section one kept me in close proximity to the other area of the city that I was most comfortable with.

Working the same section every day was beneficial and helped me to be a better police officer. I was able to get to know the citizens of my area, both the troublemakers and nontroublemakers. Often, I knew what I was heading into and who I would be dealing with just from hearing dispatched calls. I also reconnected with several of the prostitutes I had known over the years. Big Tina and Little Tina were still doing their thing, as was Blowjob Julie. I didn't allow them to prostitute themselves in front of me; if I saw them committing a crime, I would arrest them just like I would anyone else. But if I saw them just walking down the street, I would always stop to say hi and make sure they were doing OK.

The next few years seemed to fly by in a blur. My son graduated from high school and went off to college about nine hours away from home. I worked as much overtime as I could to help pay for as much of his tuition as I could. Yet, there isn't much to say about those years. There were interesting calls, of course, but I didn't participate in any special details or undercover units. Instead, I focused on keeping myself busy. I took the calls in my section and occupied my time with traffic stops when I wasn't busy. My stats were always at or near the top for calls and reports taken, arrests, and tickets written. Sadly, I was not recognized for any of the work I did. I'm not saying that anything I've done is any better than what other deputies have done, after all, it was my job, but I do know that there were many times when my good work should have been acknowledged.

One such time was when a young woman was shot in section four. It wasn't my call, but I was assisting with holding the perimeter a couple blocks away. It seemed everyone in the neighborhood was outside, wandering around to see what was happening. I stood outside my patrol car and talked to people as they went by in hopes that maybe someone would have something of evidentiary use. I talked to a teenager riding by on his bicycle and he told me that he thought he knew who committed the shooting. We continued talking for several minutes and I convinced him to pull up his Facebook account on his cell phone and show me a picture of the suspect. He showed me a picture of a group of boys and told me which ones he thought had been involved in the shooting and which one was the shooter. I tried to take the information to the detectives working the case, but I was dismissed. I don't know if they had been given different information they were following up on or if they were just ignoring me. Either way, it seemed to me that they were disinterested in what I had to say so I decided to follow up myself.

Through some extensive legwork I determined the identity of the boys in the Facebook photo and where they lived. I found an address that was associated with the possible shooter, but it turned out to be his grandmother's house. I was evasive with the grandmother about the details because I was worried that she might call and warn him that I was looking for him, but nevertheless, she gave me the address of his mother. I figured I had nothing to lose at that point, so I went to the mother's house and told her everything. I explained to her that a woman was shot and that I believed her son was the shooter. I convinced his mother to help me. She called her son and told him that she had heard that he had been involved in a shooting. He admitted to her that he had been. She demanded to know where he was and told him that she was coming to pick him up. Instead, she gave me his location. I called for a few officers to assist me, and we went to his location in section two and arrested him. I cannot explain how much respect I have for that mother. It had to be difficult for her to turn her own son in.

Unfortunately, feeling disregarded by detectives was not new to me. Once I took a missing person complaint from two people who said that their friend, Mateo, had been killed. The missing man had been at a local bar that was frequented by members of the Hispanic community. There was a verbal altercation between Mateo and another customer, Alejandro, in the parking lot. Alejandro took a gun out of his car and chased Mateo into the field behind the bar. Mateo had not been seen or heard from since. I made numerous inquiries but was unable to find any sign of him. I made it clear that I believed Mateo was dead and that the area behind the bar should be searched. Instead, detectives maintained that Mateo had fled back to Mexico to his family. Several years later a body part was located in the field behind the bar and DNA tests confirmed that it belonged to Mateo. To this day Mateo's case remains an unsolved homicide. I will always wonder if the case would have been solved if it had been investigated more thoroughly at the time.

With all that said, I'm not seeking praise for doing my job—these are the things that are expected of police—moreover, helping people is why I became an officer. However, when I saw male deputies all around me being given commendations for doing much less it was disappointing. Added to the long list of frustrations involved in working for the county, you are left with someone feeling completely disenfranchised with working in law enforcement.

The last year became torturous for me. Every day began to feel like Groundhog Day. The calls were starting to take a mental toll on me, and I felt like I was no longer making a difference. The excitement and sheer joy I once felt was now gone. It was the same people, the same calls, the same addresses, the same crimes, only now I was actually arresting children of people I had arrested in my Pontiac police days. Good grief, it made me feel so old! To make matters worse, fentanyl had made its way into the city's heroin supply with daily overdose cases. There were times that I was going on overdose calls more than once on the same person in less than twenty-four hours. Naloxone (Narcan) and CPR became almost a daily occurrence.

One summer day I was dispatched to a bleeding woman stumbling down Baldwin Road. I located a Hispanic female in her early twenties in front of the party store where I had worked the hooker detail years prior. She was clearly intoxicated and bleeding heavily from a large laceration in her hand. She was too intoxicated to explain what happened, but EMS arrived just seconds after I did. The woman was transported to the hospital, and I didn't think any more about it. Three days later I was dispatched to an overdose in section two. EMS had arrived on scene before me and had already administered naloxone and initiated CPR by the time I entered the house. My friend, Paulette, who was a paramedic pulled me aside and asked me if I remembered the girl with the cut hand from a few days ago. I nodded and she dropped the bomb on me—the dead girl was her. She had surgery on her hand and had been prescribed oxycodone for the pain. Her family said she had a history of drug use and they had tried to monitor her use of the pain medication. Sadly, they had looked the other way long enough for her to overdose on the pills.

Another woman, White and in her early thirties, was found dead by her father, face down on her bedroom floor. The heroin she had injected was so powerfully laced with fentanyl that she had died instantly. In fact, when she was found the cap from the needle was still in her mouth and the needle still in her arm. These examples aren't meant to say that only women overdosed. To the contrary. Many men of every age and race overdosed, but for some reason it was the young women that seemed to affect me the most, thus they are the ones that stand out most in my memory.

I began to realize I hated my job. I hated the county's policies, and I was sick of the unfairness, the nepotism, and the blatant discrimination of women. All the little things began to add up. The way the rules were bent for certain deputies, such as the one where subordinates couldn't work under the command of family members. The son of the Pontiac substation lieutenant was promoted from the jail to the road and came to Pontiac. Not only was he allowed to work under his father's command, but he was quickly promoted to the DPU unit, to the Narcotics Enforcement Team, and finally, to sergeant all within a few short years. That type of upward movement is virtually unheard of. To this day he continues to work under his father's supervision, which continues to provide him behavioral allowances that others don't have.

I was miserable—physically and mentally. After having back, hip, and shoulder surgery, my body wasn't holding up. I was in pain every minute of every day. I didn't understand what was going on with me mentally, but I knew that I was viewing my job differently than I ever had before. I started taking more and more time off work. I didn't do anything special during my days off; I just didn't want to be at work. I thought I couldn't hate my job any more than I already did, but then Murphy's law stepped in to prove me wrong.

11

BIG TINA

My first introduction to Big Tina wasn't the greatest, but things gradually improved over the years. Back in 2002, I never would have guessed that Tina Marie Ashton—prostitute, drug addict, criminal—would change my life. I definitely wouldn't have thought that she and I would become friends, but we did, which led to heartbreak that would stick with me forever. We began to bond when she was in my pod in the county jail and continued when I returned to working the road.

As much as I didn't like Tina at first, she was a fixture in Pontiac—a part of the landscape. I couldn't escape her, but over time she grew on me. The more I got to know her I realized that we were alike in many ways and that my alter ego, Rosie, could easily have become my reality.

It was miserable to be around Tina when she was in the depths of drug use. Her mood often depended on what drug she was high on. When she used cocaine or crack, she was irritable, hostile, high-strung, and mean. Tina on heroin was happy, hyper, cheerful, and positive. The best Tina— drug-free Tina—was amazing and a pleasure to be around. She was funny, thoughtful, kind, considerate, full of life, and willing to do anything for those she cared about. The problem? Drug-free Tina was a rare occurrence.

Over the years Tina would come and go. There were times when I would see her every day and then suddenly, without explanation, she would vanish. Days, weeks, or even months later Tina would reappear out of the blue as if nothing happened. Sometimes her disappearances were due to incarceration and sometimes because she went to stay with her sister. Regardless, I was always happy for the brief respite she received from her drug use. I honestly believe those breaks extended her life, possibly by years.

I was working in the jail one day when I saw Tina's name on the inmate roster in pod 1E. It had been a long time since I had seen her, so I immediately went to her cell to see how she was doing. Honestly, I had trouble recognizing her. She appeared to have gained at least one hundred pounds.

"Tina?"

"Oh my God. Miss Dennis?" she said as she lifted her head from the thin mat she was lying on.

"How are you doing? Are you OK? What the hell did you do to get in here?"

"I'm OK. Better when I can finally get out of here," she said, trying to smile. "The last time I was in jail I was in IE, so they said I had to be put back in here. Is there anything you can do?"

"I'll try," I promised. "You just make sure you behave in the meantime."

Pod 1E was known as the disciplinary unit for females and those that were not mentally stable enough to be in general population, max classified, suicidal, and had disciplinary problems. I hated to see Tina in that brightly lit, glass-doored cell all by herself. I made a few calls and did what I could to get her moved to general population as soon as possible.

While Tina was in jail it was a great chance for us to have one-on-one time. We had long, in-depth conversations about where her life went wrong, how hard it was to be a drug addict, and the many regrets we both had. I never told Tina all the stories of my horrible childhood, but I did tell her about a few incidents that I had never shared with anyone else. I don't know why I trusted Tina not to share them with others, but I did, and she kept my secrets. We bonded over our misfortunes, and I spent many nights lying awake thinking about how lucky I was not to have followed in her footsteps.

To understand who Tina was and why I was so drawn to her it's necessary to explain where she came from and how she ended up how she did. To piece together her backstory, I have searched my memory for information she provided me over the years and compared it to what her sister Amy gave me.

By all appearances Tina seemed to live a relatively normal life until she was fifteen years old: meaning she didn't get in trouble and exhibit outward appearances of difficulties. The fact that Tina didn't struggle earlier in life is a tribute to her resilience and strength. She certainly didn't have it easy. Rather than focus on troubles at home, Tina focused on her appearance.

She loved fashion and always wanted to dress in the latest styles and worked hard to look her best at all times.

Tina's parents were addicts. Her mother suffered from drug and alcohol abuse and her father drugs. Several of Tina's maternal uncles were also drug addicts, one of whom died of a heroin overdose. Her parents divorced when she was young. Tina's mother remarried a man who physically abused Tina, Amy, and her mother.

When she was sixteen everything in Tina's life would change for the worse. In an attempt to keep up with the fashion trends, she began shoplifting. Eventually, Tina and a friend were caught stealing clothes and Tina was sent to Children's Village, a facility that holds juvenile criminal offenders. Things did not go smoothly: she ran away, was apprehended, and brought back to the facility. Tina would never return to high school or continue her education.

During her time at the Children's Village Tina met a boy named Darius who would start her on a lifelong journey toward destruction. He was a drug dealer, user, and extremely physically abusive. Tina continued dating him after she was released from the Children's Village and moved to Pontiac with him. During this time Tina was an occasional drinker, but an avid smoker of marijuana. She and Darius went on to quickly have two children together: Ayana and Darius Jr. After the birth of her son, Darius introduced Tina to crack cocaine and she quickly became addicted.

Darius's physical abuse of Tina continued unabated over the years and would culminate in a brutal attack that nearly killed her. To save her life Tina locked herself in a room, crawled out a window, and ran away. She finally left Darius for good and moved herself and her children into the house of her friends, Caryne and Cassius. Like Darius, Cassius was a drug dealer, but unlike Darius, Cassius did not use drugs; however, Caryne did.

One day Tina was unable to find any crack in the house and began withdrawals. Caryne offered her heroin instead. From that day forward heroin was Tina's best friend, confidant, and only priority. I don't know the specifics on how it happened, but soon Caryne was out of the picture and Tina and Cassius began dating. Tina quickly became pregnant and gave birth to her third child, Sayon. She would later claim that she did not use heroin during her pregnancy, but it's impossible to know definitively. What is clear is that Tina's heroin use increased dramatically after the birth of Sayon.

In an attempt to remove Tina from that environment and get her clean, Cassius moved her and the three kids to Arkansas. Apparently, the withdrawals from heroin were too much for Tina and she abruptly disappeared from her family to continue using. Cassius called Tina's mother and told her that he couldn't care for all three children alone and that she needed to come to Arkansas and pick up Ayana and Darius Jr.—which she did. After returning to Michigan, Darius's sister heard about what had happened and filed for sole custody of the children. Darius's sister was in the military and able to provide the children a stable home. The court granted her full custody of both children.

A few months later Tina inexplicably showed up in Michigan. She told Amy that she had been staying in a drug house in Arkansas all that time. While Tina made no attempt to regain custody of her children, she did stay in contact with them for the first year that they were living with their aunt. Afterward, the children's aunt cut Tina off from all contact with them.

Tina made several attempts over the years to get off heroin. She bounced around between living with her father, mother, sister, at various rehabs, and with numerous boyfriends. It's unclear if staying with her mother and father were a help or a hindrance to Tina. She would admit to Amy years later that she had smoked crack with their mother. Tina's father eventually got clean, but not until he met his second wife and they moved to Colorado to start a family. Ultimately, nothing worked for Tina, and she always ended up in Pontiac using heroin. It was around this time that Tina was forced to resort to prostitution to finance her drug habit.

The years that would follow were not easy for Tina. She had rare moments of true happiness, but copious amounts of sadness plagued her. However, she never stopped trying to live a more productive life. Tina overdosed and nearly died innumerable times over the years, but she just couldn't break away from drugs. She would run away from Pontiac and back to the safety of Amy's house many times. Was Tina honestly looking to get off drugs or was she looking for a respite from the torment of the daily struggles of a drug-addicted prostitute? No one can say for sure. What is clear is that Tina never stopped trying.

Amy described how awful it was to see Tina show up at her house and go through withdrawals cold turkey. Even though Tina's body was ravaged by the process, she never complained. Amy told me how each time afterward she would help Tina find a job. One time Tina got a job at a Wendy's down the street from Amy's house. Amy would drop Tina off for each shift and pick her up when it ended. Amy decided to buy Tina a bicycle so that she could take herself to work and get exercise at the same time since she always put on weight when she wasn't using drugs.

Another time Tina worked at the local Kroger grocery store. Again, Tina was able to ride her bicycle to and from work. Sometimes, Amy would ride her bike to the store at the end of Tina's shift and they would ride home together. A disabled elderly neighbor of Amy's was looking for a live-in caregiver. Tina had been clean and working successfully for several months, so Amy suggested Tina for the job. Everything seemed to be going great until one day the neighbor called Amy and said that Tina had disappeared. Once again, Tina had run back to Pontiac and into the arms of her one true love—heroin.

The most successful of Tina's forays into sobriety was when Amy's daughter got Tina a job at the factory where she worked. Tina's work performance was stellar, and management took notice. Tina was told by her manager that if she kept up the good work, she would soon be promoted to the quality control department. Maybe it was too overwhelming for Tina, maybe she didn't know how to deal with success, maybe she had just become too adept at self-sabotage, but Tina told Amy that she felt like she needed to go on methadone. Amy warned Tina that going on methadone was not a good idea because Tina had struggled through withdrawals and methadone would only make her want to be high on heroin again. Additionally, Tina would be putting her job in jeopardy. No company wanted an employee who was high all the time.

Tina went behind Amy's back, went to a methadone clinic, and began taking methadone. The change in Tina's work performance was immediate: her production level fell, and she began to constantly fall asleep on the job. Tina's coworkers and managers noticed the dramatic change right away. Even after being warned repeatedly about falling asleep at work, Tina was fired, which gave Tina the excuse she needed to once again run back to Pontiac.

Throughout the years Tina was arrested for numerous crimes and developed quite the rap sheet. Her crimes were mostly nonviolent, but as with most drug addicts her need for drugs would override rational thinking. Tina, desperate for drug money, once beat her mother relentlessly when she refused to give it to her. After the assault Tina robbed her of money and stole her vehicle. Not surprisingly, Tina had many arrests for prostitution, drug and drug paraphernalia possession, trespassing, loitering, assault, probation violations, and more. Finally, the courts had enough of Tina's petty crimes and sentenced her to two years in prison for an assault that occurred while Tina was already on probation. She was released after approximately fourteen months, but because she had outstanding warrants, she was transferred to the county jail rather than being released outright.

The turning point in my relationship with Tina took place in 2015. I was working on the streets of Pontiac as a police officer again and began to see Tina on a somewhat regular basis. Whenever I would see her walking on Baldwin Road, I would pull into the nearest parking lot and talk with her. I would always ask her if she was OK and if anyone was bothering her. I would also try to get an idea of how high she was and give her a friendly reminder about getting arrested for drug possession.

"You know Tina, if I see you getting too strung out, I will not hesitate to arrest you."

"Why would you do that, Miss Dennis?"

"Because I won't stand by and let you kill yourself, Tina. Keep your shit under control or I'll make sure you have some time to clean yourself up in jail."

"Thank you for caring, Miss Dennis, but I'm OK. I promise," Tina would always say. And, honestly, she did seem OK. Long gone was the Tina of 2002 who couldn't seem to get enough drugs, who was argumentative and always ready for a fight. It was a huge relief.

The next two years continued to bring Tina and I closer. I won't say that Tina was turning her life around completely, but she was definitely taking steps toward lessening her drug use and, subsequently, her need to prostitute herself. Eventually, Tina moved into a house with her boyfriend, John, in the northwest side of Pontiac. Section one was my regular beat and it allowed me to stop in and check on her frequently.

One day I stopped in to see Tina. She had two small children with her. I asked her what was going on and she explained that her daughter, Ayana, had moved in with her and brought along her two children. While Ayana was at work during the day, Tina babysat her grandchildren. It brought a smile to my face and a warmth to my heart to see Tina so happy and proud. She had missed so much of her children's lives that she felt grateful and lucky to be a part of her grandchildren's. I was proud of Tina for taking steps to repair the relationship with Ayana, for taking on the challenge of two small children, and for having the strength to give up drugs while caring for the children.

Two things changed after Ayana and the kids moved in with Tina: she and I grew even closer and overdose cases in Pontiac continued to skyrocket. It was around this time that fentanyl made its way into the heroin supply and people began overdosing in numbers I had never seen.

I knew that Tina was using less, but I still worried for the woman who had by now become my friend. I talked to her about the rise in heroin overdoses every time I saw her. I warned her how serious fentanyl was and how even the most experienced drug users were dying easily and frequently from it. Fewer people were being saved regardless of naloxone treatment. Fentanyl was killing them too fast for us to save them. At one point I even begged Tina to go back to using crack. At least the risk of fentanyl would be gone, I thought. She always assured me that she was fine, and we would move on to another subject. I also checked to make sure Tina had enough food for the kids, and when she was struggling, I would give her gift certificates for pizza or take her some nonperishable food items.

In late August of 2017, I saw Tina walking south on Baldwin Road. I couldn't remember the last time I had seen her there and I was immediately worried. I pulled into a church parking lot and asked her what she was doing. Tina started to weep. At that moment I realized that was the first time I had ever seen Tina cry. She finally told me that her mother had killed herself and that Amy had been the one to find her. Amy called Tina and asked her to come to the house and help her. Tina promised Amy that she would head there immediately, but she never went.

Tina confided in me that she just couldn't do it. As much as she wanted to help and be there for Amy, she just couldn't see her mother like that. Amy was furious at Tina for letting her down and not showing up. Tina felt horrible. While she was trying to take care of her grandchildren, she was grieving for her mother, and dealing with the guilt of letting Amy down. Tina was not in a good place, and I didn't know how to help her. Tina and I sat on the side of the road and talked for a long time. Our conversation ended prophetically.

"I know that you are stressed right now, Tina, but please don't deal with it by using heroin," I begged her.

"I won't. I just needed to get out of the house and think for a while. Besides, if I overdosed, I know that you would come save me," Tina said with a tear-stained smirk on her face.

"That's not funny, Tina!" I snapped at her. "This fentanyl shit is serious. I may not be able to save you!"

"Sure you would, Miss Dennis," she said with a big smile. "I'll see you later." Tina turned and continued walking south on Baldwin Road. As I watched her walk away, I couldn't help but worry.

I believe it was three days later when I got the call. On August 30, 2017, at 1615 hours my police radio went off.

"8929?" the police dispatcher called.

"Go ahead for 29," I replied.

"Respond to 771 St. Clair for an overdose."

My heart stopped. I knew immediately that Tina was dead. I activated my lights and sirens and drove like a crazy person all the way to her house. I was the first responder there and I was met by Ayana who directed me to Tina who was lying on the bathroom floor unconscious, not breathing, her beautiful pale-white skin turning blue. I yelled at Ayana to help me pull Tina out of the bathroom and into the living room where there was more space to work on her.

I started CPR as the tears began to fall from my eyes. Crying at a scene was not something I normally did, but I couldn't stop. Within minutes fire and EMS personnel arrived and took over Tina's care. I put my hand on one of the firemen's shoulders and said to him, "Please, you have to save her." He had known me for years and I could tell by the look on his face that he was shocked by my request. Vial after vial of naloxone was administered to Tina, but there was no change in her status. They applied an AED to her, but it advised "no shock." Tina was pronounced dead at 1635 hours. My friend was gone.

Within minutes my sadness turned to rage. What the hell had happened? How had Tina been able to overdose with Ayana, John, and the kids in the house? My rage turned toward Ayana and John as I hurled rapid-fire questions at them.

They told me that at around 4:00, Tina said she was going to use the bathroom. After fifteen minutes went by and Tina didn't come out Ayana went into the bathroom and found Tina unresponsive on the floor. Next to her body was a half-empty syringe. Ayana called 911 and before my arrival, John threw the syringe away which I later retrieved. Even though they told me what happened, I was still full of anger. They knew Tina was a drug user. Why would they wait fifteen minutes before checking on her? The house was small. How could they not have heard the thud of Tina's body falling to the floor? So many questions to be asked, so few answers to be found. Did any of it really matter? No number of answers would bring back my friend.

I returned to my patrol car and called my sergeant and advised him of the death and then called the medical examiner's office to report it and start the process of the body removal. I then sat in my car and cried. I didn't know what to do. I wanted to go home and mourn for my friend, but I had a job to do. I decided to call Sergeant Garibaldi at home. He wasn't my direct sergeant anymore, but he had been my friend and confidant for many years. I told him Tina had died and he expressed his condolences. We talked for a little while and then he told me to call my sergeant and ask him to send someone else out to take my place at the scene. I told him I would, and we hung up.

I sat in my car thinking about making that call. I just couldn't do it. How could I turn Tina over to another officer? Leave her lying on the floor and just drive away? Tina was my friend and I owed it to her to stay until the very end. I sat in my car a bit longer trying to complete the necessary paperwork, but I couldn't stop crying.

It was around this time that Amy showed up. I had never met her before and had no idea who she was. Understandably, Amy was frazzled. She was angry, grieving, and erratic as she tried to figure out what was happening. She couldn't comprehend why her sister was lying on the living room floor and no one was helping her. Amy tried several times to get to Tina, but I held her back. I tried to explain that we had done everything we could to save her, but that Tina was dead. Amy didn't want to hear any of it, that is, until she found out that I was Officer Dennis.

Suddenly, the light bulb went off and Amy asked me if I was the Miss Dennis that Tina said was her "cop friend." Through my tears I smiled and said yes. Amy and I embraced for a long hug. I told Amy how sorry I was that I hadn't been able to save Tina and how much I would miss her. Amy then went over to her dead sister and held her hand. I walked away to give Amy some time alone with her sister.

I was useless for the rest of my shift. I spent a great deal of time sitting in my patrol car crying and remembering all the years I had known Tina. At home that night I stayed awake thinking about her. I thought about our last conversation. How sure she was that I would save her. How I let her down; let her die. How I should have done more over the years to help her turn her life around. I thought about the many conversations we had and how we confided in each other: our fears, sadness, regrets, heartbreaks. I remembered all the times she made me want to punch her and all the times she made me laugh. Our relationship had been a path along the most twisting, winding road ever, but in the end, we found similarities in one another that couldn't be denied.

When I decided to write this memoir, I knew that I wanted Tina to be included. I reached out to Amy and asked her permission. She was gracious with her time and spent many hours on the phone talking to me about Tina. She filled in the blanks and helped me remember and sort out all the things Tina had told me over the years. Most importantly, Amy told me that Tina would absolutely have loved that I was writing about her. I couldn't stop the tears from welling up when she said Tina "respected me" and that I "was a great friend to her." When we discussed whether I should use a pseudonym, Amy said, "Absolutely not. Tina would love that she meant enough to you that you would write about her."

It was such a pleasure to have someone to talk to about Tina. Someone who knew the real Tina like I did. Someone who could tell me how everyone turned out after Tina's death. Amy told me that her relationship with Ayana has become very strained. Amy took on the responsibility of paying for the funeral, burial, and headstone even though Ayana was technically Tina's next of kin. On Halloween, Tina's favorite holiday, Amy decorated Tina's headstone with decorations. Ayana removed them and claimed that Amy was practicing some sort of devil worship on her mother's grave. Amy made it clear to Ayana that she had paid for the headstone and she would decorate it however she wanted. It was the last time they spoke.

While he had wanted nothing to do with reconciling with Tina when she was alive, Darius Jr. did show up to his mother's funeral. Amy reports that Darius Jr. is doing well in life, but he's had no contact with Amy since the funeral. Tina's third child, Sayon, has not turned out so well. Sayon told Amy that he would travel north for the funeral, but he never showed up. Sadly, Sayon has a drug addiction problem.

Rescuing Tina over the years had taken its toll on Amy as well and she has struggled to come to terms with the choices that she made and how it affected those around her. Amy believes her constant need to try to save Tina led to her divorce. Additionally, Amy's daughter has told her more than once that she felt like Amy cared more about Tina than she did about her. Amy finds solace in remembering things that Tina said to her over the years. About a year before she died Tina said, "Living with you on and off through the years saved me. I've never been clean other than in rehab or jail." It's those types of memories that help Amy sleep at night.

There are conversations that both Amy and I had with Tina that we will never forget. Conversations that break our hearts and leave us feeling like we didn't do enough for her. At different times over the years Tina told us both that part of her struggle to stay clean was because she hated herself. Tina believed that when she was high, she was outgoing, happy, and fun, masking how she truly felt about herself. However, when she was clean and sober, she hated facing her true self. It was during these times of sobriety that Tina was forced to confront all the horrible things she had done and all the people she had hurt. For Tina, it was easier and less painful to stay high and forget about the destruction she had left in the wake of her drug use. This was something I could relate to. I didn't do it through cocaine and heroin, but I did use marijuana and alcohol for a time. I lashed out at the world through anger and violence. Later, I replaced it with forced amnesia. Like Tina, if I could forget about the memories, then the painful events didn't exist.

Since Tina's death I have spent a great deal of time thinking about her. I think about why I became friends with her and not any of the other prostitutes in Pontiac. I believe that I saw myself in Tina. That maybe, somewhere, deep down inside, I thought that being there for her was a way of being there for the self I could have become. Was I kind to Tina as a reminder to my subconscious that I could have easily become her had just one or two circumstances gone differently? The reality is that I will never know what brought Tina and I together, but I feel blessed to have had the friendship.

There are few people in the world who knew the complexity of what made Tina who she was. The intensity of her pain, the depth of her kindness, or her relentless determination to get clean and sober. My strength pales in comparison to hers. I will never forget seeing Tina lying dead on that bathroom floor. I will never forget the guilt that I felt in not being able to save her. But, most importantly, I will never forget that she thought of me as her friend and that my friendship was special to her.

12

ENLIGHTENMENT

With my health going downhill and my dissatisfaction with working at the county going uphill, I decided to go back to college in 2018. I enrolled at Oakland University and met with an advisor. I had no idea what I was going to do with a college education, but I had been wanting to finish my bachelor's degree for years. The love of school that I had as a child returned with a vengeance, but I once again found myself in the position of an outsider.

I was going to school with "kids" that were younger than my son and professors who were often younger than me. I knew I was on my own. My classmates didn't want to work with the "old lady," and I didn't want to study with or work on projects with students who didn't take school as seriously as I did. I worked hard and became obsessed with learning. My biggest dilemma was that I still didn't know what I wanted to do. I enjoyed different areas of academia, so much so that I wondered if I would ever settle on a major. To make my choices easier I decided on integrative studies, which allowed me the freedom to explore anything that interested me; however, it didn't help me narrow down a path for my future.

Over the summer I took the class that would change my life: Police and Society. It was taught by Professor Meehan, who, through no fault of his own, made me second-guess my entire career as a police officer. I began to learn about various policing methods, as well as the pros and cons of each. Suddenly, I questioned everything. How could I have worked in law enforcement for so long and not be knowledgeable about community policing? Broken windows policing? Problem-oriented policing? This information should be common knowledge to every person working in law enforcement, but it was completely foreign to me. More importantly, it should be common knowledge to every person working in a command position in a police department, but it was equally clear to me that wasn't the case either.

In addition to policing methods, I learned about occupational perspectives, police subculture, culture shock, and culture fatigue. John Van Maanen's "Kinsmen in Repose" and Victor Strecher's "People Who Don't Even Know You" would irrevocably change my thinking. Reading Van Maanen and Strecher felt like reading love letters written directly to me. Not only did they explain what I had been thinking and feeling for years, but they told me that those thoughts and feelings were normal.

Strecher describes policing as being fixated on "process or technique—to the exclusion of function or goal orientation."[1] Crime-reduction methods that are viewed as being outside the norm of traditional policing are often rejected. Among other things, police are trained to maintain control of all interactions, be respected by all who they encounter, and maintain order in their patrol area.[2] The police subculture perspectives make it difficult to positively interact with other subcultures. The more I think about these words, the more they resonate with me. I think about how many times I worked the prostitution detail and how it never resulted in any real change. The department was so focused on how we went about setting up and executing the detail that no one stopped to realize that the end goal should have been the most important. When it was clear that the goal of reducing soliciting wasn't being met, we should have changed strategies. Of course, at that time, I wasn't capable of verbalizing my frustrations.

Van Maanen writes about the "outsider" nature of police work: "The danger inherent in police work is part of the centripetal force pulling patrolman together as well as contributing to their role as strangers to the general public."[3] When your job is one in which you feel like most everyone hates and wants to kill you and that no one can possibly understand how that feels except for your fellow officers, your circle of friends and associates tends to become smaller and smaller. Soon, every gathering, party, wedding, game night, and social event is filled with only fellow officers. These events become filled with stories about work: grievances, close calls, angry citizens. The gap between you, the officer, and the people in your community becomes ever wider with each passing day. I quickly realized that this type of ostracization was not only accurate, but that it had permeated my life. Mine and Neil's social life became nonexistent over the years. We went to work, came home to sleep, repeat. Looking back, I realize what a detrimental effect that life had on our marriage.

As the class continued I became more frustrated, angry, and disappointed in myself. *Who was I? Was I really a good officer? Were all my perceived accomplishments actually failures?* I started to think back on my years in law enforcement and I began to see myself as a hypocrite. At times I was so kind and compassionate to the girls in the jail, but other times I can remember being cold and callous to people I interacted with on the road. It made me remember how cold the officers were to me after the hotel robbery. Suddenly it occurred to me—I had become just like them: cynical and jaded. I had forgotten why I became a cop in the first place. Not always, of course, but often enough that I was ashamed of myself when I thought about it.

The more I learned in school the more I wondered if it was time to leave law enforcement for good. I had always been so proud of my job and what it signified about who I was as an individual. Being a cop made me feel strong, almost invincible. It made me feel like I had left behind my childhood and made something of myself, like I was doing exactly what I was meant to do and that all the trauma I had been through had led me to this career. The pain and sadness was all just part of the journey to make me a better cop. John Van Maanen put into print how I had always felt about my job when he wrote, "The day a new recruit walks through the doors of the police academy he leaves society behind to enter a profession that does more than give him a job, it defines who he is."[4] But now I had no idea what to think about my job or myself. *Who would I be if I wasn't a cop anymore?* My emotions were in constant turmoil.

By this time all the joy and excitement I had once felt about going to work had turned into anger and hostility. Pontiac didn't look the way it once had. Sergeant Garibaldi was gone and nearly all of my former Pontiac officers had transferred to other areas in the county. I was one of only two women on my shift and one of two original Pontiac officers. Pontiac was a place seen as undesirable to work. No one wanted to come to Pontiac to take twenty to thirty calls a day when they could work somewhere else in the county and take ten calls a week for the same pay. Because of that Pontiac was nearly completely comprised of two types of deputies: newly hired, inexperienced officers that were forced there by low seniority and deputies that had gotten in trouble and forced to Pontiac as punishment. Deputies that were working there voluntarily and happily, like me, were a rarity.

I had been surrounded by incompetence, laziness, and youthful ignorance, not only on the road, but in dispatch as well. I missed the days of working with dependable, experienced officers and dispatchers that I trusted to have my back. Even if I didn't like them personally, I knew that I could trust them to know and do what needed to be done. Nowadays, I didn't trust anyone: not to write a decent report, not to make good decisions, and definitely not to have my back. It felt like it wasn't just me against the "bad guys," but it was also me against my coworkers.

Laws across the United States have become fairly strict when it comes to domestic assault. The law, in combination with departmental policy, means that an officer *shall* arrest when probable cause exists that an assault was committed and there is a domestic relationship between the parties. This is a fairly common call for police and one that should be easily handled in most situations. I soon learned the hard way that not all of my new coworkers were as competent as they should be regarding the law.

The first time was when I was dispatched as backup to Deputy Glass who spoke to the male party while I went into the house and spoke to the female party. The woman told me that her boyfriend, who was also the father of her children, had assaulted her. Also inside the house was the boyfriend's sister, who confirmed the assault had occurred. After gathering all the necessary information, I went outside and told Deputy Glass, "10-95," which was the code for arrest. It was a way to convey that the subject was arrestable without verbalizing it and giving them the chance to run or fight. Rather than arresting the man, Deputy Glass walked away from him and toward me. He said that if we were arresting him then we needed to arrest her as well because she had hit him. As my anger rose at his unprofessionalism, I reminded him that when someone is being assaulted that they are allowed to defend themselves and try to get away, which is what both the victim and the suspect's sister stated had occurred. The victim had injuries, but the suspect did not.

Deputy Glass continued to argue with me in front of the suspect, who was standing at least ten feet away and could have fled the scene at any time. Out of sheer frustration I finally began walking to my car and said, "Fine. It's your call. Do you what you want." Deputy Glass stopped me and said he would do as I asked. Later that night I pulled Deputy Glass aside and reminded him that I had many more years of experience than he did and if he couldn't trust my judgment, then maybe we needed to try to avoid taking calls together. Deputy Glass apologized, but I can't recall ever taking another call with him again. Whether or not he avoided me, I certainly did my best to avoid him.

Another domestic call that I was dispatched to as a backup officer was with Deputy Cortez. In this instance it was the female party that had assaulted her husband. Deputy Cortez spoke to the wife while I went to the hospital to speak to the husband who detailed the account of the assault. I also documented his injuries. I then drove to Deputy Cortez's location and relayed the information to him. I can't explain why, but he seemed completely clueless as to how to handle the call. Was it because he had been poorly trained during his FTO or because he was just lazy? The wife ended up admitting to the assault and agreed to write out a statement explaining her side of the story. I advised Deputy Cortez that I would transport the wife to the jail for him while he wrote the report and warrant request. Deputy Cortez continued to claim ignorance on how to proceed. My frustration finally came to a breaking point, and I ended up doing the transport as well as all the paperwork.

When it came to dispatch, I was equally frustrated. It seemed like a revolving door of new hires in dispatch. Dispatching for Pontiac is very different than dispatching for some of the more rural areas of the county. For example, the roads in rural areas tend to be longer and further apart. When a deputy is calling out a pursuit in a rural area the dispatcher always repeats over the air everything the deputy says. In Pontiac, an urban area, the streets are shorter and much closer together. If a dispatcher tries to repeat everything the deputy says they will tie up the airwaves. By the time the deputy gets back on the air the responding deputies may have missed several turns that have taken place in the pursuit or that the pursuit terminated, and the deputy is now on foot chasing or fighting with the suspect. In Pontiac, once a chase starts the dispatcher should remain silent and just document what is being said so that the airwaves are open for the deputy to relay information.

While it is considered unprofessional to "argue" with a dispatcher over the radio, sometimes it was impossible not to speak up. One day I was dispatched to a civil complaint with no backup. The only information that the dispatcher gave me was that a man was arguing with his nephew about money. As I was driving I tried to read the comments that were in the call. I soon discovered that this call wasn't just an argument, but that they were actually fighting. I called dispatch.

"8929 to radio."

"Go ahead."

"Are the comments in the call correct that the people are physically fighting?

"Yep, that's what the comments say."

I was furious. Since when do we dispatch deputies to physical altercations without advising them and without backup?

"Maybe you could have let me know that?" I said as I approached the address. Then I noticed that there were three grown men in a physical altercation in the front yard of the house. I again called dispatch, advised them of what I was seeing, and requested another unit. Later that day I was given a "verbal reprimand" from the sergeant for my argumentative radio behavior. The more I thought about these and other incidents, along with my newfound academic knowledge and medical problems, the more I realized it was time to leave law enforcement for good.

It became clear that I would never view policing the way I had before going back to school. In August 2018, I was finally given the push I needed to leave policing for good. I had my second spinal fusion surgery. The recovery went nothing like the first. Instead of immediate relief, I found myself in pain every minute of every day. I received a call from a county lieutenant in November who demanded that I return to work the next day. I had been going to physical therapy since surgery, but by November the therapist said there was nothing more she could do for me. I spent my days doing homework from bed in too much pain to do anything—even sit upright at the table. Sitting through classes was torture. Household chores would enflame my back and put me in so much pain that it would often bring me to the brink of tears. There was no way I could return to work where I had to sit at a desk between eight and sixteen hours a day. I made the decision to end my career and officially quit my job. I was forty-five years old. I had no idea what was next for me.

Today, I am a different person. My view of my career in law enforcement has been forever altered. The only thing that keeps me from falling into a black hole where I completely succumb to the guilt of the many times I failed as a police officer is remembering the many good things I did in the years before I forgot how important compassion was. There are people who will remember me positively, which helps me realize that it wasn't all for nothing. I did make a difference in the lives of some, and since I can't change the past that will have to be enough.

There was the little girl whose mother caught her stepfather molesting her and then fled the scene. I tracked him down in Ypsilanti, had him arrested, stayed after my shift to drive to Ypsilanti personally and take him to jail. After dropping him off I went back to the apartment to let the mother and the little girl know that they could sleep safely knowing that he wasn't coming back to hurt them. The rape victim who laid her head in my lap and cried while I stroked her hair and tried to reassure her that she was strong and could get through this. The elderly woman whose hand I held for hours while she tried to process the fact that her adult son had just shot himself in the head in front of her and me. The young woman in her early twenties who was devastated after finding her alcoholic mother dead on the floor of her apartment. I must have spent over an hour comforting her and assisting her with making the necessary arrangements for removing her mother's body. Fortunately for me, there are more positive memories from my career than there are negative ones.

Charles Ramsey said that "fate and circumstance are the only things that separate us from one another as human beings."[5] Many times I had told the girls in the jail that the only difference between them and me is that I was lucky enough not to get caught for the many stupid things I did as a kid. I'm not sure why, but it was easy for me to recognize that fact when I worked in the jail, but somehow, over the years, I seemed to forget it when I was on the road. It's one of my biggest regrets in law enforcement.

One of the most important things I ever learned in college was culture shock syndrome. Victor Stretcher wrote that culture shock is usually experienced by people traveling to foreign lands, but police officers experience different phases of it when they work in areas that subject them to new subcultures. Antagonism toward the community and its citizens are early signs of culture shock in officers. If left unchecked culture shock can turn into culture fatigue, where every interaction with a citizen is tainted and seen through a negative and judgmental lens.[6] I knew immediately that was me—of who I had become those last couple years. Most days, I had forgotten about relating to the citizens of my city, remembering that I was one of them once, understanding that it was my responsibility to protect and serve them, knowing that I could make a positive difference in their lives. I grew contemptuous of the people that I dealt with regularly. Instead of trying to find solutions to their problems so that I wasn't called to them repeatedly, I tried to appease those citizens as quickly and with the least amount of effort possible. One of the clearest examples of this was my many interactions with the homeless population.

There was a large, open field directly across the street from a liquor store that became known as "the pit." The pit became a place for the homeless, mentally ill, prostitutes, and drug addicts to congregate. They tended to create a lot of police calls. I was frequently responding to that location for overdoses, medical calls, stabbings, fights, and more. Rather than make any attempt to help these people, policing them became a game.

My section partner and I would often make plans to simultaneously arrive from different directions to box them in and engage in needless overpolicing. We knew most of the people by name and knew who had outstanding warrants. Trespassing, loitering, open intoxicants, warrants— take your pick. Either way, it gave us the ability to conduct a search of their person where we often located drugs and/or weapons. Sometimes we issued citations, sometimes we arrested them, but we always we told everyone to leave the area.

I never thought of myself as an agent of the state⁷ or someone who enforced laws on the poor to benefit the wealthy, but I would learn that, for many people, that is exactly how police officers are viewed. Ultimately, that's what matters: how does the public, the people living in your jurisdiction, view you as a police officer? I began to ask myself why I arrested and/or ticketed so many people that were homeless. Loitering. Trespassing. Soliciting. The honest truth is that I don't have a good answer for my overpolicing actions, but I believe I did it because I thought it was my job. I did it because I didn't understand then, as I do now, that in many cases these people had nowhere to go and no one to reach out to. Could I have at least tried to help them? Yes. Was I ever trained and instructed to do so? No. Is that my fault? Maybe, maybe not. But these questions will haunt me for the rest of my life.

I threw myself into school with every ounce of my being. The longer I was away from the county the happier and less stressed I was. I thought I would miss the comradery, the excitement, the sense of self-satisfaction in making a difference, but I found that I didn't miss any of it. In fact, as I thought about the bias, the unfairness, and the harassment that I had experienced, I grew more hostile and angrier toward my former profession. The veil had been lifted and it felt like, for the first time ever, I was seeing my job for what it really was.

One particular memory that I began to ruminate over frequently involved a deputy that had been charged with criminal sexual conduct for having a sexual relationship with an inmate. Deputy Bowman had worked in the jail for nearly twenty years, and he was approaching retirement when accusations came forward claiming that he and an inmate were having sex in the pod closet while he was on duty. All the deputies were talking about it and many recalled unusual circumstances that had surrounded Deputy Bowman and that particular pod. One deputy told me how Deputy Bowman had asked her to switch pods with him on several occasions. Regardless of evidence, all the deputies proclaimed his innocence and disparaged the inmate for being a lying drug addict. The subculture stuck together, but I knew better.

My relationship with the inmates was different. I knew who could be trusted to tell me the truth and I could usually tell when they were lying to me. Throughout Deputy Bowman's trial I was approached by a variety of inmates who told me stories that not only confirmed Deputy Bowman's guilt but provided more information that I believed even the prosecutor wasn't aware of. I'm ashamed to say that I never spoke up. I was already an outsider who was being harassed endlessly by my coworkers. I knew that if I came forward and revealed what I had been told, which would be considered hearsay and not admissible in a criminal trial, I would become a full-on pariah.

Eventually, Deputy Bowman's trial ended with a hung jury. While the deputies all around me cheered, I felt angry. I knew he was guilty, and I knew I didn't speak up. The prosecutor's office announced it was going to retry the case and I held onto hope that the right outcome would happen next time. Unfortunately, Deputy Bowman's victim died of a drug overdose before the second trial started. The gossip was that her death all but assured Deputy Bowman's exoneration in his upcoming trial.

In the middle of Deputy Bowman's second trial an inmate that I had become acquainted with came back into the jail. She pulled me aside one day and asked if she could talk to me about Deputy Bowman. I was hesitant but agreed. Privately, she told me how she absolutely knew that Deputy Bowman was guilty and that she had proof. I was shocked, but I also knew that I shouldn't be discussing this with her. She told me that Deputy Bowman had also initiated a sexual relationship with her, and it had continued after she was released from jail. Her cell phone, she claimed, which was currently in the jail's property room, was full of phone calls and text messages between her and Deputy Bowman.

It was time for me to make a decision: was I going to stand by and do nothing out of fear (again) or was I going to come forward and tell what I knew? I chose somewhere in between. I made an anonymous call to our special investigations unit and told them what I knew. I refused to give my name but provided the investigator the name of the inmate who provided me the information and advised them that she was currently in our jail and ready to talk. Honestly, I don't know if the information I provided to them was used in the trial, but I do know that they spoke to the inmate and that Deputy Bowman was found guilty and sent to prison.

I took no pleasure in seeing a fellow deputy go to prison, but I also couldn't stand by and support someone who was abusing the inmates, abusing his position, and abusing the trust placed in him by the citizens. I felt an odd mix of anger, guilt, and pride. It might have taken me a while, but I finally did stand up and do what was right. The problem, as I look back on it now, is that I shouldn't have been afraid to step forward. What kind of profession has members who seek to actively protect coworkers who have committed egregious criminal acts? That isn't a profession I want to be a part of. Actually, it isn't what most people in the profession want, but the pressure and coercion that is placed on the many by the few can be overwhelming.

I graduated with my bachelor's degree in May 2019 and was strongly encouraged by several of my professors to go on to graduate school. I decided to reach out to Professor Meehan and ask for his advice. That conversation would ultimately dictate the next steps in my life and future.

Professor Meehan was beginning a research project with colleagues from Wilfrid Laurier University in Canada studying how the use of video affects the trials of police officers involved in on-duty shootings. To my utter shock Professor Meehan asked if I would be interested in joining the project as a graduate research assistant. Not only that, but he worked to get me a graduate assistant position that would provide me with free tuition and a modest stipend. I was excited at the prospect, but it meant another two years without a job and income. It was definitely something I was going to have to discuss with Neil before making such a big decision.

Several years prior to this time my marriage with Neil cracked under the many pressures of life and fell apart. While we were both partially to blame for the breakdown of the relationship, I was stupid and impulsive and filed for divorce prematurely and we ended up apart for about two years. Luckily, Neil and I found our way back to one another. The only good thing that came out of our divorce is that when we reunited, our relationship became stronger and healthier than it had ever been. We both realized how much we loved each other and that no matter how hard things got, life apart was worse.

After discussing school and our future, Neil agreed to financially support me for another two years. I applied and was accepted into the master of arts in liberal studies program. I got the graduate assistant position and began the next phase of my life. It had been a long time since I had felt fulfilled—proud of myself—like I had purpose. The more involved in the research I became, the more my life took on new meaning. One of those moments of clarity came during a meeting when I was relating stories to our research team about treatment I received during my days on the road. A member of the group asked me, "Why don't you want to burn this institution to the ground?" I knew that the answer was that I didn't, but I couldn't quite explain why. However, it was a question that really made me think. I wrote the question down and continued to ponder it for months. The questions and doubts I had struggled with throughout my law enforcement career were becoming clearer. As I spent more time reflecting, I began to understand what the problems were with my former profession and why it was so important that changes had to come.

The world all around me was changing. Police shootings and deaths were all over the news. Breonna Taylor, Atatiana Jefferson, George Floyd, Rayshard Brooks—the names were on protest posters and the lips of newscasters countrywide. Through it all I wanted to defend my former colleagues. I wanted to offer up valid, logical reasons to explain some of the behaviors that I was seeing on television and in our research. Sometimes it was easy to offer explanations, but other times I found myself at a loss to justify behavior that was clearly wrong.

One case that troubled me, in fact, still haunts me, is the Patrick Harmon shooting out of Salt Lake City, Utah. A big part of our research has been to systemically accumulate and analyze a collection of police-involved shooting videos. While there are approximately one thousand police shootings per year, only a small percentage have body camera footage available, and an even smaller percentage have video that is usable for our research. The Patrick Harmon shooting happens to be one of those cases.

Harmon was stopped on the street by an officer for not having a light on his bicycle. Eventually, it was determined that he had a felony warrant out for his arrest and two additional officers arrived to assist. When the officers attempted to take Harmon into custody, he fled from them on foot. The shooting officer claimed that Harmon, while running, reached into his pants pocket and presumably retrieved a knife. The officer then claimed that Harmon turned toward them and yelled, "I'll fucking stab you."[8] While I am not making any accusations, I have viewed the body cam video repeatedly and have been unable to see or hear what is alleged by the officers.[9] I was immediately skeptical about the shooting after viewing the video, but when my research uncovered that the officers were not criminally charged, I was shocked. To this day, I'm saddened that Patrick Harmon's name isn't on protest signs or newscaster's lips along with the other high-profile cases.

Over time I began to understand that some of what was happening in policing was due to a lack of education, a lack of training, a lack of transparency, and biases. Initially, I struggled to be critical of the police officers I was watching in the videos. To me, they were still my coworkers, my people, my family. After all, I had been in situations where I had come close to shooting people. I wanted to believe that people would have supported me had I taken the shot. Didn't these officers deserve the same from me?

A personal close call that stands out in my mind was an incident where a suspicious-looking man with a gun was in a woman's backyard. I assumed he would be gone before I arrived, so I didn't wait for my backup officer, which was a poor tactic and goes against training. But the sad truth is that officers do become lax at times, especially in busy cities where precincts are understaffed and officers overworked. I walked into the backyard and, sure enough, there was a Black male wearing a white t-shirt and blue jean shorts with a black semiautomatic handgun in his right hand. I can't tell you what his face looked like because tunnel vision kicked in and I was completely focused on his right hand. His arm was hanging down at his side and his index finger was on the trigger. I unholstered my gun, pointed it directly at the center of his chest, and screamed, "Drop it! Drop the gun, now!"

The man didn't move. I told myself that if I saw his hand move, even slightly, that I would shoot. I don't know how long we stood there staring at each other, but it felt like an eternity. Time seemed to freeze. I slid my index finger onto the trigger and slowly began to squeeze as I continued to scream at him to drop the gun. While I could hear myself yelling at him it felt like it was coming from someone else. Abruptly, the man dropped the gun to the ground, turned, and ran. I ran over where the gun lay, picked it up, and ran after the man. It finally occurred to me that I hadn't told dispatch what was happening, so I called out my location, the man's description, and his direction as I ran. Between stopping to pick up the gun and then being further slowed down by hopping the fence at the back of the yard, I lost sight of him. The whole shift converged on my area, but it was summertime and there were people everywhere wearing white t-shirts and blue jean shorts. We never found the man, but I learned a valuable lesson about waiting for backup. Later that night I lay in bed thinking about how close I had come to killing someone. All these years later that incident is still seared into my memory and I'm grateful that I didn't have to pull the trigger.

It was moments like those that impacted my research in the early days. It was difficult for me to cast aspersions on the decision-making of another officer. It's easy to make judgments after the fact, but it's another thing when it's happening to you in the moment. I knew that feeling intimately and it felt like a betrayal to criticize the actions an officer took when I was not in their shoes. Luckily, those days faded as I became more educated and learned to look objectively at what I was seeing on the videos of the police shootings. Rather than focus on the feelings of betrayal, I instead focused on being a knowledgeable observer. I was able to utilize my prior experience to more fully understand the circumstances the officers were faced with while still maintaining an objective perspective. There were so many times when I thought to myself, *Who trained that officer to do that? Don't they know there's a better way to handle that person/situation?* At the same time, I became stressed and saddened by how I was seeing police officers portrayed in the media, haunted by my own actions as a police officer over the years, and frustrated by my inability to share the newfound knowledge that I accrued to introduce positive changes in police departments everywhere.

So, how do we fix the problems in policing? Well, there are no easy answers, and I would never suggest that I have all the solutions. However, based on my experiences, education, and research, I have a few suggestions. First, policing is called a "profession" so it's time for officers to start acting like it's one. Professionals are educated. How many other professionals out there are expected to deal effectively with such a wide variety of problems, people, and serious issues with training that includes, in most cases, less than six months? Police officers need to learn critical thinking skills that come with a formal education, not to mention writing skills. I've seen and read too many reports written by police officers that read like they've been written by illiterate children. Police reports are viewed by prosecutors, judges, juries, and sometimes by the media—they should be well-written and comprehendible.

Why are there so many police agencies that still don't require their officers to have a four-year criminal justice degree? I can only speak of those agencies in Michigan, but I'm aware that Michigan isn't much different than most other states. The standards for the State of Michigan require police officers to have sixty college credits; however, those credits can be in any subject. There is no requirement that they be accrued from criminal justice courses. Worse yet, Michigan offers many exceptions to this rule.

Sheriff's offices, like the one I worked for, have no requirements. A sheriff can deputize anyone, such as their family members, or send anyone they want to the police academy—educated and trained or not. The same is true with the City of Detroit, which runs its own police academy and therefore makes its own requirements. Detroit can send kids right out of high school to the police academy. No one will ever convince me that an eighteen-year-old has the maturity, temperament, education, or life experience to be working as a police officer. For those who claim a degree isn't necessary, at minimum, police academies need to be transformed into more of a trade school format where prospective officers receive one to two years of extensive training in order to become certified.

Another issue that needs to be addressed is the "good ole' boys club" culture in police work. I'm not saying this is a problem in every agency, but it's prevalent enough to affect officers directly, as well as the profession overall. Some of the problems relate to the way women are treated. I've related some of my stories of mistreatment and bias based on my gender, but there are so many others. The longer I worked at the county the more it became glaringly apparent that female deputies would never be given the same leeway in discipline or career opportunities as their male counterparts.

Regrettably, gender bias isn't the only issue. Policing tends to be a job that people get into and stay until they retire. Some will be promoted, and others won't. But one thing that doesn't change with those promotions is the close friendships that are formed in the early years of one's career. Why is this a problem? Let's say my old partner, Carlos Luna, got promoted to lieutenant and I stayed on the road. One day I violate a serious policy—so serious that I should be fired. When that paperwork lands on Lieutenant Luna's desk what are the chances that he finds a way to make it go away? Sadly, these types of incidents occur every day and that's precisely how bad cops are allowed to continue on the job until something so big happens that it goes public and there is no one to save that officer from a reckoning.

During my years at the county, I witnessed this type of bias repeatedly. For example, two deputies, one male and one female, went out drinking and drove home. Both got into accidents. The male deputy caused serious injury in the driver of the car he hit and fled the scene. The female deputy hit a pole and caused no injury. Both deputies were demoted, but the male deputy was allowed to return to his position on the road within a few months; the female deputy went to jail and remains there to this day, more than two years later.

A deputy got caught drunk on duty. He was sent to rehab, allowed back to the road afterward, and received a special assignment (in effect, a promotion) shortly thereafter. Another deputy was discovered abusing prescription drugs and was forced to quit or be threatened with criminal charges if he didn't.

A deputy used a taser on a handcuffed subject. He was given no punishment, not even a written reprimand. In fact, the deputy received a special assignment (promotion) shortly after the incident. During my Pontiac years, an officer did the same thing and was fired and criminally charged. Of course, I could go on, but you get the point. Many of these punishments, or lack thereof, are due to the relationships those deputies built over the years with their superiors.

None of these examples are given to paint police officers as bad people. Nor am I suggesting that any of these behaviors are acceptable. Police are like everyone else and have faults and make mistakes like people in all professions. What I'm trying to point out is that there is a better way. Prospective officers need to be educated so that they can start their careers with knowledge that will provide them with the best possible foundation for success. That education should continue throughout their careers so that when they become supervisors, they will be able to recognize signs of culture fatigue in their officers, such as what I was unknowingly experiencing. Further, holding officers accountable and making the discipline process transparent and equal is the professional way of conducting business.

Eliminate bias. Provide female and minority officers with an environment that allows them to feel comfortable enough to come forward when they are being mistreated and harassed. Discipline officers who are responsible for the mistreatment and, again, make that discipline equitable. Less than equal discipline makes officers feel less than, which leads to bitterness and resentment.

Stop favoritism and preferential treatment. Every agency should hire an outside entity with the appropriate expertise to handle all citizen and disciplinary complaints. Many agencies have an internal affairs division, special investigations unit, or other internal mechanisms for handling complaints. As I've pointed out, this practice is ripe for abuse. Those agencies that don't have a special unit rely on shift sergeants to evaluate citizens' complaints. If someone completely unknown to the agency and its officers was brought in to handle those complaints, it would eliminate all bias and complaints would be handled professionally and fairly. Most importantly, the community and tax-paying citizens could be sure that the "bad apples" are being dealt with early on and not allowed to continue damaging the good work of officers everywhere.

The same could be said for bodycam video. While there is a general consensus that bodycams are a good thing, many police unions worry that agency command staff will utilize the videos to "fish" for something that can be used to fire officers they don't like. Hire someone with proper education and experience from the outside who has no relationship with the agency to review the videos. That person could look for egregious abuses of power that need to be addressed, as well as situations that officers are repeatedly experiencing and could benefit from additional training. Those videos could then be used to design and implement specific training programs. It's not about punishment but making everyone better. There would be no favorable treatment, no bias. Someday, I hope that these outside experts could lend credibility and equitability to agencies that choose to implement these ideas.

While it may seem like I am bashing police and policing, that couldn't be further from the truth. I will always be a fervent and dedicated supporter of law enforcement because I know that the vast majority of police officers are doing their absolute best. I do not support or endorse inappropriate, abusive, or illegal behavior by law enforcement. However, I firmly believe, and statistics demonstrate, that unjustified uses of force are exceptionally rare. There are no organizations that run perfectly, and to expect law enforcement organizations to is unreasonable. All we can do is try to put forth positive changes that will make law enforcement more professional, fair, and customer (citizen) driven. Neither police officers nor law enforcement agencies can do this alone. These changes need to come from a group effort that must include government intervention with help related to mental illness resources, mandated minimum training standards, and adequate funding to provide the appropriate level of ongoing training.

As for the "Defund the Police" movement, again, there is a better way. One issue that I think most police officers would agree on is a problem with the lack of funding for mental health treatment. Deinstitutionalization has had disastrous consequences for the mentally ill, their families, and communities because the promised dollars for community-based treatment never fully materialized owing to political decision-making. While everyone seems to agree that deinstitutionalization was a mistake, no one can agree on a solution.

As it relates to police officers, deinstitutionalization has made dealing with mentally ill individuals a daily occurrence. The problem is that police officers are not trained or equipped to effectively manage the mentally ill, which makes their job more difficult, as well as leading to many unfortunate circumstances. Not to mention, deinstitutionalization has led to an explosion of mentally ill individuals being caught up in the jail system where they receive little to no treatment, and the costs associated with housing them are substantially more than if we still had appropriate institutions.[10]

There is one mentally challenged person who I will never forget: Natalie. I met her early in my career when I was still in FTO. She was a young White female in her early twenties, severely mentally ill, and lived with her mother on the southwest side of Pontiac. Natalie was prone to have violent outbursts when she was angry, and her mother frequently called 911 when Natalie would threaten her—often with weapons. My first interaction with Natalie came from a call described as "family trouble." Many officers arrived on scene indicating that they were familiar with Natalie. I noticed that no one liked her. All the officers seemed to be very short and hostile with Natalie. I took a different approach and tried to soften my voice and speak kindly to her. To my surprise it worked. Natalie calmed down and agreed to allow me to transport her to the hospital for a mental evaluation.

My kindness toward Natalie ended up being a curse. Instead of the future calls coming from Natalie's mother, they instead came from Natalie. Not only that, but Natalie specifically requested that I be sent to her call.

When Natalie didn't get her way and another officer was sent in my place Natalie would then call 911 and tell the dispatcher that she was going to kill herself if I didn't show up. Of course, I was always dispatched. This became a weekly event, then twice a week, then whenever Natalie was high, drunk, stressed out, or just wanted someone to talk to. It was a difficult couple of years dealing with her constant calls, but it all sadly ended when Natalie was finally sent to prison.

I have no way of knowing if Natalie's version of events was true, but we had built a solid rapport over the years, and I had no reason to doubt her. Natalie told me that her roommates had gotten high and drunk and accidentally set their house on fire. She said they convinced her to take the fall for it knowing she would get a lighter sentence due to her mental illness, and she agreed. I felt bad for her, but there was nothing I could do. I had tried unsuccessfully to help her over the years. I even took her to the hospital and filled out involuntary commitment papers on her more times than I can count, but she was always released within hours.

Defunding the police isn't the answer: officers, including corrections deputies, need more training on how to deal with the mentally ill. More importantly, deinstitutionalization needs to be reversed. There must be hospitals and institutions where people can go to receive humane mental health treatment and not a quick evaluation and sent home with the hope that they will follow health care instructions. I can confidently say that most police officers would be willing to give up some of their funding if they knew that the money would be going toward appropriate facilities to house the mentally ill.

As I bring this book to a close, I ponder all that has happened to me. I think about my life, how much I overcame, and where I would have ended up had it not been for the amazing people in my life who took on the roles and responsibilities of family. I think about all the people I interacted with in my law enforcement career—both as a dispatcher and as an officer. Whether I treated them kindly or harshly, whether I saved their life or helped their family while processing their death scene, I realize that I had a permanent impact on their life and they on mine. It hurts me to know that the impact I left with some people was negative. That, like me with the officers at the hotel robbery, they would have deleterious memories of that interaction forever. I am ashamed and embarrassed to admit that I became that officer.

It would be easy to blame my lack of compassion on culture fatigue and the subculture at work—the expectation of being strong and stoic. The reality is that when I worked in the jail, I spent more time with the inmates than I did with my coworkers. It was easy to dismiss the deputy's harassment by secluding myself in the pod with the inmates. It was difficult not to see myself in their stories and want to help them overcome their challenges. Everything was different when I was back on the road. I worked with people who didn't have the passion for the job that I did, people that were young and hadn't experienced the life struggles that I had or that the citizens of Pontiac had. Showing compassion (weakness in the eyes of my coworkers) was a quick way to be teased, harassed, and ostracized. The funny thing is that I'm not generally a follower, but somehow I lost my way. The truth is that there is no one to blame except myself. I forgot who I was, where I came from, and why I became a police officer. It means nothing now, but I sincerely apologize to every citizen who ever had a negative encounter with me—every citizen who I didn't give my best effort to help.

Conversely, I would like to thank the citizens of Pontiac for giving me some of the best years of my life. I feel blessed to have been allowed into your lives and hearts. Lastly, to all my girls from the jail: you don't know it, but each of you had more of an impact on my life than I had on yours.

NOTES

CHAPTER 6

1. "City History." City of Pontiac Michigan. Accessed July 2020. http://www .pontiac.mi.us/about/history/city_history.php.
2. George Kelling and James Wilson. "Broken Windows: The Police and Neighborhood Safety." *The Atlantic*, March 1982. https://www.theatlantic.com /magazine/archive/1982/03/broken-windows/304465/.
3. Kelling and Wislon, "Broken Windows."
4. Kelling and Wislon, "Broken Windows."

CHAPTER 7

1. Louis Shimmel Jr. "The City of Pontiac: A 'Going' Concern?" *Michigan Privatization Report*. December 2006, https://www.mackinac.org/8125.

CHAPTER 12

1. Victor Strecher, "People Who Don't Even Know You," in *The Police and Society*, ed. Victor Kappeler (Long Grove, IL, 1995), 203–19.
2. Strecher, "People Who Don't," 203–19.
3. John Van Maanen, "Kinsmen in Repose: Occupational Perspectives of Patrolmen," *Policing: A View from the Street*, eds. Peter Manning and John Van Maanen (Santa Monica, CA, 1978), 220–37.
4. Van Maanen, "Kinsmen in Repose," 220–37.
5. Charles Ramsey, "The Challenge of Policing in a Democratic Society: A Personal Journey toward Understanding." National Institute of Justice, June 2014.

6. Strecher, "People Who Don't, 203–19.

7. William Garriott, ed., *Introduction to Policing and the Project of Contemporary Governance* (New York: Palgrave Macmillan, 2013), 1–28.

8. Gregory Gregory, "Police Civilian Review Board: Investigation Report." Internal Affairs Case Number S2017-0016, Salt Lake City, Utah, 2017.

9. Graphic: Bodycam Footage of Patrick Harmon Fatal Shooting. Police Activity. October 5, 2017. Video, 2:42. https://www.youtube.com/watch?v=Enn EiWDrnxo.

10. D. Sisti, A. Segal, and E. Emanuel, "Improving Long-Term Psychiatric Care: Bring Back the Asylum." *Journal of the American Medical Association* 313, no. 3 (2015): 243–44; A. Primeau, T. Bowers, M. Harrison, and XuXu, "Deinstitutionalization of the Mentally Ill: Evidence for Transinstitutionalization from Psychiatric Hospitals to Penal Institutions," *Comprehensive Psychology* 2, no. 2 (2013): 1–10; A. Pustilnik, "Prisons of the Mind: Social Value and Economic Inefficiency in the Criminal Justice Response to Mental Illness," *Journal of Criminal Law & Criminology* 96, no. 1 (2005): 217–65.

INDEX

ABOUT THE AUTHOR

Ann Marie Dennis spent twenty years working in various areas of law enforcement, including dispatch, corrections, courts, and road patrol. After leaving law enforcement, she returned to college. As of this writing, she is completing her second master's degree in social work and a member of a research team researching police-involved shootings and the legal concept of the reasonable officer. In her free time, you can find Ann Marie enjoying a glass of German Riesling, snuggling with her cats, Mia and Marcellus, or exploring her creative side through abstract painting and jewelry-making. *Behind Her Badge: A Woman's Journey into and out of Law Enforcement* is Ann Marie's first book.

Ann Marie Dennis
Used with permission of Gil Garrett at Garrett
Group Media

CPSIA information can be obtained
at www.ICGtesting.com
Printed in the USA
BVHW040025010623
665136BV00001B/1